Praise for *The Screenwriter's Legal Guide*

"As hard as it is to write a good screenplay, it's still only half the game. What's in this book is the other half—and to ignore it is to risk being eaten alive. Steven Breimer is the exception to every lawyer joke I've heard, and you'd be crazy not to soak up everything he has to offer in these pages. Unless you want to see your ship finally come in and then sail away without you, you should march to the counter right now, take this *Legal Guide* home, and start reading!"

  —Jeff Arch, screenwriter, *Sleepless in Seattle*, *Iron Will*, and *Sealed with a Kiss*

"Navigating the shark-infested waters in a litigious world where fortunes change hands based on legal mistakes, this extraordinary handbook is a guide for anyone in or contemplating entering the entertainment business. It's a must for those wishing to avoid or minimize problems before they impact, a primer in basic deal flow and structure from a man with decades of experience at the highest levels of the business."

  —Peter J. Dekom, entertainment attorney

"*The Screenwriter's Legal Guide* demystifies screenwriting contracts. An unsurpassed and imperative reference for screenwriters, their attorneys, agents, and managers!"

  —Marc H. Glick, entertainment attorney

"Short of having a brilliant idea for a movie, this is one of the best resources for the aspiring as well as the professional screenwriter."

  —Michael Peretzian, Creative Artists Agency

"This book answers every question that a writer could ask and some he or she should ask."

  —*The Beverly Hills Courier*

"Here is expert advice on the legal issues involved in screenwriting, with an overview of a screenwriter's place in the industry and the role of producers, agents, and lawyers."

  —*The Writer*

The Screenwriter's Legal Guide

Released.
Studio.
Running Time.
Director.
Producers.
Screenp

THIRD EDITION

Stephen Breimer

**ALLWORTH
PRESS**
NEW YORK

© 1999, 2004 Stephen F. Breimer

All rights reserved. Copyright under Berne Copyright Convention,
Universal Copyright Convention, and Pan-American Copyright
Convention. No part of this book may be reproduced, stored in
a retrieval system, or transmitted in any form, or by any means,
electronic, mechanical, photocopying, recording, or otherwise,
without prior permission of the publisher.

08   07   06   05   04   5   4   3   2   1

Published by Allworth Press
An imprint of Allworth Communications
10 East 23rd Street, New York, NY 10010

Cover design by Derek Bacchus, New York, NY
Page composition/typography by SR Desktop Services, Ridge, NY

Library of Congress Cataloging-in-Publication Data
Breimer, Stephen F.
    The screenwriter's legal guide/Stephen F. Breimer, Esq.—3rd ed.
        p.   cm.
    Includes index.
    ISBN 1-58115-352-X (pbk.)
        1. Motion picture industry—Law and legislation—United States.
    2. Authors and publishers—United States.   3. Screenwriters—Legal
    status, laws, etc.—United States.   I. Title.

    KF4302.B74 2004
    343.73'07879143—dc22

                                                    2004006524

The first edition of *The Screenwriter's Legal Guide* was published in 1995 as *Clause by Clause:*
The Screenwriter's Legal Guide, by Dell Publishing (ISBN 0-440-50561-5).

Printed in Canada

For all screenwriters, and, in particular,
for my writer clients,
whom I am proud to represent.

Contents

HEY THERE!
YOU WITH THE STARS IN YOUR EYES!
HAVE YOU HEARD ABOUT:

- How to protect yourself if the studio buys your screenplay and sits on it . . . that is, never makes the picture?

- Why bonuses only increase your chance of being *kicked off* a project at an early stage if the studio can find a cheaper writer?

- What two important provisions you should negotiate and will get, *if you ask for them,* when you are entitled to a percentage of profits?

- What payments you can get if the studio produces a sequel picture or a television series based on your script . . . *if you ask for them?*

- What up-front guarantees you must negotiate if you are commissioned to write a screenplay—with payoffs that can *add thousands* to what you make, along with pension payments and other extras?

- How to get a 75/25 percent book deal for novelizations of your screenplay—and the right to use the artwork from the movie and its title?

- Why you must *never* blurt out an idea at a cocktail party?

· · · · · ·

Preface

How often have newcomers to Hollywood—and old-timers, too—wished that they could put the expertise of a Hollywood lawyer to work for them, without the high price tag? Here is a book that explains the vocabulary of lawyers and agents when they're talking about the various terms of a screenwriter's contract.

As Robert Altman's famous movie *The Player* indicated, a writer's life in Hollywood can be a hazardous one. (The hapless writer in that movie is murdered by his producer!) When writers gather in Los Angeles, they often spend the entire evening regaling each other with horrendous can-you-top-this stories. The Writers Guild maintains a busy docket hearing the grievances of members who allege exploitation. And various computerized bulletin boards around town make sure that everyone knows about the latest contractual wrinkle, new level of option money or sales price, and unscrupulous producer behavior. If you are already established and on the grapevine, that is one thing.

But what if you are just starting out? What if you have sold a few screenplays and suspect that you could be doing better? Or, perhaps you are a smart attorney who wants to break into this fascinating branch of show biz. Or a literary agent.

The Screenwriter's Legal Guide is for all of you. This book will take you through various types of film and television negotiations, explaining the terminology in clear, layperson's language. By keeping this book close at hand, you will see what is possible, will understand industry norms, and have a better grasp of the process.

· · · · · ·

Acknowledgments

I would like to thank some of the people who have helped so generously in the preparation of this book:

CHARLOTTE SHEEDY, my agent, who inspired me to write this book. Her passion for books is unparalleled.

PETER DEKOM, my former partner and teacher. His advice and encouragement, as always, were invaluable.

ELLEN GEIGER, who gave me many wonderful ideas.

MARC H. GLICK, who gave so generously of his time, sound advice, always, and constant friendship.

RONALD PARKER, for his many helpful suggestions.

CHRISTOPHER PHILLIPS, my good friend, who is always there.

PATRICIA BARRY, my godmother, for her steadfast and loving belief in me.

MY PARTNERS at Bloom, Hergott, and Diemer, LLP, for their constant support.

TAD CRAWFORD, my publisher, for this tasteful and complete edition of the book.

NICOLE POTTER and NYIER ABDOU, my editors, for their terrific notes.

NANCY KESSLER, my assistant, for her great help on this edition.

ELIZABETH STOULIL, my former assistant, who graciously coordinated the entire process for the first edition.

THE WRITERS GUILD OF AMERICA, west, Inc. (WGAw), for their permission to publish portions of the WGA Schedule of Minimums.

Many thanks also go to:

> Stephanie and Mark Agnew
> Howard Askenase
> Miranda Barry
> Philip Barry, Jr.
> Leigh Brecheen
> Bruce Cohn Curtis
> Bobbie Edrick
> Nancy Gray
> Ari Greenburg
> Earl Greenburg
> Judith Karfiol
> Fred Leopold
> Jeffry Melnick
> Bruce Moccia
> Regula Noetzli
> Gail Shatsky
> Martin Singer
> Jay Statman
> Carol Vogel
> Richard Weiss

for their help, encouragement, and patience.

. . . . . .

Introduction

I am a partner in one of Los Angeles' better-known entertainment law firms. We have conducted thousands of negotiations over the years—everything from a fledgling writer's first deal to a top screenwriter's negotiations with a major studio, and screen rights deals ranging from blockbuster bestsellers to that tiny, precious novel. I know how important it is for the writer to understand what is being negotiated. Fewer surprises mean more satisfied clients; more satisfied clients have more successful careers.

I always make it a point to involve my clients in the negotiation of their deals. For me, it is important that my clients understand their rights and why they need to be protected. Most enjoy the process. Unfortunately, I do not have the time to review every clause of every deal with every client. I also recognize that the time involved to do that would be costly.

I have often wished that I could refer my clients to a reference book that would explain the process of negotiation and the meaning of the many terms that appear in sales and services agreements. Based on the questions that I am most commonly asked, and based on the questions that *should* be asked, I am writing this book.

Art Buchwald has shown that in the world of Hollywood the elusive term "net profits" has often been interpreted as if seen through a funhouse mirror. Indeed, Hollywood has historically held a rather cavalier attitude toward writers' services. For these reasons alone, writers and their agents need all the knowledge they can get.

Understand that I am not advocating that you negotiate a deal all by yourself. But by using this book, together with the right professional, you will learn a great deal about what you need to know to interpret a contract and what to expect in the process.

Imagine now that you are a working screenwriter—one of the fortunate ones whose efforts are finally paying off. You have worked hard to create a piece of material that someone wants to acquire. Or, you have worked hard to develop your writing talent and someone wants to hire you. Negotiations have begun, and, if all goes well, you will be asked to sign a contract—a legal, binding contract in which the rights to your labor of love will be owned and controlled by someone else. If you have never read a writer's contract, or, even if you have, you will probably have many questions.

As negotiations continue, you will be pressured. You do not want to lose the deal. Your agent or lawyer explains the terms. All sorts of new phrases are thrown at you—options, representations, warranties, passive payments, obligations, bonuses for sole writing credit, sequels—as are lengthy "Buchwald-type" profit definitions. You are advised that the proposal is a good one or a bad one. You are not sure. You have a hundred questions. There is no time to explain it all. You are confused. Finally, you decide to rely on your advisor's recommendations. That person knows. You do not. But it is a deal. As time goes on, you will become knowledgeable. For now, ignorance is not bliss, but it will do. You need the money.

I have been in your shoes. Before I was a lawyer, I produced movies. I also did some writing. In the beginning, I did not have enough money to hire a lawyer, and I did not have an agent. I sometimes worked without a contract. I got burned. When I finally started demanding contracts, I asked a few questions and signed without fully understanding. I still did not have a lawyer. Luckily, it turned out all right.

Finally, I retained a lawyer, a great lawyer, Peter Dekom, who later became my partner. His best advice to me at the time was to read my contracts and to *understand* them. A contract is one's guide to the level of performance expected and certain conditional bonuses. Reading a contract should not be hell, and it will not be, if you understand it. Nothing should be a secret to you. A lawyer or agent can make recommendations and great deals, but the best deals are made with the full participation of the client. You want to be able to participate in the negotiation of your contract. At the end of the day, it is *your* contract, your obligations, your money. Remember: You are signing it, not your agent or your lawyer.

You will be asked to make decisions, and you'll want to make those decisions intelligently. You should not be asked to sign something you do not understand. Inevitably, you, the writer, will be asked to sign a lengthy contract based on an agent's and/or lawyer's advice and expertise. But many questions, I am sure, will go unanswered. I understand this. Business must go on. Agreements have to be finalized quickly or deals may be lost.

You may decide to leave it to the lawyers and agents to make decisions on your behalf. The problem with that approach is not so much that the decision may be wrong for you, but that you may be *surprised*. Many contracts have quirky provisions. Take the following example: In most cases, when a writer options a script to a studio for one year, it is for one year. At one studio, however, that one year can be extended without the studio paying more for the extension. I had a client who was astonished when he realized how this provision works. He optioned his screenplay to a major Hollywood studio for one year and he was hired to rewrite the script. That particular studio has a policy that for purposes of computing the one-year period, the one-year period does not *begin* until the writer turns in all rewrites. My client took more than the allotted time for his rewrites, with the studio's blessing. What they knew, and he did not, was that the studio still had one year to go on the contract, no matter when he finished his rewrites. He had forgotten that this provision was in his contract, and it came as a complete (and certainly unwelcome) surprise.

Another provision many writers overlook: Contracts often put you in breach for behavior that is commonplace. For example, when hiring a writer, the studio will almost always require that the writing services be exclusive. The writer is not supposed to be working on two scripts at once or for different people. Do writers do it? Yes. Do they get away with it? Sometimes, by not talking about the other project that they are writing. It is usually not a problem, but it *might* be. In fact, it may be grounds for termination. You need to know that before you decide to take the chance. I always advise my clients of the risk. I also point out that if it becomes a problem, the studio may be compassionate—as long as you can deliver your draft on time. If studio officials are extremely compassionate, you might get more time. It depends on the circumstances and how much you're in their good graces. Ultimately, you will have to make the decision, but you should know that you are at risk and that by working on two scripts at once for different employers, you are in breach of your contract. For that reason, I do not recommend it.

I assume that you have chosen to read this book because you *do not* want to be surprised. The other major benefit of understanding the various clauses in your contract is that you will be able to follow the negotiations and participate in the process. And you probably want to be assured that your representative is acting in your best interests. I will never forget one particular negotiation that took place when I was a producer. In that negotiation, I felt the lawyer on the other side was *not* representing his client's best interests. The negotiation was a nightmare. The writer's lawyer had unrealistic demands and asked for extraordinary provisions. I finally closed the deal, but the negotiation left such a sour taste that I later abandoned the project. Looking back, I realize that I blamed the writer for these demands and I shouldn't have. He was poorly represented. You want to make sure that doesn't happen to you.

I was asked to write this book by a good friend of mine, an extraordinary literary agent named Charlotte Sheedy. She told me there was no such book on the market at the time. We agreed that such a book was needed, and I was pleased to fill the gap. This is the third edition. If you want to learn more about the negotiation and terms of your contract (and you should), this book is your guide. It will also help you and your advisor to speed up the process, an essential step in running your own unique business.

By using this book and working together with the right professional(s), you should learn just about everything you need to know about interpreting a contract and what to expect in the negotiating process. While I am certainly not suggesting that you negotiate a deal all by yourself, it is your responsibility to understand the process.

The best contracts are written in plain English. Unfortunately, most are not drafted that way. "Legalese" is the vocabulary and it often intimidates nonlawyers. This book is designed to help you understand these contracts in plain English. I have delineated some of the best deals one can get. At the very least, you should understand what is possible, what essential protections you must have, what you can reasonably expect, and what is dreaming. I have found that the most successful artists in Hollywood read their agreements and participate in the negotiation of their contracts. They understand what is expected of them and what special perks they have been given. That understanding, invariably, helps to create strong professional relationships between writers and their employers.

Yours is an exciting business. With knowledge, you will find that the process of negotiation is a challenging and rewarding one. You have arrived. Someone is excited about your work. The work has value and you have some negotiating power. Remember: Until you finish negotiating, your work cannot be used, duplicated, or ripped off (provided it is more than an idea—a concept discussed at length later in the book). Your dreams are coming true. I want you to enjoy the process.

1

The Screenwriter Holds a Unique Position in Hollywood

In order for you to understand the basic philosophy of the studios (the main buyers of writers' scripts and main employers of writers' services), it is important to appreciate the historical position of the screenwriter in Hollywood.

HISTORY

Since the inception of the film *business*, studios have considered the screenwriter a disposable employee. *Hired help*. In the early days, studios employed stables of writers. These writers were exclusive to a particular studio and the studios were thus able to commission scripts using many contributors, each with his own specialty. A writer known for structure would be brought in to help if the problem was structural. If the problem was romance, a romance writer would come on board to write a love scene. Sometimes a writer would be brought in just for one scene. *Gone With the Wind*, for example, had sixteen different writers.

Famous playwrights like Ben Hecht and John Van Druten were brought in to write words and scenes. F. Scott Fitzgerald was hired to edit and reshape the structure of the screenplay. Producers like David O. Selznick (who produced *Gone With the Wind*) were the contractors; writers were the laborers.

Most writers of feature films today are hired freelance, but the philosophy is the same. Like their predecessors, writers are often replaced. New writers are often brought in for drafts, rewrites, and polishes. Scripts might go through ten drafts and ten writers. *Tootsie* is one such example. Three writers were credited. Many came in just to write scenes and even lines.

The same philosophy prevails even if you sell a script. Unlike book writers or playwrights, who usually do their own rewriting and often have the last word (indeed the Dramatists Guild for playwrights *insists* that the playwright must be the only writer unless he consents to bring someone else in), Hollywood writers are almost always rewritten, even the best of them, even those who sell finished scripts. Virtually no script sold is *ever* the final draft. The buyer of an existing script (commonly known as a "spec script") usually assumes the same attitude as if such script had been commissioned from the start. Often, writers of such scripts are never consulted again, and, invariably, they are cut out of the process of making movies. This reality constantly reinforces the attitude that writers are hired help.

Of course, if you sell a spec script, you will try to ensure that you are hired for at least one rewrite and maybe more. This all depends on leverage and how "hot" the screenplay is ("hot" meaning that there is more than one buyer out there when it is sent out).

In short, no matter how good the deal is, once the deal is made, most writers accept the fact that they will have to walk away from their material, just as in the days of the old Hollywood.

A WORK-MADE-FOR-HIRE

The studios' attitude toward writers derives, in part, from the fact that Hollywood is a *business*. When studios and producers pay writers to write, they own the writers' script(s). The notion that the writer is an artist, while recognized, has little or no bearing on the writer's legal relationship to her work.

Under the 1976 Copyright Act, a "commissioned work," meaning that the writer is paid to write something (as distinguished from being paid for an already existing piece of material such as a spec script), is called a "work-made-for-hire." A work-made-for-hire is, specifically, material prepared within the scope of an employment relationship or "work specially ordered or commissioned for use as a contribution to a collective work, as part of a motion picture or other audiovisual work" (17 U.S.C. §101 [1976]). You will actually see this language in your employment agreements. All writing assignments are works-made-for-hire. And what that means essentially is that the written material belongs to the studio or employer. It works that way because, under the Copyright Act, the employer, by paying for the material to be written, *owns* that material. "In the case of a work-made-for-hire, the employer or other person for whom the work was prepared is considered the author . . . and, unless the parties have expressly agreed otherwise in a written instrument signed by them, owns all of the rights comprised in the copyright" (17 U.S.C. §201). Here is a sample "work-for-hire" provision from a studio contract:

Results and Proceeds

Artist acknowledges that all of the results and proceeds of Artist's services hereunder are and will be created by Artist as a "work-made-for-hire" and/or a work specially ordered or commissioned by Studio *for use as a part of a contribution to a collective work, as part of a motion picture or other audiovisual work, with Studio being deemed the sole author of all such results and proceeds.* Artist acknowledges that Studio is and shall be the sole and exclusive owner of all rights of every kind and nature in, to, and with respect to Artist's services hereunder and the results and proceeds thereof and that Studio shall have the right to use, refrain from using, change, modify, add to, subtract from, and to exploit, advertise, exhibit, and otherwise turn to account any or all of the foregoing in any manner and in any and all media (including, without limitation, in and in connection with theatrical and nontheatrical motion pictures [including, without limitation, *remakes and sequels*], all forms of television, radio, legitimate stage, videodiscs, videocassettes and all other home video devices, phonograph recordings, publications and merchandising), whether now known or hereafter devised, throughout the world, in perpetuity, in all languages, as Studio in its sole discretion shall determine.

Since the studio owns all material from the start, studio executives believe in the philosophy that they can do anything they want with the material, subject, of course, to the terms of the writer's contract. While I have many problems with the prevalent Hollywood attitude toward writers as disposable manpower, I cannot in good conscience put all the blame on the Hollywood financiers. The choice of words contained in our copyright law emphasizes the disposable role of the writer. The employer is not treated *as if it is* the author, but *is considered to be* the author. This language certainly did not help writers! By treating the employers—the studios—as *authors*, our own laws have helped to reinforce the philosophy that the employed writer can be forgotten. He is not even the *author* of his own work. The choice of words was, to say the least, unfortunate. Designed to give the employer the same ownership rights that the nonemployee writer has, it does more. By adding credence to the mentality that an employed writer is just a hired hand, it takes away much of the respect that he may have had as an author and serves to justify the studio attitude.

FILM IS A DIRECTOR'S MEDIUM

The other factor that contributes to the placement of writers at the bottom of the Hollywood hierarchy is the utmost respect given to directors. You have probably heard the expression that film is a "director's medium." Studios clearly validate and promote the notion that directors are the stars (aside from the cast).

For one, star directors tend to be paid much more than star writers and star producers. The minimum for a star director today is $1.5–$2 million, and that is low. I have a director client who was just offered $6 million for his next film. Few writers have ever been paid that much.

In addition, directors customarily receive profits in the form of "adjusted gross," as compared to the writer's "net profits." "Adjusted gross" is much better and, indeed, there is a major financial difference between adjusted gross and net profits (see discussion in chapter 6).

That is not to say that writers never receive adjusted gross, but it is extremely rare, and some studios categorically refuse to give writers adjusted gross, even if the writer's last script was turned into a movie that generated more than $100 million at the box office. The studio prefers to reward a successful writer in other ways, so as not to destroy the precedent in Hollywood that star writers are lower on the totem pole than star actors and star directors. For example, the studio may hire a successful writer as a "producer" (in name) and give that writer a piece of the adjusted gross for the writer's so-called services as a "producer." This is a clever fiction—designed almost solely to deal with the precedent problem.

Always keep in mind that the director is considered the visionary in Hollywood, the person whom the studio is ultimately banking on to shoot the film, cut it, and complete it. While it is true that directors are replaced, the studio attitude at the outset is that the director will be on the picture until delivery of the director's cut. If anyone is going to be replaced, based on a disagreement between director and writer, invariably it will be the writer. It is built into the system, and as long as a particular director is on the project, the studio will bow to the director's wishes when it comes to the choice of which writer stays or goes.

When a director is replaced, however, it sometimes helps the original writer of a screenplay. During the process of developing a screenplay, directors come on board and are sometimes replaced. Many a director has been unable to "lick" a script—take it to the point where she feels comfortable directing it, notwithstanding his desire initially to get involved with the project. A new director may very well choose to go back to the original screenwriter. *The Verdict* was one such example. David Mamet was the original writer. At one time, Robert Redford was set to star; James Bridges to direct. They chose a different writer, then abandoned the project. When Sidney Lumet came on board, he went back to Mamet's original screenplay. *War Games* had a similar history. The writers of these screenplays were lucky survivors of the system.

As you read this book, you will undoubtedly come across customary provisions for writers which seem outrageous. You will say, "How can they do that?!" Always remember the historical place of the screenwriter in Hollywood. It will help you to comprehend what might otherwise seem illogical or unfair. It also helps to remember that the film industry is a big business. And thank God it is. As films get more and more expensive to make, we need the conglomerate media companies to continue financing them. In short, do not bite the hand that feeds you. Understand the system, accept it, and you can be a success within it. Whine about it and you will be labeled as a whiner. That is not an attractive posture. Of course, changes can and will be made within the system. But the system is the system. It is unlikely to change overall. Your negotiations should be about getting the best there is to offer within that system, not changing it.

2

Contracts:
A Brief Overview

The working writer needs to be knowledgeable about two kinds of contracts—"employment agreements" (when you are hired) and "literary acquisition" or "option agreements" (when you grant someone else the rights to one of your existing works). Of course, many screenwriter agreements may combine the two, but I want to make sure you understand the particulars of each type of agreement. Then we will examine the combination agreements. Always remember that negotiation of these agreements is about leverage, and leverage for the screenwriter, even the best, is limited by the attitude I identified in chapter 1.

If you are a Writers Guild member, you will be entitled to certain valuable protections accorded by the Writers Guild Basic Agreement (sometimes referred to as the "MBA," the "Minimum Basic Agreement," or the "WGA Agreement"). Many of the provisions I cover in this book are automatically accorded to you because you are a member.

However, the Guild protections are minimum protections and writers are often able to obtain better terms by negotiation and by contract. If you are a beginning writer, you will have the most leverage when someone approaches you about a script that you have written. Remember: You do not *have* to sell it unless you are comfortable with the deal. The same holds true if you are a seasoned writer. If you have something that someone else wants, you can hold out for the best deal. If not, you may have to take whatever is offered.

As mentioned in chapter 1, an existing script that is sold or optioned (not a "work-made-for-hire") is called a "spec script." The "spec script" comes by its name because the writer has written it with only a speculation that someone might buy it. From time to time, studios pay high prices for what they believe is a hot property. In such instances, studios bid against each other and the writer may walk away with over $1 million in cash and a promising deal. The *Sixth Sense* is one such example. I represented the writer of that script (he is also the director) and the process was very exciting. The deal was closed very quickly. The package, including purchase price, bonuses, and fees totaled several million dollars. The film went into production within one year after the sale. Such a sale is a writer's dream.

The spec script market today is more limited than it was several years ago because studios realized that a huge outlay of cash did not necessarily ensure a hit. Today, the studios are all on a budget kick. That is not to say that scripts are not purchased outright, but don't count on it.

To begin with, there is a lot of competition. Agents, readers, and executives spend mornings, evenings, and weekends reading and pouring over new submissions. To put this business in perspective for you, an agent friend of mine at a large major agency told me that he had spent the weekend with his favorite relative. He had not seen her in a long time and he wanted to carve out as much time as possible over the weekend to spend with her. She was old. He also had to deal with his normal workload. "I obviously couldn't get all my weekend work done," he said to me, "but I did spend ten hours reading." I said, "You must have read a lot of scripts." "Scripts?" He shook his head. "I spent ten hours reading *coverage*." "Coverage" in Hollywood terms is a reader's short summary of a screenplay (usually a couple of pages) with a rec-ommendation at the end: Read, Pass, Consider. Ten hours spent read-ing coverage means coverage of at least two hundred scripts, probably more. In short, there is a lot out there. If someone wants to *buy* your script, consider yourself lucky. All in all, the percentage of spec script sales compared to the number of screenplays offered for sale in a given year is low.

More likely, if you have written a spec script, it will be optioned. The next chapter explains in detail the basic provisions of what is commonly called the "Option/Purchase Agreement."

3

Option/Purchase Agreements: Negotiating the Price

N ow I want you to sit back, relax, and pretend that your agent and lawyer are about to begin discussions. The main concept to grasp is that your script is an asset—a bundle of various rights. Naturally, the buyer's goal is to obtain as many of those rights as he can get, for as little money as possible.

Because of the competition and the reluctance to spend huge sums of money, studios and producers usually take an option on spec scripts. The option literally gives the buyer the option to purchase the material at a later date for a specific price. This agreement is called an "option/purchase agreement."

The option price is the price the producer pays to gain exclusive control of a certain piece of material. That option will be for a certain period; when the period expires, the producer must "exercise" his option (acquire the rights—see discussion in chapter 4 on Transfer of Rights) or lose his right to buy rights in that material. The price paid for the material is usually called the "purchase price." The option agreement stipulates certain requirements for exercise of the option. Usually there is a requirement of notice to the owner and payment of a set purchase price established at the time the option/purchase agreement is negotiated. Note that the purchase price is generally paid at the time of exercise (the end of the option period) but sometimes the purchase price is paid at other times (see discussion in chapter 4).

Options may be for any length of time. The standard option is for one year, and often there are renewal or extension periods. It takes a long time to get a movie made. Studios want the time to develop the script and to bring the right director and stars on board. Thus, they will insist on at least one additional year, sometimes more.

MAJOR STUDIOS

Option prices are very low in comparison to purchase prices. There is no rule. A standard option payment for a feature film from a major studio is $10,000–$25,000 for one year—sometimes more, sometimes less.

You should be aware that studio producers also receive very little money during the development period. Contrary to what you might think, they usually receive less money than the writer during this period. While it is true that many producers of studio pictures receive high salaries if a picture gets made, they do not get these salaries if the project does not get made. The customary studio producer development fee (the producer's salary during the development stage before the picture is shot) is $25,000. This salary is paid only at the point when the project is set up with a financier *and* the first writer begins to render services. If the first writer to be hired cannot start working for six months, the producer does not get paid for six months. Half of the development fee is payable on commencement of the writer's services and half when the studio decides to either abandon the project or produce it.

Remember: Producers have to live on that money until a project is "greenlighted" (the Hollywood expression for the point when the studio decides to finance the movie). This could be many years away. In short, until the studio decides to make a project, you and the producer are in the same boat. The option is going to be low and the salary of the producer is low. And you will probably receive some sort of writing fee on top of the option payment (see discussion in chapter 4).

Independent Producers

When an independent producer options a script, he usually pays a much lower option fee than the studio does—customarily, $2,500–$5,000 for one year. The independent producer's argument, and it is a fair one, is that his most valuable contribution is the effort to get the studio interested in the project and to get the picture made. If you agree to give an independent producer an option for little money, however, you should protect yourself with what is called a "set up bonus." Your best argument when dealing with an independent producer who will only give you a low option fee is to say: "Okay, if I accept your low offer and I believe you will get the picture made, then I want another payment when you do set it up at a studio. Say, another $10,000." This is quite customary. Studios will accept it and you should insist on it. You will be paid your set up bonus when the producer sets the project up at the studio. Legally, this may be when he makes the deal with the studio or, more commonly, when he *signs* the deal with the studio. This is negotiable. Each studio has its own policy in that regard.

Application against the Purchase Price

Another main area of bargaining with respect to option payments is whether the option payment is applicable against the purchase price or not. Thus, for example, if the option price for the first year is $5,000, the purchase price for the script is $200,000, and the $5,000 option payment is applicable against the purchase price, you would receive $195,000 at the time of purchase. Generally, the first option payment for the first option period is applicable. Subsequent payments are not. Of course, it is all negotiable. The set up bonus may also be applicable or nonapplicable. The payment of the set up bonus might also extend the option.

Example: The producer has a one-year option for $5,000, renewable for a second year for $5,000, and renewable again for a third year for

$10,000. (Keep in mind that the longer the producer wants to hold onto the material, the better your position is to raise the option payment in the later option years.) The purchase price is $200,000. The first option payment is applicable against the purchase price, the second and third payments are not applicable against the purchase price. There is a set up bonus of $10,000, which extends the option until the date that is one year past the set up date (the date on which you are to receive the set up bonus), but the set up bonus is not applicable against the purchase price. Let's say the option begins on January 1, 2004, and the producer sets up the project on June 6, 2004. You will receive $5,000 on January 1, 2004. You will receive $10,000 on June 6, 2004. The initial option period would have expired on December 31, 2004, if it had not been set up. With the set up fee extension, the first option period expires on June 5, 2005. The option may be extended two more times according to the contract. You will receive another $5,000 before June 6, 2005, and $10,000 before June 6, 2006. The option expires on June 5, 2007. If the script is purchased, how much will you receive? Since the only applicable payment is the first one, you will receive $195,000 at the time of purchase. You will have received in this example a total of $5,000 (first option payment) + $10,000 (set up bonus) + $5,000 (second option payment) + $10,000 (third option payment) + $195,000 (purchase price) for a total of $225,000.

FREE OPTIONS

Sometimes producers look for a free option. Most writers believe that if the producer is really committed, the producer should put his money where his mouth is. Something, at least.

I have found, generally, that producers who ask for a free option do not get the picture made any faster than those who pay. Producers are generally juggling many projects. They have to. And just because it is free does not mean they will give it any more attention. In fact, they may give it less attention because they have not spent any money on it (other than legal fees, of course, to draft the option, which, depending on the length of the negotiation, may be costly).

My attitude is that you probably should not give anyone a free ride, unless the producer has a tremendous track record, is a good friend, or you have no other offers. The option is worth something. You are taking the script *off* the market for the option period (and it will probably be shown and *covered* everywhere, possibly destroying its future value). No other producer can touch it. Producers are in business—remember, it *is* a business—and they should treat the transaction that way. They will buy a refrigerator for their house—they should pay for your material. Also keep in mind that if you use a lawyer, you will be out of pocket unless you use a percentage lawyer—a lawyer who receives a percentage of what you receive. If you do not use a percentage lawyer, it will cost you money to negotiate the deal at the time you negotiate it.

Also note in chapter 15, below, if the producer is a signatory to one writer's guild, he is not allowed to exclusively option material for free.

TELEVISION OPTIONS

Television options are usually much lower than feature options and there is a reason for this. Producers who option projects for television, and features for that matter, generally expect the network or studio to reimburse them for option payments when they set up the project at the network or studio. The networks keep option reimbursement payments low, $1,500–$2,500 for six months to one year. Studios, on the other hand, will generally reimburse the full cost of an option for a feature, within reason, and do not impose artificial ceilings. If the producer of a television project has already paid you a $5,000 option, the networks do not care. The producer may have to eat it. That does not mean you cannot fight for a higher price. Try.

TV-movie producers, known as "supplier producers," own the right to exploit their movies after the initial network order, which is generally two runs. They earn a lot if the picture is made, sometimes up to $750,000–$1 million, if you include all sales of the picture over the years. They can earn that much because, until recently, the networks (unlike the studios for features) have been prohibited from owning most of the products they put on the air. The general rule, however, is that most producers will not go out of pocket and, if they do, option prices in TV are rarely over $5,000.

TIME

Your other major bargaining point with respect to options is time. If the producer is only going to pay you $1,500, then make it a short option (six months instead of the customary one-year period). That is enough time for a producer to cover the networks and/or the studios and to find out if there is any interest. If he cannot set it up in six months, then you should get your project back.

NON-NEGOTIATED OPTION EXTENSIONS

Most option contracts give the purchaser the right to extend the option under certain unusual circumstances for no additional compensation.

Force Majeure Events

The option may be extended for a "force majeure event." A force majeure event is usually defined as "an act of God, war, a labor strike which affects (shuts down) the motion picture, television, and theatrical industry." More specifically, a force majeure event is an event beyond the studio's control, such as a writers' strike. (Arguably, however, a writers' strike could be viewed as within the control of the studio: If the studio would only give in to the applicable demands, there wouldn't be a strike. Studios, of course, do not look at it that way!). From the studio's perspective, if there's a writer's strike, studio executives cannot develop your script. So they get an automatic extension.

Your representative should try to make sure that the contract stipulates that the force majeure event has to be one that directly affects the development of your project. A hurricane in Florida is a force majeure event, but if it doesn't affect your project, why should the studio get an extension?

You can also ask for a limit on the amount of time for such extensions. Some studios will agree to six months (in some cases, one year), in the aggregate, for any and all force majeure extensions during the option period.

Your representative should also ensure that, even though such extensions are automatic, the studio will notify you in writing of the extension, so that you can keep track of the option period.

Claims

Studio contracts also provide that if there is a claim made against your script, the studio gets an extension. Suppose another writer claims that you have stolen her material? Suppose someone else claims that he has rights in your script? Studios usually will not put a cap on these extensions. Claims such as these put the whole project in jeopardy. They are treated very seriously.

In fact, a standard clause states that if there is a claim, you will have to repay all the money you have received. Generally, I am able to get this provision deleted. The studio always has the right to prove that you did steal someone's material and, if you did, then you will have to pay damages. The concept of automatic repayment is an insulting one. There may be several bad eggs in Hollywood, but the presumption should not be that you have stolen someone else's material just because someone has made a claim. In a highly visible and lucrative business, there will always be people making claims to see if they can get something out of it. These are called "nuisance suits."

SHOPPING BEHIND YOUR BACK

Unfortunately, some producers may express interest in a script, drag out the negotiations, and, in the meantime, shop your script to the major buyers (that is, the studios). If all the studios pass on it, the negotiations fall apart and you are left with a script that may become worthless.

As I mentioned above, scripts are "covered," particularly by the buyers. A reader reads the script and makes a recommendation. If it is a pass, the whole episode is recorded in the studio's ledger. If the script is resubmitted, the studio simply looks at its records and gives the same response. Some writers change the name of the project or their names when resubmitting a script. This usually doesn't work. Records are such that someone at the studio will probably be able to find or remember the coverage of the earlier submission before the script is actually read by an executive, so don't count on this route to get a second chance. Once it is a pass, most studios will not take a second look at a script unless the project is resubmitted with a major "element" (star or director) signed on.

The Writers Guild recently added a provision prohibiting the submission of scripts without an option/purchase agreement in place or without specific permission. Article 49 of the Guild Agreement provides:

A. TELEVISION

Company may not shop literary material to a third party or parties without first obtaining in a separate written document the writer's consent that the literary material may be shopped to the designated third party or parties.

B. THEATRICAL

The Company may not shop literary material to a third party or parties if the writer requests, in writing, that the material not be shopped. If the writer requests, in writing, that the script be shopped only to designated third parties, Company will not shop to any other third party.

If the Company shops any literary material to any third party or parties in violation of the above provisions, it shall pay to the Guild for the benefit of the writer involved the sum of seven hundred fifty dollars ($750.00) for each person or company to whom the literary material has been shopped in violation of the above provisions.

"Shopping" is defined to mean submitting the literary material to a third party or parties and specifically does not include submitting the material to individuals within the Company. If the Company has an option to acquire motion picture or television rights in literary material, or has acquired motion picture or television rights in literary material, the Company may submit such literary material to any third party or parties without restriction or penalty, except as may be otherwise provided in the agreement granting such option or rights.

As a result of this provision, to a certain extent, this behavior has been arrested, but most writers do not want to take on the producer—even if the project has been shopped—for fear that the producer will close doors to their other projects. This is a reality, alas, and relationships are important. The old saying, "Don't burn your bridges," is very pertinent in contemporary Hollywood. With fewer buyers nowadays, writers are often unwilling to take on major producers, and this is a factor that must be considered.

4

Option/Purchase Agreements: Negotiable Rights

If you have written a screenplay (other than as an employee-for-hire or on a commissioned basis), you hold the copyright in that screenplay. The most important point to keep in mind is that your screenplay, by virtue of your copyright, comprises many rights. The Copyright Act of 1976 provides the copyright holder with five different categories of exclusive rights in a copyrighted work. These are the rights of reproduction, adaptation, public distribution, public performance, and public display (17 U.S.C. 106 [1976]).

The *reproduction* right allows the copyright holder (or the person or entity to whom the copyright owner has licensed or sold her rights) to make copies. The *adaptation* right allows the holder to prepare a new or derivative work based on the copyrighted work, such as a motion picture based on a play, a new screenplay based on an existing screenplay, a sequel motion picture, television series, and so on. The *public distribution* right allows a work to be sold or rented, such as a book or a videocassette. The *performance* right allows the copyright holder to have her work performed publicly, as when a play is staged or a motion picture is screened for an audience. The right to *public display* of the copyrighted work applies to the individual frames of a motion picture, such as a still photograph. The photograph is not being performed—yet it would still be entitled to copyright protection as a form of display.

COPYRIGHT: DIVISIBLE BY LAW

A copyright is divisible under the copyright law. Not only can it be broken down into the rights noted above, but it can also be divided by medium. Thus, you can convey motion picture rights in your screenplay and the copyright in the motion picture rights, yet retain live stage rights and the copyright therein. Or you can convey television rights and retain publishing rights. There are numerous commutations and permutations.

This concept is a newer addition to copyright law. The older Copyright Act of 1909 referred to a single copyright (17 U.S.C. 10 [1909 Act]), which belonged to the author of a work. The 1909 Act addressed only a single copyright proprietor. While different rights could be *licensed* to different parties (not *granted* to different parties, as they are today), there were certain limitations. Most prominent among these limitations was the inability to sue for copyright infringement, because this right belonged only to the original copyright proprietor or someone to whom the copyright proprietor had assigned all his rights (M. Nimmer, *Nimmer on Copyright*, §10.01[A], Volume 3, 1992).

Today, the right to sue for infringement is one of the most important rights to be conveyed under copyright law. A motion picture studio must have the right to sue in its name for infringement of its motion picture's copyright. A motion picture is a valuable asset (now costing sometimes in excess of $100 million dollars), and it must be protected.

Under the current Copyright Act of 1976, the previous doctrine that copyright was indivisible has largely been abolished. Section 201(d)(2) of the 1976 Copyright Act provides an explicit statutory recognition of the principle of divisibility of copyright. "Any of the exclusive rights comprised in a copyright, including *any* subdivision of any of the rights specified in Section 106, may be transferred . . . and owned separately. The owner of any particular exclusive right is

entitled, to the extent of that right, to all of the protection and remedies accorded to the copyright owner by this 'title" (17 U.S.C.
§201(d)(2) [1976]). The term *transfer* is interpreted broadly. Thus, a
hardcover trade book edition may have its own copyright and the
transfer might be limited to a particular time and geographic location
(M. Nimmer, *Nimmer on Copyright*, §10.02[A], Volume 3, 1992).

RIGHTS GENERALLY GRANTED

The rights you sell are the rights *granted*. The rights you retain are the
reserved rights. A big part of the negotiation process involves which
rights you will hold on to as reserved rights. Your ability to reserve rights
is always limited. Producers—and particularly studios—like to acquire
and retain all rights, exclusively. Very rarely is a deal made for a one-pic-
ture license. Many successful motion pictures have generated sequels (*Die
Hard, Lethal Weapon, The Fast and the Furious*). Many have actually been
developed into franchises (*Friday the 13th, Nightmare on Elm Street, Terminator*).
Thus, inevitably, sequel rights must be given away. The studio's argument
is that it invests large sums to launch the first picture. Studios want the
right to participate in other productions. Remake rights are treated the
same way. Their argument is logical, but keep in mind that you are also
entitled to additional compensation for these uses. That is the subject of
a different chapter. For now, I want you to understand the studio mentality and the essential rights you must convey in any studio deal.

To help you understand these essential rights, it is useful to read the
granted rights section of any long-form studio contract. Here is an
example:

> The rights (granted) shall include, without limitation, the following
> rights:
> 1) The right to produce motion pictures or other productions
>   based upon or adapted from all or any part of the screenplay.
> 2) The right to produce sound records. [*The studio always
>   wants the ability to make money from a tie-in sound recording.*]
> 3) The right to adapt, use, dramatize, arrange, change, vary,
>   modify, alter the screenplay and any parts thereof; to add
>   to, subtract from, or omit from the screenplay, characters,

language, plot, theme, scenes, incidents, situations, action, titles, dialogue, songs, music and lyrics [*this right to make changes is at the heart of the screenplay contract—derived from the prevailing attitude toward screenwriters, as discussed above*], to include in motion pictures, sound records, and other items, such language, speech, song music, lyrics, plot, sound, sound effects, action, situations, scenes, plot dialogue, incidents and characters, characterization, and other material as Purchaser in its uncontrolled discretion may deem advisable; it being the intention hereof that Purchaser shall have the exclusive, absolute and unlimited right to use the screenplay and each and every part thereof for motion picture purposes in any manner it may, in its uncontrolled discretion, deem advisable with the same force and effect as though Purchaser were the sole author of the screenplay, specifically including, without limitation, the right to produce motion pictures as sequels, series, serials, or otherwise. [*As you can see, the studios do not mince words—they want it all.*]

4) The right to broadcast the screenplay by radio and television or otherwise.

5) The right, for the purpose of advertising and exploiting motion pictures produced hereunder, to produce and publish stories, synopses, excerpts, summaries, fictionalizations, and novelizations.

6) The right to write and prepare screenplays, teleplays, treatments, storyboards, and musical compositions.

7) The right to manufacture, sell, distribute products, byproducts, services, facilities, merchandise, and commodities of any nature and description, including, but not limited to, still photographs, drawings, posters, artwork, toys, games, items of wearing apparel, foods, beverages, and similar items which make referral to or are based on the screenplay or any part thereof and the right to make trade deals and commercial tie-ins of all kinds. [*Again, the studio wants to be able to exploit the picture and recoup its substantial investment in many ways. Batman, for instance, generated millions in merchandising sales.*]

8) The right to copyright motion pictures, sound records, musical compositions, screenplays, teleplays, and all other items contained in the rights granted section, together with the right to manufacture copies thereof and to distribute, sell, vend, lease, license, exhibit, transmit, broadcast, project, reproduce, publish, use, perform, advertise, publicize, market, exploit, turn to account, and derive revenue in any form or manner therefrom, without any territorial restriction whatsoever by any and all means, methods, systems, and processes now or hereafter known.

9) The right to use the title by which the screenplay is now known and the right to use any other title as producer may deem proper in its uncontrolled discretion.

10) All rights of every kind and character whatsoever not specifically reserved to owner. [*This catch-all almost always goes to the buyer. The buyer wants you to spell out exactly what you are reserving. Simply put, the studio wants to know that if something is left out, they get it, not you.*]

RESERVED RIGHTS

The rights that are typically reserved by the writer of a spec screenplay or book (if you are hired to write, there are usually no reserved rights) are stage rights, live television rights (a holdback from the 1950s—there is virtually no live television today, but it is still a common reserved right), and radio rights.

Some screenwriters are able to reserve novelization rights, and, as you will see in the discussion below, even if they are not reserved, the writer may end up with these rights anyway. Of course, the author of a book always reserves publishing rights. Some screenwriters are also able to reserve the right to publish their own screenplay. Generally, the studio will allow this only if the screenwriter is the only writer on the project. The reason: The movie may be very different than the writer's spec script. If the movie fails, the studio does not want to be embarrassed by having some critic point out that the original screenplay was better. I was recently involved in a negotiation concerning this issue, and, believe it or not, the studio actually articulated the reason!

Book authors also reserve the right to create what are called author-written sequels, that is, a sequel or prequel book (a prequel consists of events that took place before the events in the book that is being sold). Here is an example of a typical reserved rights provision:

RESERVED RIGHTS: The following rights are reserved to Owner, including the copyright therein, exclusively for Owner's use and disposition, subject, however, to the provisions of this agreement:

(a) Publication Rights: The right to publish and distribute printed versions of the Work owned or controlled by Owner in book and play form, including photonovels, comic books, microfilm, microfiche, computer database, whether hardcover or softcover and in magazines or other periodicals, whether in installments or otherwise (subject to Purchaser's 7,500-word publication rights and ten (10) minute excerpt rights for advertising and promotional purposes). Such publications by Owner may be copyrighted in the name of Owner.

In no event, however, shall such publisher have the right to use the title of a motion picture produced hereunder (if different from the title heretofore used for publications of the Work) or any still photographs, artwork, trademarks, logos or substantial literary material owned or controlled by Purchaser without Owner negotiating for said rights and Purchaser's specific written approval, which such approval shall not be unreasonably withheld.

(b) Radio rights (subject to advertising and promotion rights granted to Purchaser);

(c) Live television (subject to advertising and promotion rights granted to Purchaser);

(d) Legitimate dramatic stage rights, including cast album rights and merchandising rights in connection with such stage productions only, provided nothing contained herein shall in any way limit Purchaser's album or soundtrack rights and/or merchandising rights in connection with the Rights granted hereunder and Owner shall not be entitled to use any of Purchaser's material with respect to said rights;

The stage rights reserved by Owner hereunder do not include (and Owner shall not have) the right to authorize or permit the transmission or projection, dramatization, or adaptation of the Work by means of television, disc, cartridge, cassette, computer, satellite, or any process analogous thereto for the purpose of exhibition or reproduction at any theater or place of public assembly, or for exhibition or reproduction in private homes, theaters, or elsewhere where any viewing fee or charge is imposed or collected as consideration from the persons observing such transmission or projection, whether paid directly or indirectly by means of cash, tokens, credit, or any other manner now known or hereafter devised;

(e) All rights in Owner-written sequels (includes prequels). All references in this subparagraph to "Owner" shall be deemed to include any author of an Owner-written sequel who writes such material under authority of Owner or Owner's successor in interest.

If you are at an impasse with the studio concerning reserved rights, then there is another alternative: to "freeze" certain rights. That means that the studio cannot do anything without you, and you cannot do anything without the studio. You and the studio will negotiate a deal if there is interest at a later date in something involving these rights. Since the primary goal is to get a movie made, there is logic in the argument that you can worry about these rights at a later time.

Novelization and Publication Rights

It was common in the 1970s for studios to market novelizations of their movies. Writers fought to retain novelization rights and, depending on their leverage and their ability to write a novelization, often won what was considered in those days a valuable right. Today, the novelization market is practically dead, but, again, tradition allows certain writers to reserve this right.

Even if you are not successful in reserving novelization rights, if you are a member of the Writers Guild, under certain conditions you are automatically given the first opportunity to go out and obtain a book deal based on your screenplay. This right is yours, even if you are *commissioned* to write the screenplay. The main conditions are that you must have *created* the material that is turned into a movie and that the actual screenplay for the picture cannot be so different from your original material as to have a substantially different plot or different characters (under the WGA Agreement, this essentially means that you are entitled to "separated rights"). If you meet these criteria, you are then given a window of time in which to sign a book deal. That window is very short—thirty days after studio executives notify you that they want to make such a deal. However, if you are successful in obtaining a novelization deal within this time period, you are allowed to retain the major share of the book revenues—they are split 75 percent/25 percent in your favor. If you are unsuccessful, then the Guild still protects your interests. If the studio makes a novelization deal, the book revenues are shared 65 percent/35 percent in the studio's favor and you are accorded a $3,500 advance against your share. What is important is that, under this arrangement, you will receive a separate payment for these rights. The revenues are not part of the net profit definition, which, as you will see below, is basically meaningless.

I generally try to improve these numbers as follows: If you make the book deal but do not write the book, 50 percent/50 percent. If the studio makes the deal and you write the book, 65 percent/35 percent in *your* favor. If the studio makes the deal but you do not write the book, 50 percent/50 percent. I also try to improve on the period granted to the writer to make a deal. Instead of thirty days, I ask for sixty to ninety days.

Even if you are not a member of the Writers Guild, you can still ask for the same provisions. In fact, I generally try to have the producer treat my non-Guild clients as if they were members of the Guild. That way, all the benefits of the Writers Guild Basic Agreement, including provisions such as these and payment of residuals and other perks, may be integrated into the deal.

If you are successful in reserving the novelization or other publishing rights, you must make sure that you obtain the right to use the artwork from the movie and the title of the movie, if it is different than your original title. In other words, you should be able to duplicate the ads and poster logos so that the tie-in with the movie is clear. Basically, a novelization is a promotional tie-in, just like a T-shirt or soundtrack album. And that is why studio executives argue that the studio is entitled to a share of the proceeds for the use of the artwork, title, and logo of the movie, and why the studio usually gets it.

Sometimes you can even obtain the right to publish stills from the movie in the novelization. This can be a sticky point, and studios are reluctant to give it away, even when they are getting a share. If you are stuck on this point, pass on it in favor of getting the right to use the logo, artwork, and title. You must have those.

When you are selling a book that you have written, of course, you must insist on reserving all publication rights, including the right to continue to sell your book and the right to write novelizations or any other publications springing from a movie production of your book. You do not want any competing books in the marketplace that could cut into the sale of your already existing book. Assuming your book has been published, it is *you* who established a recognition of the material in the book world. Since the studio is interested in your material based on your success in that medium, you should reap all the rewards of *that medium*. The right to use the title and logo for free is sometimes hard to get, but it is worth trying. Studios do recognize the merits of the argument that they should not share in the proceeds of a book if they have purchased a successful book to begin with, but more often than not they want their piece, too, based on the added value that a motion picture will bring to the book. Their argument is not without merit.

If you have written a book, you also want to protect all other forms of publication rights, such as photonovels, comic books, microfilm and microfiche rights, and computer database rights, including electronic publishing rights.

Note that if your book is actually made into a movie, even if you do reserve electronic publishing rights, the studio will not allow you to use portions of the movie. Invariably, you will have to negotiate with the studio to obtain such rights and, of course, the studio will want its share.

Finally, if you are selling a book, you will want to reserve the rights for books on tape. This medium has emerged as a viable marketplace. I always ask to spell out these rights separately. It is a hybrid form of media combining audio rights and publication, but it does not really fit neatly under either category.

No matter how strong your bargaining power is, the one thing you must give the studio if you are successful in reserving publication rights is the ability to publish excerpts of your material for advertising and promotional purposes. This is important. The advertising and marketing departments need some flexibility, including the right to quote different passages from your work. Generally, 7,500-word excerpt rights are acceptable, although now the trend is toward 10,000-word excerpt rights. Of course, if your material is only a short story, the excerpt rights should be considerably less. In that case, you might limit the excerpt privilege to a percentage of the total work—say 5 percent to 10 percent.

Merchandising Rights

Merchandising rights may be extremely profitable. *Jurassic Park* merchandising is one such example. The typical studio "net profits" definition, however, usually includes only a small amount of the revenues actually received by the studio from the exploitation of these rights. Studios do not like to give away any merchandising profits separate and apart from their net profits definition. Still, there are exceptions and, sometimes, the studio is forced to account separately to the original author for merchandising revenues. This separate accounting is sometimes referred to as a "separate revenue stream." In such cases, either the work has been merchandised already, or it has the enormous and obvious potential to launch a very profitable merchandising business, such as *Star Wars* or *E.T.*

For instance, if you are selling motion picture and television rights to a comic book character that has already been established in the marketplace, you have a lot of leverage. Studio representatives will still argue that the motion picture they are going to produce will increase the merchandising potential and they want their piece. I do not know of any instances in which a studio is willing to walk away from some share of the merchandising business.

Such negotiations are usually very difficult and take months. I have resolved several very difficult negotiations with the following formula: First, we establish a baseline level of merchandising revenues that existed before the studio bought any rights. That amount should *always* belong to the original creator. Studio executives certainly cannot argue that they are adding to an already existing market. The studio then will participate in all revenues *after* that level has been reached for a certain period of time, linked to the release of the picture—usually at least thirty-six months, starting six months prior to release of the picture. As an example, if *Batman* merchandising grossed $1 million annually for the three years preceding release of the picture and grossed $3 million annually after release of the picture, the studio would share in the additional $2 million per year on merchandising and characters already created prior to the production of the movie during the time period that the studio is entitled to share in such revenues. Any merchandising based solely on the movie—such as any new characters created for the movie—will usually belong solely to the studio and those revenues are included in the "net profit" pool, although sometimes the writer is able to get a separate piece of this merchandising as well. It is all negotiable.

The other big issue is who is actually going to do the merchandising. If the comic book character is already being produced and merchandised, doesn't it make sense to have the same manufacturer merchandise the character for the movie? That is usually not a factor. Studios always want control and will usually demand that the movie merchandising be arranged by the studio. Studio executives have their own relationships with merchandising companies and they prefer to work with their own people. At the very least, you should be able to continue the merchandising efforts already in place with the companies currently handling it. Any new merchandising items might be handled through the studio.

What if you have created material that you know has tremendous merchandising potential, but you have never done anything with it? In this case, it is doubtful the studio would let you reserve merchandising rights. You would be lucky to negotiate a separate merchandising royalty based solely on the merchandising revenues. Under this arrangement, if the picture was a flop but the merchandising was profitable, the losses of the picture would not influence your right to receive money. However, in many instances, if you are successful in getting a separate merchandising royalty, the royalty may not be payable until the rest of the picture costs have been recouped by the studio. Your merchandising profits will accumulate based only on merchandising revenues and costs, but they do not actually get paid out unless the picture is successful in covering its costs.

The top royalty that the studio may pay is 15 percent to 20 percent of *the studio's* merchandising profits for characters that have already been merchandised. If the merchandising has never been exploited, the royalty will generally be much less. In defining merchandising profits, keep in mind that studios usually take a 50 percent fee for their services (!) in addition to a deduction for all the merchandising costs. That fee may be justified or not. Some studios do license their own merchandising. Most use outside licensing agents. The licensing agents also take a fee on the revenue they receive—between 35 percent and 50 percent. As an example, if $1 is received by the licensing agent and the licensing agent is receiving a 50 percent fee, he will take out $.50 for his fee and his costs of $.20. Thus, $.30 would be remitted to the studio. The studio will take off $.15 (50 percent fee) and costs of, say, $.05 from the $.30. That leaves $.10. You get a piece of that. The trick is to put a cap on the combination of the licensing agent's fee and the studio's fee—maybe 65 percent. After all, only one of them is doing the real work; the other is just a middleman. This is a difficult area of negotiation, but if you have a lot of leverage, you may be successful. Note that the Writers Guild Basic Agreement provides that a writer who has created a character that is merchandised must receive some separate compensation. (However, the character must be sufficiently detailed in its description so that any merchandising efforts involving that character clearly differentiate it from any similar merchandise on the market.)

Theme Parks

No matter how great your leverage is, you probably won't be able to reserve these rights. Almost all the studios are now in the theme park business—Disney, Paramount, Warner Bros., Universal—in one way or another. By creating a ride, the studio creates another way to recoup its investment for an extremely costly motion picture. The studio certainly does not want to produce a motion picture only to see some other studio capitalize on it by opening a theme park ride. What you might ask, though, is give the studio a certain period after the movie has opened within which to build a theme park attraction. If the studio does not build an attraction within that period, then the studio would lose its *exclusive* rights, although studio executives will still want to retain the option to create an attraction at some point. The other point of negotiation is to define what constitutes building an attraction. Putting up a lemonade stand in the middle of a theme park should not. On the other hand, a significant expenditure of at least $3 million probably should.

If you have great leverage, can you get a piece of any ride or other attraction based on your material? Unfortunately, studios will not give you a percentage of ticket sales for the theme park or allocate a specific sum for each visitor to an attraction for the simple reason that such formulas are too difficult to monitor. I know of only one instance when the studio did agree to this method of accounting. All parties ultimately agreed that it was unworkable and eventually came up with a different formula: a guarantee that the studio would provide shelf space to sell the picture's merchandising, which was controlled in part by the owner of the rights. These provisions are extremely rare and would be entertained only if your property had already been successful in another medium.

Unfortunately, most studios take the position that theme park revenues are totally excluded from the "net profit" definition for a movie, and, thus, they do not have to account at all for revenues derived from the exploitation of the movie in the form of a theme park ride or the merchandising sold there. That is a reality for most writers. Barring unusual circumstances, writers have to live with the fact that they will not participate in any revenues derived from a theme park attraction based on their character(s) or story.

General Comments

Today, with the cost of producing and releasing a picture so high, studios are reluctant to allow an author to reserve any rights. They want to be able to recoup their revenues from the so-called ancillary markets. If you are a writer-for-hire, the norm is that the studio will own everything. If you wrote the script on spec, then it is possible to reserve stage, radio, and live TV rights. Novelization rights are harder if your work has never been published or you have never written a book before, but if you are a Guild member, you have certain protections in this area, and, even if you are not, you can ask for them. Reserving the right to publish the screenplay is usually acceptable (but only if you are the sole writer), as there is not much money in it. Studio executives will usually allow you to reserve the right to books on tape if you have written a book that they are purchasing.

With the cost of producing movies constantly going up, the studio's attitude toward reserved rights might change. And even though revenues are also going up, as of the end of 2003, *net* motion picture revenues were not rising significantly. Regardless, if the studio is buying a piece of your material that you have invested numerous hours in creating, then you should be entitled to reserve all heretofore customary reserved rights of authors. It's worth a fight.

HOLDBACKS

If you are successful in reserving certain rights, there are certain restrictions you must be willing to accept. If you have reserved production rights, such as stage rights, the studio will insist on a holdback of time before you are permitted to exploit your reserved rights. The rationale for the holdbacks is logical: If the studio is going to produce a picture based on your screenplay, the studio doesn't want a competing stage production to be playing at the same time. Studio representatives want their picture to be the focus. This is a legitimate concern (unless they have purchased the rights to an existing play such as *A Chorus Line*, in which case, obviously, they will not ask you to stop the run of the play). You, on the other hand, do not want to be held back forever by the studio from exploiting your reserved rights. This is also a legitimate concern. Both concerns are usually addressed. Studios customarily ask that you hold back granting stage rights for five years from release of the picture or seven years from exercise of the option, whichever is earlier. That way, if the picture is never made, you will eventually be able to exploit these rights. You can sometimes knock this down to three (or four) years from the release of the picture or five (or six) years from exercise of the option, whichever is earlier. It is negotiable. The same holdbacks usually apply to live television and radio rights.

The restrictions concerning novelization rights are different. If there is no movie, there is no novelization. And if there is a movie, the studio does not want to hold back publication of the novelization based on the movie. The studio does want to ensure, however, that you coordinate your novelization with the release of the picture. The publisher will have to agree to consult with the studio, use the studio graphics in the book, use certain language on the cover of the book (such as, "See the upcoming Warner Bros. release") and release the book in conjunction with the release of the movie.

If you are successful in reserving merchandising rights, these will also have to be coordinated with the release of the picture, even if you are already merchandising a related product.

FIRST NEGOTIATION/LAST REFUSAL/FIRST REFUSAL
Studio executives will usually insist on the right to negotiate first to purchase your reserved rights when you offer those rights for sale. They have a vested interest and they want to know that they will have the first crack. This a called a right of *first negotiation*. But the right of first negotiation is usually not enough. You might ask $1 million for the stage rights, a price they think is ridiculous. They do not want you to offer it to their competitor for $100,000, so they will ask for the right to match *any other offer*. This is called a right of *last refusal*.

Many writers feel that the right of last refusal effectively kills their ability to negotiate with anyone else. Other studios do not like to make an offer if someone can simply match it and pull the rug out from under them. While it is difficult to get around this, sometimes, again depending on how much leverage you have, you might be able to limit the studio's right to what some people call a right of *first refusal*.

Keep in mind that there are many definitions of first refusal floating around, and, thus, the meaning should be carefully delineated in any negotiation. (Sometimes studios define the "last refusal" discussed above as a "first refusal.") Here is usually what is meant by it: You offer your stage rights to Warner Bros. for $1 million and they counter with $500,000. You cannot then sell it to another studio for less than $500,000. If Columbia offers you $400,000, you have to go back to Warner Bros. and give them the right to match the offer. If someone offers you $550,000, on the other hand, you can sell it. In that scenario Warner Bros. goofed. They miscalculated the value of the rights, thinking that no one else would make a higher offer.

Today, it is very difficult to get any studio to accept a first refusal right. However, sometimes they will accept a first refusal right with some room for error. No matter how sophisticated the studio is, it is hard to predict exactly what price a literary property will command in the marketplace. Thus, studios will ask for the right to match any other offer, provided no one offers more than, say, 20 percent or 25 percent above their price. If an offer is made above that level, then the writer is free to take it. The studio was sufficiently off in its guess and loses its right. This provision is also difficult to get, but the argument does have some sound logic behind it, and it is always worth a try.

There is one other variation on last refusal and first refusal rights: The studio gets to match any other offer, but it has to pay 5 percent or 10 percent over that other offer. In other words, the studio has to pay a premium for this right.

Here is an example of a first negotiation/last refusal provision with a holdback:

First Negotiation/Last Refusal Rights With a Holdback

A.   Owner agrees not to exercise, license, sell, exploit, or otherwise dispose of, or permit or authorize the exercise, license, sale, exploitation, or other disposal of, any of the rights reserved by Owner in the Work hereunder until the expiration of seven (7) years after the date hereof or five (5) years following the first general release of the Picture, whichever shall first occur, or any of the other rights reserved to Owner in the Work until the expiration of seven (7) years after the date hereof or five (5) years following the first general release of the Picture, whichever shall first occur.

B.   All rights and interests herein granted may be exercised, exploited, or enjoyed by Purchaser at any times hereafter, whether or not in competition with any or all of the Reserved Rights.

C.   If at any time Owner shall propose to make a bona fide offer to sell or license any of the Reserved Rights set forth above (any such proposed rights hereinafter referred to as "Affected Rights"), Owner shall give Purchaser written notice thereof, and the terms and conditions of the proposed transaction. Purchaser shall have the exclusive right and option during the thirty (30) day period following receipt of such notice to acquire the Affected Rights upon the terms and conditions set forth in the notice; provided, however, that Purchaser shall not be required to meet any material term or condition of the proposed transaction which may not be as easily met by Purchaser as by any other party. Purchaser may exercise said right and option by giving Owner written notice of Purchaser's election to do so within the aforesaid thirty (30) day period. If Purchaser shall exercise said right and option, Purchaser shall be deemed to have acquired the Affected Rights and appropriate documentation shall be prepared, executed, and delivered, and the terms and conditions thereof shall be performed, by Owner and Purchaser. If Purchaser shall fail to exercise such right and option as aforesaid, Owner may make a bona fide offer to another party; provided, however, that if the transaction contemplated by such offer is for any reason not consummated upon the material terms and conditions set forth in Owner's notice to Purchaser with respect thereto, Purchaser's right and option shall revive and shall apply to each and every further offer relating to the Affected Rights, except that Purchaser shall be obligated to pay a sum equal to fifteen percent (15%) more than any third party offer received by Owner after the first third party offer in order to consummate its purchase of the Affected Rights. With respect to the first third party offer made, Purchaser shall have the right to match said offer. Without limiting the generality of the foregoing, Owner shall not have the right to dispose or license any Reserved Rights in any instance at a price less than or upon terms and conditions other than those set forth in the aforesaid written notice from Owner to Purchaser, without first offering Purchaser the opportunity to acquire the same on such terms as set forth above. Owner's exercise of author-written sequel reserved rights shall be governed by paragraph D below.

D.   In the event the Owner shall create or desire to create or cause to be created or written an Owner-written sequel based upon the Work, Owner agrees that he shall not so exercise, sell, license, exploit, and/or dispose of any motion picture, television, or allied rights in said Owner-written sequel without first complying with the terms of the following right of first negotiation and right of first refusal and preemption with respect thereto:

(i)   If Owner desires to exercise, sell, license, and/or exploit any of the above-referenced Owner-written sequel rights, Owner shall first give Purchaser written notice thereof and Owner and Purchaser shall thereupon negotiate in good faith for thirty (30) days for the purposes of reaching an agreement whereby Purchaser would undertake such exercise and/or exploitation of such rights.

(ii)   If the parties fail to reach a written agreement with respect to such exercise and/or exploitation within the thirty (30) day period referred to in subparagraph (D)(i) hereof, then Owner shall be free to deal with third parties, provided that Owner shall first give Purchaser written notice of his desire to exercise, sell, license, exploit, or otherwise dispose of any rights listed in this paragraph or of any bona fide offer which Owner has received and intends to accept for any such rights, setting forth in such notice the name of the third party and the basic terms Owner desires to secure or the basic terms of such offer. Purchaser shall have the right to purchase and acquire any of such rights upon the same terms and conditions as set forth in such notice; the terms and conditions which Purchaser shall be obligated to accept in order to exercise such right of first refusal shall not include terms and conditions specified in said notice which cannot be met as easily by one person as another (such as required employment or use of a certain writer, director, star, etc.). At any time within thirty (30) days after receipt of such notice, Purchaser shall notify Owner that Purchaser wishes to acquire any such rights upon the terms and conditions so specified, and Owner shall grant such right or rights to Purchaser upon said terms and conditions. If Purchaser fails to so notify Owner, Owner shall be free to dispose of any such right to any third party in a bona fide, armslength transaction, but only upon terms previously specified in Owner's notice to Purchaser, it being understood and agreed that any such right may not be offered or disposed of by Owner to any third party on any more favorable terms and conditions than previously so specified in Owner's said notice, without Owner first again offering such right to Purchaser as hereinabove provided.

(iii) All references in this subparagraph (D) to Owner shall be deemed to include any author of an Owner-written sequel who writes such material under authority of Owner or Owner's successor in interest. Any disposition of motion picture and allied rights in any rights listed in this paragraph made to any person or company other than Purchaser shall be made subject to the following limitations and restrictions:

(1) Such motion picture and allied rights shall not be exploited or turned to account until after a period of five (5) years from the date of first general release of the first motion picture produced in the exercise of rights assigned by this Agreement or seven (7) years from the date of exercise of Purchaser's option with respect to the Work and the Screenplay, whichever is earlier, unless Purchaser advises Owner in writing that such rights may be disposed of at an earlier date;

(2) Inasmuch as the characters of the Work are included in the exclusive grant of motion picture rights to Purchaser, no sequel rights or television series rights may be granted to such other person or company who purchases the rights to an Owner-written sequel, but such characters may be used in motion pictures whose plots are based substantially on the plot of the respective Owner-written sequel (or, in the case of rights terminated pursuant to the Copyright Act, the plot of the Work);

(iv) Motion picture and allied rights in not more than one (1) Owner-written sequel may be disposed of, subject to subparagraph (i) above, in any respective three (3) year period, the first such period being the three (3) years starting with the date of this Agreement, and each succeeding three (3) year period commencing, respectively, three (3) years after the date on which the next preceding Owner-written sequel shall have been submitted to Owner pursuant to subparagraph (i) above.

It is expressly agreed that Owner's reserved rights under this paragraph relate only to material written or authorized by Owner, and not to any screenplay, teleplay, music, lyrics, or sequels written or authorized by Purchaser, even though the same may contain characters or other elements contained in the Work.

REVERSIONS

How do you protect yourself if the studio buys your screenplay and sits on it—that is, never makes a picture? Your goal is to have your screenplay turned into a movie—not to gather dust. What you want is a *reversion*, the ability to get your script back after a certain period of time if a picture is not produced.

Studios *hate* these! Thus, it is very difficult, nearly impossible with respect to theatrical motion pictures, to get this right. One basic reason is that the studio has already paid for your material. Studio executives feel they should get what they paid for, which means the rights. They also do not want to be embarrassed. The studio may have been indecisive. If you can take your material elsewhere and the next studio makes it a big hit, they look like fools. Studio executives do not like to look like fools, particularly when they are being paid huge bucks not to. Still, if you have leverage, you can ask for it. Reversions are much more common if you are selling a published book. At least you can argue that you had established a market for your material before the studio got involved and they cannot take forever to exploit it.

If the studio is open to the concept at all, it will probably want to hold on to your material for at least ten years, sometimes even a minimum of fifteen years after the option is exercised, before your rights revert. It takes time to get a picture made and fewer are made each year. The studio's executives have paid you what you wanted (remember you did not have to sell your script to them) and they want time! They do not want a gun to their heads.

If you are lucky enough to get a reversion, then the studio is bound to ask for its money back at some point in time. At the very least the studio will want back the money it has actually paid to you plus interest. And not at the interest rate that you get paid in your savings account. The norm is 125 percent of the prime rate—in other words, a premium on top of the average interest rate charged over the period that the studio has expended money on the project. In the 1970s, with interest rates in excess of 15 percent, that sum could have been double or triple the amount paid.

What the studio will also ask for is to be paid back all of its costs—costs for messengers, writers, typists, et cetera. Try to eliminate these and to limit the payback to the money that has been paid to you only. If you have to pay for all these costs, then be sure that all rights in your material revert, including *all* of the subsequent screenplay drafts that the studio has commissioned. If you are paying for these rights, you should get them.

"Wait," you say, "the cost of this payback could be well in excess of my net worth! Do I want this provision?" Do not worry. The studios are not interested in having you pay the bill. They want the next studio that you make a deal with to pay—when you set it up again. "But that may make it impossible for me to set up the project!" you say. Again, do not worry—the next studio will negotiate with the first. Let Studio #2 cut down the price if it is too much. The studios negotiate among themselves all the time and they will work it out if there is real interest. The studios have their own relationships with each other and what is good for the buyer is also good for the seller when the seller is on the buyer's side.

There are several types of reversions. Each is more difficult to get than the previous one. As noted above, the first reversion you should ask for is if the studio never makes a picture. What if the studio makes a picture, but does not make a sequel? What if there's a sequel, but no television series? What if a TV series is made, but not a movie? Look at *Batman*, *Dennis the Menace*, and *Star Trek*. Each project has been produced in several different media. Remember, also, that it took more than twenty years to make a movie out of the TV series in the case of *Batman* and *Dennis the Menace*. This is all negotiable, but if you believe your project has sequel or series potential, you might try to get some protection as follows: Studio executives, in essence, will get a rolling right to produce sequels and/or a television series. They have to commence production of a new film or television series within, say, ten years after release of the earlier production (in the case of a television series, the time period would commence after production of the last episode produced) or they lose all subsequent production rights.

If you are a WGA member, you should be aware that in 1988 the Guild added a provision that allows the writer to get his rights back.

Keep in mind that this right is very limited. It only applies to work that is original (not based on any pre-existing material) and work that has not been exploited in any medium. The rule for literary material acquired after August 8, 1988, is that the writer may reacquire such material upon the expiration of five years following the later of (1) the studio's purchase or license of the material or (2) after the last draft is written *if* such literary material is not in active development and the studio still owns the first draft of the material. Note that once the studio is no longer actively developing your project, it has a certain period of time to resume development again. If it does, then the cycle repeats itself. Once active development ceases, the writer can then proceed to reacquire the material (Writers Guild Basic Agreement, Section 16.A.8).

The best thing about the WGA provision is not just that it exists, which is a major accomplishment in itself, but that it covers commissioned works as well as material that is purchased. If you are hired to write a script, you will *never* see a reversion in a studio *contract*. The Guild provision is the only way to get your material back. The other good thing about the WGA provision is that the cost of acquistion is limited to the cost of creation of the material only, with no overhead charge or costs of any other kind.

The Guild also added a provision recently with respect to a commissioned rewrite that the studio owns in a situation where the option on the original script has lapsed. This applies only to material which was optioned on or after May 2, 2001. The writer of the optioned material may reacquire revisions within a two (2) year period commencing upon written notice from the writer to the company of the writer's intent to reacquire. Such notice may be given no earlier than one (1) year and no later than six (6) years after the date of the expiration of the option.

You should also be aware that in the television arena the rules are even better for a writer. For MOW's and pilots, writers get a non-exclusive reversion, in some cases as early as thirty to forty-eight months after the script is complete, depending on how actively the purchaser is developing the project.

TRANSFER OF RIGHTS: EXERCISE OF THE OPTION

The most important aspect of any option/purchase or purchase contract (should you be lucky enough to sell a spec script outright) is the *transfer of rights* provision. Note that when you option your screenplay, the effective purchase will take place if and when the option to purchase your screenplay is *exercised* and, at that time, the rights that you are conveying to the other party will, in fact, be conveyed. What you want to ensure is that payment *accompanies* the transfer. In other words, the transfer of rights should be *subject* to your being paid the correct sum under the contract. If you do not get your money, the contract should not allow a transfer of rights. If the contract is worded poorly (I have seen contracts, for instance, that stipulate that the only requirement for exercise is notice to the author!), and a transfer of rights occurs without your being paid, then all you will end up with is a breach of contract suit for the purchase price. In other words, the buyer will own the rights and all you will have is the right to sue, which, believe me, will cost a lot of money for you to enforce. You, of course, may argue that the failure to pay the purchase price voids the contract, but this is an argument, not a clean bill of health, so to speak, and under such circumstances, it would be difficult to enter into an agreement for that screenplay with another party.

Therefore, I always strive to ensure that transfer will occur *at the time* payment is made. One major studio insists that it must have up to five days *after* the option is exercised to pay. I do not like this provision. On the other hand, since it is a major studio with major assets and since it will not change the provision, the provision is universally accepted. The major studios are trustworthy in this area. They would not be in business if they failed to pay for the rights they acquired. But you should *never*, ever, accept this provision if your contract is with an independent company. I've seen transfer of rights provisions stating that transfer occurs on exercise of the option with payment on commencement of principal photography—in essence, a right to pay only when and if a movie is made. I've also seen contracts that include a provision that a transfer occurs on execution of the contract with a reversion if the studio doesn't pay a negotiated amount within a certain period of time. These provisions are to be avoided at all costs.

Payment *must* accompany the exercise of an option, or, if your contract is for the outright purchase of rights without an option, then with the transfer of rights. In short, purchase should only be effective if the requisite payment has been made.

Many option/purchase contracts are structured in two parts. There is a separate option contract and a separate purchase/transfer of rights contract that is attached to the option contract. You must sign *both*. While the purchase agreement states that you *are* transferring rights (the contract has language that states, "I *hereby* grant Buyer the following rights"), there is also a provision in the option contract (at least there *should* be one) stating that the purchase contract is effective only *when the option is exercised*. (As noted above, this paragraph should also say when the option is exercised *and when the purchase price is paid*.) The provision usually goes on to say that the signature of the writer to the purchase contract will be void and have no effect unless the purchase price is paid. If you negotiate nothing else in your agreement, this concept must be crystal clear. Otherwise, you may end up in years of litigation, and your project will be tied up.

Sometimes, the owner of a screenplay is able to negotiate further requirements for a transfer of rights to occur, among them, the purchaser must not only pay the purchase price, but also commence principal photography of a motion picture or hire a star or a director. These provisions are rare and you must have extraordinary bargaining power to get them. You should be aware, however, that such provisions exist.

SHORT FORM DOCUMENTS

You will be asked to sign what is called a "short form option agreement" and "short form assignment," along with the option/purchase agreement. The purpose of the short form option is for the purchaser to be able to file with the copyright office a short summary of the fact that your project is tied up and for how long. Once filed, it puts other buyers on notice of the agreement that has been entered into. The purpose of the short form assignment is to record the fact that rights have been granted. The main reason that a short form document is filed, instead of the longer contract, is (1) for simplicity and (2) so that the terms of the agreement are kept confidential. Studio executives do not want anyone to know what they have paid for their option and what the purchase price is, and, for that matter, neither do you.

The short form option indicates the option periods. It usually looks something like this:

Short Form Option Agreement

KNOW ALL MEN BY THESE PRESENTS: that in consideration of the payment of One Dollar ($1.00) and other good and valuable consideration, receipt whereof is hereby acknowledged, the undersigned, _____, does hereby sell, grant, assign, and set over unto _____ ("Purchaser"), and its heirs, representatives, successors, and assigns forever, the exclusive and irrevocable right and option to purchase and acquire from the undersigned all rights throughout the world in perpetuity, in and to that certain original literary work described as follows:

Title:
Written by:
Publisher:
Date and Place of Publication:
Copyright Registration No.:

including all contents thereof, all present and future adaptations and versions thereof, and the theme, title, and characters thereof and in and to the copyright thereof, and all renewals and extensions of such copyright.

The option herein granted may be exercised by Purchaser or his or its heirs, representatives, successors, licensees, or assigns at any time on or before _____ or, if extended, as provided in that certain option agreement entered into concurrently herewith between Purchaser and the undersigned, at any time on or before _____, or, if further extended, on or before _____, and this agreement is subject to all of the terms, conditions, and provisions contained in said agreement.

IN WITNESS WHEREOF, the undersigned has executed this assignment this ___ day of _____, 20___.

_____

[Name]

The short form assignment looks like this:

Short Form Assignment

For good and valuable consideration, receipt whereof is hereby acknowledged, the undersigned hereby sells, grants, and assigns to _____ ("Purchaser"), and its representatives, successors, and assigns, all right, title and interest, including the entire copyright and exclusive motion picture, television, and allied rights throughout the world in perpetuity, in and to that certain original screenplay described as follows:

Title:

Written by:

including all contents thereof, all present and future adaptations and versions thereof, and the theme, title, and characters thereof, as well as all subsequent production rights, and in and to the copyright thereof, and all renewals and extensions of such copyright.

The undersigned and Purchaser have entered into or are entering into a formal Agreement dated as of _____ relating to the transfer and assignment of the foregoing rights in and to said original screenplay, which rights are more fully described in said Agreement, and this Short Form Assignment is expressly made subject to all of the terms, conditions, and provisions contained in said Agreement.

IN WITNESS WHEREOF, the undersigned has executed this Short Form Assignment this ___ day of _____, 20___.

_____

[Name]

Both documents should refer to the long form agreement that you have entered into and be *subject* to all terms of that agreement. These documents are not meant to modify in any way the terms that you have already negotiated. These documents are solely for recording purposes. Indeed, it is crucial that these documents state that they are subject to the terms of the longer agreement and, in the event of any inconsistency between the short form and long form documents, the longer form contract prevails. As discussed previously, for instance, you want to make sure that no rights are assigned unless the purchase price is paid. Having taken the time to see that this provision is in your contract, you certainly do not want the short form assignment to upset the apple cart and negate all of your negotiations.

Once these documents are recorded, anyone can check with the copyright office concerning your project. The easiest way to do this is to call one of the handful of law offices that specialize in copyright searches and to order a copyright report. Studios routinely order copyright reports when they option and/or purchase literary properties. The reports will give the name of the project and the name of the writer. If the short form option and assignment have been filed properly, then these documents will be duly noted on the report.

On a nonrush basis, such a report costs about $600, depending on the complexity of the report. If you want an opinion from a lawyer regarding the status of the rights based on the copyright report, it will cost approximately $650 more.

Option/Purchase Agreements: Fixed Compensation

How much you will be paid for your script is, of course, negotiable. If you agree to option your script, you can try for a higher purchase price than if it is to be purchased outright. Argument to the producer: It's been taken off the market for the option period and will probably be shopped to everyone. Once shopped, a screenplay may lose its luster. (Many writers do not comprehend this and keep trying to sell the same old scripts. As a word of advice, once your script has been shopped, you must be selective about who you go to next with it. You do not want to pitch it to someone who has already passed on it. All that person will remember you for is that same old script that they didn't like the first time and, believe me, that will not enhance your reputation.) The other argument to use in asking for a higher purchase price is that you have optioned your script for very little money. You gave them a break. Now they should give you one.

The amount you are to be paid for your script is the purchase price (also referred to as "fixed compensation," as distinguished from "profits," which are referred to as "contingent compensation," because "profits" are contingent on the film's generating sufficient revenues).

EXERCISE PRICE

The purchase price may also be split up into several components based on factors such as the budget of the movie, your final writing credit, and so on. The most important component, in my opinion, is the "exercise price." This is the price that must be paid by the end of the option period in order to purchase the rights. In my mind, this is the true purchase price. Once paid, you can never get your script back again unless you have a reversion (see discussion in chapter 4). Many deals, however, do not include the entire purchase price in the exercise price and provide that the purchase price may be increased based on factors such as the budget of the picture and writing credit. These increases are really bonuses. But, in Hollywood jargon, these bonuses are actually spoken of as part of the purchase price. It makes it that more difficult to figure out what is really being offered. Bonuses based on the budget of the picture and writing credit are nice, but they are paid when the picture is made, not at the time of exercise. The main thing to keep clear in mind is *what you will get paid if the picture is never made*, and that is the exercise price. Ideally, you want as much of your ultimate compensation as possible included in the exercise price.

Sometimes a deal is structured so that a bonus is paid if the picture is made as a feature motion picture, as distinguished from a television movie. The producer may not know when he options the script whether the picture will be turned into a television movie or a feature. He might want to make it as a feature but keep his options open. If, after shopping the script, he cannot make a feature, then he wants the ability to make a television movie, and that means a much lower price. In order to do this, the producer will set a low exercise price as the purchase price, which corresponds to the ultimate price to be paid if the picture is to be made as a television movie or a low-budget movie. If the picture is eventually made as a feature or for a higher budget, then the producer will pay you more money at the time the picture is made. Of course, any such subsequent payments are all *speculative*. The picture may never be made.

Prices for network television spec scripts usually range from $55,000 to $75,000–$100,000 tops. Prices for other television productions are variable. For instance, a producer should pay more for a pay cable movie (usually just HBO) than for a network movie. Budgets for network movies are generally $2.5–$3 million on average. Budgets for pay cable movies are around $3.5 million and go up to $5–$7 million and higher for special projects. Thus, if your purchase price for a network TV movie is $60,000, try to get $65,000–$70,000 for pay TV. The producer might ask for a break for a nonpay basic cable movie (like one produced for USA Network). Budgets for such movies are less— around $2.2 million. Thus, he might offer only $55,000 or WGA minimum for such a movie.

As an example, a producer might ask that the purchase price for network television be $60,000; pay cable (usually just HBO), $65,000; basic cable, $55,000; and for features, $150,000. If, at the time of exercise, the producer knows he is probably going to make a network television movie, then he will pay you $50,000 at the time of exercise. If he ends up making the movie as a feature, he will pay you the balance when and if it gets made. (Remember: If you do not want to sell your script as a television movie, then do not even get into the distinction. That way, if the producer wants to make a television movie, he will have to pay you the feature price.)

Bonus Based on Budget

Assuming you will not be paid the maximum purchase price on exercise of the option, the easiest way to approach the issue of different media (feature versus television, pay TV versus network TV) and different budgets is to base the ultimate purchase price (including all bonuses) on the budget of the picture. You still need to establish a base exercise price to protect yourself if the movie is never made—a minimum price that must be paid by the end of the option period. The bonus based on a percentage of the budget will be paid when the budget is finalized.

Example: A producer has optioned your screenplay for three years. At the end of the three-year period, he must pay $100,000 to exercise the option or he loses his rights. If a picture based on your property is made and it is a $50 million movie, you will feel cheated if all you get is $100,000—so you build in some protection: 2.5 percent of the budget, with a floor of $100,000. The studio also insists on some protection, called a ceiling. The ceiling is usually no more than three times the exercise price. Of course, that's negotiable. Let's say the ceiling is $300,000. In this example, you would receive $300,000 for your script ($100,000 on exercise of the option, the balance when the final budget is established for the first picture based on your screenplay). You should always base the percentage on the "final" budget, or, if possible, the final cost of the picture. Most studios will not base your bonus on the final cost because if the picture goes over budget, they do not want to give you a premium based on their misfortune. They will usually agree to base your bonus on the final budget, excluding from that budget such items as interest and overhead, contingency and bond.

Bonus Based on Credit

Another common provision is to give a bonus based on credit. There are usually two bonuses—one for sole screenplay credit and one for shared screenplay credit. If you end up with either of these credits, a bonus should be paid. While this is an absolutely essential part of an employment agreement (for instance, when you are hired to write a script, as discussed in the next chapter), often the studio will argue that the bonus is already built into the purchase price, so you may not get this in an option/purchase situation. And, quite frankly, you want to get as much as you can up front (on exercise of the option). You are selling the rights—if studio executives want to hire another writer, that is their business. Your argument: You will not be happy unless you walk home with a guaranteed sum if the picture is made, no matter what credit you end up with. Bonuses, particularly a high sole screenplay bonus, only increase your chance of being kicked off the project at an early stage if the studio can find a cheaper writer.

If a screenplay bonus has to be part of the deal, meaning that some of your compensation will be paid based on credit, the number to focus on is the shared screenplay bonus. Nine times out of ten, you are going to be replaced, and if you wrote the original script, odds are you will get shared screenplay credit (the Writers Guild usually favors the original writer). The shared screenplay bonus is usually one-half of the sole bonus. If you are worried about not getting any screenplay credit and, therefore, no bonus, then sometimes you can negotiate a bonus simply for story credit. This sum will be lower, of course, than the screenplay bonuses.

In short, think about how much you are willing to accept if the picture is never made, how much you want guaranteed if the picture is made, and how much you are willing to risk based on credit, budget, and the like. Be clear in your mind what your bottom line is in each instance.

6

Option/Purchase Agreements: Contingent Compensation

G enerally, writers who sell spec scripts are accorded 5 percent of 100 percent of the net profits. You always want to make sure it is "of 100 percent of *the* net profits." Otherwise, you will receive 5 percent of something that could be considerably less than 100 percent.

PITFALLS OF PERCENTAGES

One pitfall you want to avoid is accepting a definition that says you will receive 5 percent of the "producer's share of net profits." Remember: The producer may only retain a small share. (Generally, producers receive 50 percent of 100 percent of the net profits, reducible by participations granted to actors, directors, and the like. These people are called "third party profit participants.") The producer may or may not have a floor. As an example, if the producer's share of the net profits—50 percent of 100 percent—were reduced by third party profit participants to 10 percent, you would receive 5 percent of 10 percent, or ½ percent of 100 percent of *the* net profits—a far cry from the 5 percent of the profits that you thought you were getting. The producer may also be participating in the studio's gross and may not receive net profits at all from the studio. Thus, a percentage of the producer's net profits may be nonexistent.

You also want to make sure that the corporation you are contracting with is the corporation receiving the revenues from the picture. Let's say you are to receive 5 percent of 100 percent of the profits of Corporation A. Corporation A might be a so-called shell corporation— a corporation with no assets, designed principally to shield the individual producer from liability. The company with the assets may be a parent corporation of Corporation A, or the parent company might be a separate company with no legal relationship to Corporation A whatsoever. When contracting with Corporation A, therefore, you should try to broaden the scope of the profit definition for purposes of defining your net profits. One solution is to say that you will receive 5 percent of 100 percent of the net profits of Corporation A, "its parents, subsidiaries, affiliates, and related companies." This language takes into consideration the revenues that may be received by other companies not cited in your contract. Parent and subsidiary corporations have a definite legal and corporate relationship to the contracting entity. Affiliates and related companies may not, but the language is used as a catchall to prevent the producer or studio from squirreling away revenues without accounting to you for them. You will also want a guarantee from the parent corporation to protect any other compensation you are entitled to receive under the contract. If the small corporation goes bankrupt, you will probably be out of luck without that guarantee.

It often happens that you think you are going into business with a famous company. When you call the producer, the phones are answered indicating you have reached the famous company. You make a deal. Your contract arrives. The contracting entity is a company you have never heard of. Obviously, there is some relationship. The famous company may even have issued a press release that it is making your picture. But the contract makes no mention of this famous company whatsoever. More likely than not, it is a related or affiliate company. The added language ("its parents, subsidiaries, affiliates, and related companies") takes into account that company's revenues as well. You will probably want to spell out the name of the famous company in your definition to avoid any doubt, but still use the affiliated or related company language to encompass companies that you may not be aware of. In this instance, you should receive "5 percent of 100 percent of the net profits of Corporation A, its parents and subsidiaries, famous company, its parents and subsidiaries, and their respective affiliates and related companies." You should also have the famous company guarantee all obligations under the contract.

Sometimes the studio will not agree to give 5 percent of 100 percent of the profits to the seller of a spec script. But, it will almost always agree to at least 2.5 percent of 100 percent of the net profits and might stipulate that you will receive another 2.5 percent of 100 percent only if you get sole screenplay credit. If you have leverage, you should be able to get 5 percent of 100 percent of the "net profits" without regard to credit. You should also be able to get 5 percent of 100 percent of the net profits from the sale of a book. Since the book writer is usually not the writer of the screenplay, the book writer will not be able to get extra points for sole screenplay credit. So the norm has been 5 percent.

NET PROFITS DEFINED

You have probably heard that "net profits" in Hollywood are almost nonexistent. For the most part, this is true. But extremely successful pictures have generated net profits, so it is important for you to understand how they are defined. Many people incorrectly think that the studios keep different sets of books and do not report the actual earnings of a picture. If you understand what a net profits definition consists of, however, you will quickly realize that the studios do not have to hide anything. The definitions themselves make it almost impossible for a picture to reach the point where net profits are paid.

One could probably write a whole book about net profits definitions. Many definitions are more than forty pages long—and in very small print. Since very few people in Hollywood have the leverage to negotiate them, and since those who *do* have leverage also have the clout to receive some type of gross definition (a definition based on the gross of the picture without all the deductions charged off in a net profit definition, in particular the higher distribution fees), it is not necessary for you to understand every provision because you will not be able to change many of them anyway. What you should understand is why net profits are so elusive.

Net profits and gross participations are called "contingent compensation." Unless it is what is called a dollar one gross participation based on the studio's gross (see discussion later on in this chapter), these participations are payable *contingent* on the picture making enough money to "breakeven" and may never be payable. They are also referred to as the "back end" or "points."

The studio does not pay profits until it reaches what is called "breakeven"—in simplistic terms, when it has made back its money. But making back its money does not mean that if it has spent $10 million for a feature, the picture has grossed $10 million at the box office. First of all, box office receipts are different from studio receipts. The studio (distributor) makes a deal with the movie houses (exhibitor) to screen the picture. While there are many types of deals that exist between distributor and exhibitor, the general rule is that the distributor will end up with 50 percent of the U.S. and Canadian box office receipts. The distributor's receipts are called "film rentals" or "studio gross."

As you will see from the following example, if a picture costs $10 million to make and makes $20 million at the box office, it will still not reach breakeven. First, the distributor deducts its distribution fee. This is usually 30 percent for U.S. theatrical distribution. (The fees are higher for other media and foreign revenues.) Then it deducts the costs of distributing the picture (the costs of checking the receipts at the box office, the costs of collecting receipts, trade association dues, taxes [other than corporate income taxes], conversion costs, residuals, licenses, duties and fees, and co-op advertising charges [meaning ad costs that the studio and theater owners share]). These costs are referred to as "off the tops." Then it deducts the costs of prints, advertising, marketing, and other distribution expenses. A major film today is launched with a $10 million-plus campaign. The studio imposes an overhead on advertising costs of usually 10 percent. Thus, if advertising costs are $10 million, add another $1,000,000. This fee is for the running of the studio ad department. (In the studios' minds, the distribution fee of 30 percent is not enough!)

Studio Deductions

Here is a sample provision of the type of expenses that the studio deducts:

(a) As used herein, the term "Distribution Expenses" shall mean all customary, direct, out-of-pocket, and reasonable costs and expenses paid or incurred and thereafter paid by Studio or its subdistributors to the extent charged to Studio by its subdistributors, in connection with the distribution, advertising, exploitation, and turning to account of the Picture of whatever kind or nature or other exercise of any of the rights granted to Studio under the Agreement, and shall include, without limitation, the following:

(i) All costs and expenses of release prints, replacements, duped and dubbed negatives, fine grains, interpositives, internegatives, sound, music or effects tracks, including re-recording of soundtracks, matrices, cassettes, tapes, duplicating material and other Picture material manufactured for use in connection with the Picture, and television and theatrical trailers thereof net of any rebates, discounts, and credits accorded to Studio, and all sums actually expended or incurred and thereafter paid by Studio in processing, inspecting, repairing, and renovating said material, including, but not limited to, the repairing and renovating of reels, cans, containers, and cassettes, all packing, shipping, storing, transportation, and insurance costs, and all other expenses incurred in connection therewith; it being understood that Studio and its subdistributors may manufacture or cause to be manufactured as many or as few duped negatives, positive prints, and other material for use in connection with the Picture as it or they, as the case may be, in their sole and absolute discretion, may consider advisable or desirable.

(ii) All costs and expenses of advertising, publicizing, promoting, and exploiting the Picture and all rights therein, by such means to such extent as Studio may, in its sole discretion, consider advisable or desirable. Such advertising, publicity, and exploitation expenses shall include, without limitation: payments in connection with the preparation, supervision, and/or execution of advertising plans and campaigns; the preparation, supervision, and production of theatrical and television trailers, teaser trailers, recordings, and radio transcriptions; the preparation, supervision, printing, and distribution of trade advertising, and advertising for regional and national fan magazines and newspapers (including charges for space in such newspapers and magazines); the preparation, supervision, and distribution of press kits and all publicity, promotion, and exploitation items, advertising accessories, lobby displays, slides, novelties, and tie-ins; pre-release advertising and publicity, screenings and personal appearances by actors and/or other production personnel; so-called cooperative and/or theater advertising (other than for or by studio directly); the salaries, costs, and expenses of publicity and advertising personnel allocated on the basis of time spent on the Picture in relation to other films; artwork, posters, and other accessories, still photographs and other advertising material used in connection with the Picture; the salaries of field exploitation personnel allocated on the basis of time spent on the Picture and their expenses; any film festival or market expenses, or other selling or nonselling activities related to the Picture; and any such expenses incurred in connection with "four-wall" exhibition, and any excesses of "four-wall" expenses over "four-wall" film rentals received. All marketing costs to be advanced by Studio are to be recouped as a distribution expense from the balance of monies due after deducting distribution fees. Except as set forth in this paragraph, no salary or fee paid to any permanent executive of Studio shall be deductible as a Distribution Expense;

(iii)   All costs and expenses of preparing and delivering the Picture for distribution in any and all media, now known or hereafter devised (including, without limitation, salaries and expenses of parties not regularly employed by Studio), including, without limitation, all costs incurred in connection with the production of foreign language versions of the Picture, whether dubbed, subtitled, superimposed, or otherwise, as well as any and all costs and expenses in connection with the changing of the title of the Picture, the recutting, re-editing, dubbing, redubbing, shortening, or lengthening of the Picture for release in any territory of television sales, and exhibition on television or in any other media, or for videogram sales or renting, or in order to conform to the requirements of censorship authorities or to the peculiar national or political prejudices likely to be encountered in any territory, or for any other purpose or reason, subject to the Agreement. The costs and expenses referred to in this subparagraph (iii) shall (A) include all studio charges for facilities, labor, and material, whether or not incurred at a studio owned or controlled by Studio, and all costs and expenses of delivery materials; (B) be net of laboratory negative and print discounts for only the Picture and advertising agency commission rebates relating to only the Picture; and (C) not include any mark-up for Studio's own benefit. Except as set forth in this paragraph, no salary or fee paid to any permanent executive of Studio shall be deductible as a Distribution Expense.

(iv)   All sums paid, incurred, or accrued on account of sales, use, receipts, income, excise, remittance, and/or any other taxes or license fees, however denominated, imposed, assessed, or levied by any governmental authority or duly constituted taxing authority, imposed, assessed, or levied upon the negatives, duplicate negatives, prints, or sound recordings of the Picture, or upon the use or distribution of the Picture, or upon the revenues derived therefrom or any part thereof, or upon the remittance of such revenues or any part thereof but not including any taxes based solely on Studio's net income or accrued on account of duties, customs, and imposts, costs of acquiring permits, and any similar authority to secure the entry, licensing, exhibition, performance, use, or televising the Picture in any country or part thereof, regardless of whether such payments, charges, or accruals are assessed against the Picture or the proceeds thereof, or against a group of motion pictures in which the Picture may be included or the proceeds thereof. In no event shall the recoupable amount of any such tax (however denominated) imposed be decreased (nor the Gross Receipts increased) because of the manner in which such taxes are elected to be treated by Studio in filing net income, corporate franchise, excess profits, or similar tax returns. Subject to the foregoing, Writer shall not be required to pay or participate in (A) Studio's own income taxes and franchise taxes based on Studio's net income or (B) any income tax payable to any country or territory by Studio based on the net earnings of Studio in such territory or country and which is computed and assessed solely by reason of the retention in such country or territory by Studio of any portion of the Gross Receipts. Gross Receipts shall include an amount equal to any refund received by Studio of taxes paid by Studio and deducted as a Distribution Expense pursuant to this paragraph (iv), and, to the extent Studio shall have not deducted a distribution fee on Gross Receipts inclusive of such taxes, Studio shall not deduct a distribution fee on such refund.

(v)   All costs and expenses of converting and transmitting to Los Angeles, California, any funds accruing to Studio in respect of the Picture from foreign countries, including, without limitation, cable expenses, and any discounts from such funds taken to convert such funds directly or indirectly into United States Dollars or Pounds Sterling;

(vi) All costs and expenses of contesting any of the matters described in subparagraphs (iv) and (v) above, with a view to reducing the same, which costs shall be fairly apportioned to the Picture (on a mathematically justifiable basis) if done on an industrywide basis or with respect to motion pictures distributed by Studio generally;

(vii) If the Picture is distributed theatrically, all costs and expenses paid or incurred in collecting Gross Receipts, including, without limitation, attorneys' fees and all costs and expenses of checking attendance and receipts at any and all theaters where studio may be exhibited and all costs and expenses of checking and analyzing percentage engagements, accountings, and payments of film rental in connection with the Picture under percentage engagements with exhibitors of the Picture; provided, however, that if the expenses of such box office analysis of motion pictures other than the Picture are included with such expenses in connection with the Picture, then the amounts set forth in this reasonable and customary basis, and to the extent Studio (rather than a subdistributor or licensee of studio) shall make such allocation, such allocation shall be made in good faith and on a mathematically justifiable basis;

(viii) All amounts paid or incurred to or for the benefit of actors, writers, directors, and others pursuant to applicable collective bargaining agreements by reason of any exhibition or exploitation of the Picture in any media in the Territory, or by reason of, or as a condition for, any use, reuse, or rerun thereof for any purpose or in any manner whatsoever including, without limitation, royalties, participations, and reuse fees (hereinafter collectively referred to as "residuals"), and all taxes, pension, health, and welfare fund contributions, and other costs and payments computed on or payable in respect of any such residuals. To the extent reasonably practicable, all residuals paid by Studio in respect of a particular exploitation of the Picture shall be included on the accounting statement(s) in which Studio accounts for the Gross Receipts derived from such exploitation, it being agreed that Studio has no obligation to pay any residuals;

(ix) All costs and expenses of errors and omissions insurance incurred by or on behalf of Studio and thereafter paid (including, without limitation, any extensions Studio obtains of Producer's errors and omissions insurance or additional or supplementary coverage), it being understood, however, that Studio shall not be obligated to secure or maintain any such insurance;

(x) All costs and expenses of securing and maintaining copyright protection for the Picture throughout the Territory, including, without limitation, the cost of copyright and title reports and copyright registrations and renewals and extensions thereof;

(xi) Dues, fees, assessments, and contributions (to the extent paid, incurred, accrued, and allocated to the Picture or the distribution thereof) to the Motion Picture Association of America or other motion picture and/or television industry trade organization of which Studio or any subdistributor may now be or hereafter become a member.

(xii) All costs and expenses paid or incurred (and thereafter paid) in connection with any claims, actions, suits, proceedings, litigation, arbitration, or other disputes (hereinafter collectively referred to as "Claims") arising out of or in connection with the Picture, including, without limitation, Claims relating to infringement, unfair competition, violation of prints or other material, violation of any guild provision, material on which the Picture is based or otherwise in connection with the exhibition of the Picture. Without limiting the generality of the foregoing, the expenses described in this subparagraph (xii) shall include all outside attorneys' and accountants' fees, investigative costs and fees, losses, costs, damages (including the gross amount[s] paid for the settlement of any Claims or on account of any judgment, decree, or decision relating to any Claims), or other liabilities paid or incurred (and thereafter paid) in connection with any such Claims;

(xiii) If any person or entity shall make a claim relating to the Picture against Studio and/or any of its licensees, which claim, in Studio's judgment, is of sufficient merit or constitutes a reasonable probability of ultimate loss, cost, damage, or expense, Studio may deduct as a Distribution Expense the amount of any liability, loss, cost, damage, or expense suffered as a result thereof. Subject to the Agreement, Studio shall have the right to settle and pay any such claim. After the settlement of any such claim or after the final judicial determination thereof, the amount previously deducted hereunder shall be adjusted accordingly with the next accounting statement rendered hereunder. Nothing herein contained shall be construed as a waiver of any of Writer's representations or warranties contained in the Agreement to which this Exhibit is attached, or as a waiver of any right or remedy at law or otherwise which may exist in favor of Studio, including, but not limited to, the right to require Producer to reimburse Studio on demand for any loss, liability, cost, damage, or expense arising out of, or resulting from, any breach by Writer's of its representations, warranties, covenants, and/or other agreements, or any right on the part of Studio to set-off, recoup, or recover any such cost or expense out of or against Producer's share of any monies payable hereunder other than the Purchase Price, rather than treating such costs or expenses as Distribution Expenses hereunder.

(xiv) All other costs and expenses actually paid or incurred (and thereafter paid) by Studio in connection with the distribution, promotion, advertising, publicizing and/or exploitation of the Picture or any rights granted to Studio in the Agreement.

(b) Whenever Studio makes an expenditure or incurs (and thereafter pays) any liability in respect of films, including the Picture, or any right therein, pursuant to any agreement or arrangement which does not specify what portion of the expenditure or liability applies to the respective films in the group, then in any and all such situations, Studio shall deduct as a Distribution Expense such sums as Studio shall determine reasonably in good faith.

(c) To the extent the Picture is distributed by a subdistributor, the term "Distribution Expenses" shall include (in addition to any of the foregoing costs and expenses which may be incurred by Studio) all costs and expenses incurred by Studio in connection with entering into and administering the contract with each such subdistributor. To the extent the Picture is distributed by a subdistributor, all Distribution Expenses of the type or nature described in this Paragraph incurred by such subdistributor and passed on to Studio or which Studio otherwise accepts for purposes of its account-ings with such subdistributor shall be deducted by Studio from Gross Receipts for purposes of determining Producer's Profits hereunder, as if Studio had incurred such expenses without any cap. Notwithstanding the foregoing, the term "Distribution Expenses," as used herein, shall not include any cost or expense paid or incurred by a subdistributor of the Picture if:

(i) such cost or expense was applied against and deducted from Gross Receipts derived in respect of the Picture by such subdistributor; and

(ii) the Gross Receipts against which such costs and expenses were applied were excluded from the com-putation of Gross Receipts.

Let's say that these expenses total $13 million. Using our example, here is where we're at:

If the picture has grossed $20 million at the box office and distribution costs equal $13 million ($5 million of that for advertising), then:

Film Rentals = $20,000,000 × 50%	=	$10,000,000
Distribution Fee (30%)	=	− 3,000,000
		7,000,000
Costs		−13,000,000
Ad Overhead (10% × $5,000,000)		− 500,000
		−$6,500,000

Suppose the film grosses $10 million at video stores. You probably think the film has reached breakeven. *Wrong!* The studios have an obnoxious policy regarding video revenues. Only a small portion of those revenues go into the pot for purposes of calculating profits. The norm is that the studios will include a 20 percent royalty into gross. Twenty percent of the *wholesale* selling price, not retail. Let's say of the $10 million grossed at retail video stores (through sales and rentals), $6 million represents the wholesale selling price of those cassettes. Twenty percent of $6 million = $1.2 million. Studios sometimes take a distribution fee off that. Let's use our example of 30 percent.

	$1,300,000
Less Distribution Fee	
(30% × $1,300,000)	− 390,000
	$ 910,000

Out of $10 million in video revenues, only $910,000 is calculated into gross. Using our example:

Film Rentals	$10,000,000
Less Distribution Fee	− 3,000,000
	$7,000,000

Add Video Royalty	+ 1,300,000	
		$8,300,000
Less Video Distribution Fee	− 390,000	
		$7,910,000
Less Costs	−13,000,000	
Less Ad Overhead	− 500,000	
Studio Gross		−$5,590,000

You now see why the notion of net profits is an elusive concept.

The other major killer deduction is the interest that is charged until the picture breaks even. Interest is charged on the unrecouped cost of the picture. (The entire interest charge is recouped first before the other deduction, unlike a mortgage on a house.) Sometimes the studio also charges an overhead fee on top of the cost of the picture. Let's say film rentals, video monies, and other revenues derived from the picture, less costs and distribution fees equal $10 million. In our example, that is also the cost of the picture. Has the studio broken even? No way. By that point our $10 million picture cost (the industry term for picture cost is "negative cost") is not a mere $10 million. Say the studio charges a 12.5 percent overhead fee (some charge as much as 17.5 percent). The $10 million negative cost is now $11.25 million, without adding the interest charge. Interest charges may be quite high. Keep in mind that the studio does not charge the actual rate of interest charged by its bank. It usually charges 125 percent of the prime rate charged by the bank. In other words, it makes a profit on the interest! If the prime rate is 5 percent, the interest rate charged is 7.5 percent on the *unrecouped* portion of the negative cost until all receipts less distribution costs are enough to pay back the negative cost. Interest charges are recalculated as additional revenues are received, but until recoupment, interest is always charged on the unrecouped portion of the negative cost. As you can see, the interest cost could add up, thus pushing the point of recoupment further and further back. Most studios charge interest on overhead; some charge overhead on interest (the latter not as common).

Gross Participations

There is one other key deduction that also makes it almost impossible ever to net profits. In order to understand this deduction, first you must understand the basic difference between a "net profit participant" (one who is entitled to a share of net profits) and a "gross participant" (one who is entitled to a share of gross, as opposed to net). There are several types of gross participants. The best gross participant definition is for the participant who receives gross from the first dollar. This person receives a share of the studio's gross, less *only* the off-the-top deductions (listed above). Such "off the tops" usually amount to approximately 5 percent. Thus, if the studio gross is $10 million and the off the tops are $500,000 (5 percent × $10 million), the dollar one gross participant will receive a percentage of the initial $9.5 million that the studio receives. The net participant, on the other hand, receives a share of $9.5 million less a 30 percent distribution fee, less all the other deductible costs. Using our example, this amounts to a share of nothing.

There are few "dollar one" gross players. Most people who receive gross receive what is called an "adjusted gross" after breakeven. Adjusted gross is basically the same as net profits with one major exception. The distribution fees are lowered, in some cases to 15 percent or 10 percent. As noted above, the distribution fee for theatrical rentals is usually 30 percent (for U.S. rentals); the distribution fee for foreign theatrical receipts is usually 40 percent. Distribution fees for television may be higher. The distribution fee on U.S. cable receipts is usually 35 percent. The general rule is that the *average* full distribution fees on all receipts (domestic and foreign, theatrical and television) is 34 percent. Thus, reducing the fees to 15 or 10 percent on all receipts may make a huge difference.

As an example, consider net profit participants on a project with a studio gross of $10 million. You normally deduct 34 percent for distribution fees (the average of all distribution fees), or $3.4 million, leaving $6.6 million to be applied toward recoupment of expenses and negative cost. If only 15 percent of $10 million, or $1.5 million, is deducted, that leaves $8.5 million going toward recoupment of expenses and the negative cost, which means the picture will reach breakeven much earlier.

Now that you understand the basic difference between net and gross participants, you should be aware that *gross* participations are also deducted in calculating *net* profit participation breakeven. Using our example above:

Video Rentals & Sales	$10,000,000	
Less Distribution Fee	− 3,000,000	
		$7,000,000
Add Video Royalty	+ 1,300,000	
		$8,300,000
Less Distribution Fee (Video)	− 390,000	
Studio Gross		$7,910,000
Less Costs	−13,000,000	
Less Ad Overhead	− 500,000	
		−$5,590,000

Now let's say gross participations of $1 million were paid out before net profit breakeven was reached. The studio charges interest and overhead on these participations too, so the $1 million could easily turn into $1.3 million or more. You deduct that from the bottom line too, so the −$5.59 million becomes −$6.89 million.

There are other provisions that are just as egregious, if not more so. (For instance, the distribution fee for merchandising is 50 percent and the studios sometimes hire an outside merchandising agent to take care of the licensing. That outside agent also takes a fee. If his fee is 30 percent, you have, in essence, close to an 80 percent fee on merchandising receipts!) I could go on for pages—that could be the subject of another book. Even in this brief synopsis, however, you can see why artists are outraged about not sharing in profits.

NEGOTIABLE PROVISIONS

There are very few provisions that you can negotiate in a net profits definition, particularly if you are just beginning your career. However, there are two important provisions you should negotiate, and can get, if you ask for them.

Double Addback

Most net profits definitions provide for a penalty if the picture goes over budget. This provision is basically designed as an incentive for the director and producer to bring the picture in on budget. The provision is called a "double addback" because the studio adds twice the over-budget amount to the negative cost in its calculations. Writers have absolutely nothing to do with whether a picture comes in on budget or not, so this provision can be deleted.

Cross-Collateralization and Abandonment Charges

The other provision concerns cross-collateralization and abandonment charges. Some producers and directors have what they call "overall deals" at a particular studio. They are called overall deals because they envision that these producers or directors will make or be involved in more than one picture at that studio. The producer may be exclusive to that studio or he may have an obligation to bring the projects to that particular studio first. Some studios link the pictures (total or partial) for purposes of recoupment, although this is uncommon. If picture #1 is produced and unrecouped, the studio may require that the second picture earn enough revenues so that it gets back its money on the first picture out of revenues from picture #2 before it pays profits on the second picture. Or the studio may simply want to recoup from picture #2 the monies that it *paid* the producer or director with an overall deal on picture #1. For a producer with an overall deal, the studio may also allocate a portion of the overhead expenses to each picture he produces. These charges also may be charged to the writer: secretaries, office messengers, and the like. The recoupment of one picture's losses from another picture's profits in the calculation of a film's profits or the recoupment of a producer's fees and overhead expenses is called cross-collateralization. As the writer usually does not have an overall deal, the cross-collateralization charges that may be charged to a director or producer should not be charged to the writer.

Finally, the producer with an overall deal may have developed a project that was abandoned. The studio may charge off all the costs of this abandoned project to a different picture that is produced by that producer for purposes of deferring the producer's profits on the picture so produced. These charges are called "abandonment charges," and the writer should not be penalized with abandonment charges in the calculation of his profits on that picture.

Time

Another point you can usually negotiate in a net profits definition is the time period you have to sue with respect to profit participation statements (that is, if you think the revenues reported are inaccurate or the calculations are wrong). The studio definition usually gives you twelve months. This can be increased up to twenty-four to thirty-six months. Accounting periods are usually the same for everyone (quarterly for at least the first year, semiannually thereafter for several years, then yearly).

Caps

Producers, directors, and some high-level writers can also negotiate other provisions in a net profits definition, which may or may not make a difference in the bottom line. Some studios accept a cap or a ceiling on collection and checking costs (1 percent of gross revenues for each). Some studios accept a cap on Motion Picture Association and other trade association dues. Studios pay dues for all their pictures, so it is unfair for them to charge off all these costs against your picture. (Caps are sometimes $250,000 for U.S. trade dues and the same for foreign trade dues.) Although it is rare, some studios put a cap on the overhead. Some studios agree not to charge overhead on interest charges and interest on overhead charges. Some studios eliminate the distribution fee on the video royalty. Some studios agree not to charge off the salaries of their in-house employees (arguably, that is what the distribution fees and overhead charges should cover). Or, sometimes, studios will agree not to charge interest or overhead on gross participations. I know of one instance where this particular clause meant the difference between my client actually receiving net profits on a successful picture and another net profit participant on the same picture (who had a greater percentage of net profits) not receiving a cent! Some studios agree that their fees include subdistributor and subagent fees. This is an important provision because subdistributors may charge the same or a greater fee than the studio, in which case you have fees on top of fees, which gets ridiculous! Recall the discussion at the beginning of this chapter regarding parent, subsidiary, affiliates, and related companies. At the very least, you want to ensure that each affiliate company is not taking a separate distribution fee. Just as the catchall is used to ensure that your net profit definition takes into consideration the revenues derived from all such companies, the definition should also ensure that the distributor fees set forth in the net profit definition include the fees of all such companies.

Advances

The other big issue concerns the inclusion of advances into gross (what we often call "the pot") for purposes of determining the net. Many companies will receive an advance for the sale of pay cable rights or home video rights. They may receive this when the picture is completed. Most definitions do not include these advances in the calculation of gross when they are received. Rather, they include the revenues from these sources when and if they are *earned*. For example, pay cable receipts will be included when the movie is broadcast on pay cable. Similarly, the company may have received an advance against home video sales. This will not be included in the gross for two reasons. First, the calculation of home video revenues for you is different than it is for the studio (see discussion above). For the most part, the studio receives 100 percent of the wholesale video revenues from the retailer—not the 20 percent royalty you will receive. Second, your calculation will be based on videocassettes actually sold. The company may receive an advance, representing sales of 100,000 cassettes. It is a nonreturnable advance, but you do not get the benefit of it. If only 20,000 units are sold, your definition only takes into account sales of 20,000 cassettes and not the 100,000 that the studio received monies for. These provisions will not be changed. However, sometimes the studio will agree, as a compromise, that for purposes of calculating interest charges only, the money that the studio receives as an advance will be deemed received, and, therefore, you will not be charged interest on the money. In other words, for purposes of calculating your share, the studio did not receive the money, but for purposes of calculating interest charges, it did. Now you see why studios do not have to keep various sets of books. Lopsided bookkeeping is built into the very definition of profits.

Producer's Net Profit Definition

The producer is usually in a better position to negotiate, so many writers ask to be tied to the producer's definition. If you make a deal with a producer before he takes a project to the studio, you have no way of knowing which studio definition, if any, you will be stuck with. If the producer agrees to tie you to his net definition (which most will), make sure you will not be charged any over-budget penalties or cross-collateralization charges. Remember, too, that you will only be tied to the producer's *net* definition. If he gets gross, his gross definition will not apply to you. Try to find out if the producer you are going into business with is a "gross player"—one who receives "gross" as distinguished from "net." Your agent or lawyer will probably know. Note that if you are tied to the producer's definition, you might not get your own audit rights. The producer may agree to give you the same definition of profits he has, but say to you that he will not let you audit the studio separately. In that case, you want to be able to "piggyback" on his audit rights—in short, to join him when he audits the studio and pay the proportionate costs. You also want to be able to prompt the producers to audit the studio, even if he doesn't want to. But in this case, you will have to bear all the costs, unless the producer decides to join in.

DEFERMENTS

Deferments are delayed payments. They can either be fixed—in which case they are payable on a certain date—or contingent—in which case they are payable contingent on certain circumstances, such as the film earning enough money to reach net profits.

An example of a fixed deferment would be a payment of a certain amount that is required to be made within one year after the option is exercised, regardless of whether a film is produced. If the option is exercised, it *must* be paid. Such deferments are rare in writers' deals. The only reason for you to take a fixed deferment, in lieu of cash on exercise of the option, is to give the purchaser a breather with respect to his payment obligations.

An example of a contingent deferment would be a payment of an agreed-upon sum out of the first net profits of the picture. The deferment would be paid before any net profit participations are paid out of the first monies that are available to net profit participants. Suppose you are a net profit participant entitled to a 5 percent share. If, for example, $100,000 in net profits are generated, you would be entitled to $5,000. But if there are any deferments, these have to be paid first. If you have a $100,000 deferment payable out of the first net profits and $100,000 in net profits are generated, then, assuming you are the only person entitled to a deferment, you would receive the $100,000. (This also assumes that there are no other charges tacked onto the deferment—such as overhead and interest charges!) No net profits would be payable because the net profits generated would be eaten up by the deferment in this example. If others are entitled to deferments, then usually all deferments are paid out on a pro rata basis. Thus, if another person is also entitled to a $100,000 deferment and $100,000 of net profits is generated, you would each receive $50,000 out of the first $100,000 and the second $100,000. You would also each receive another $50,000 out of the next $100,000 of net profits.

This tradition of only giving writer's "net profits" has given way slightly. Recently, Sony Picture Entertainment pacted with thirty-four established screenwriters in a historic agreement that was touted by the *Hollywood Reporter* as "an arrangement that shatters a glass ceiling for writers"[1] and was reported by the *Daily Variety* as "opening up the gross participation concept to hundreds of people for whom it was previously a pipe dream."[2] The deal guarantees each writer at least 2 percent of the applicable picture's gross receipts in all media in perpetuity for sole credit, and 1 percent when the credit is shared with another writer or writers. According to the *Daily Variety* article, the studio will recoup its negative cost, print and advertising (P&A) costs, and certain miscellaneous off-the-top costs, but no distribution fee. The writers will receive their monies before the studio gets its fee or other participants kick in. To qualify, a writer must have earned at least $750,000 as a front-end payment for a feature (this requirement goes at the rate of $50,000 per year), sold a spec script for at least $1 million, or received a nomination for an Academy Award® or a Writer's Guild of America award. Each writer of this first group has agreed to write one script for the studio in the next four years. Unfortunately, so far most other studios have not followed this example.

---

[1]"Unprecedented Col deal gives 31 writers percentage of gross," by Kirk Honeyoutt. The *Hollywood Reporter* (5–7 February 1999).

[2]"Sony's Scribes: Historic deal gives writers gross deals," by Benedict Carver and Dan Cox. *Daily Variety* (5 February 1999).

7

Option/Purchase Agreements: Sequels, Rewrites, and Reversions

When you sell a script to a studio or write a screenplay for a studio, the studio will purchase *all* rights, other than the limited reserved rights generally allowed, and, specifically, the ones that you have negotiated. What if the studio produces a sequel picture or a television series based on the script? Shouldn't you be entitled to something? The answer is yes and studios will give you something if you ask.

PASSIVE PAYMENTS

A production following the initial production is commonly called a "subsequent production." The payments for these subsequent productions are called "passive payments," because you do not have to *do* anything to receive these payments. Payment is automatic, but there are usually conditions.

If you sell a screenplay, passive payments should be unconditional, but often they are not. Certainly, if you are commissioned to write a screenplay and often if you sell a screenplay, the studio will require that the first picture produced essentially reflects your story and characters in order to receive passive payments. Under the WGA rules, you must be accorded what are called "sole separated rights." If the script has been dramatically changed in its plot and characters by the time the picture is produced, you may only receive "shared separated rights," which, in most cases, will *not* entitle you to passive payments or, at best, will entitle you to a reduced royalty. Some studios require also that you receive sole "written by" or sole "screenplay by" credit. There are numerous permutations and combinations. The general rule is that, in order to receive passive payments, you must at least receive sole separated rights.

If the studio does give passive payments for shared separated rights, the payments are usually one-half of the payment accorded for sole separated rights. If the studio does accord payments for shared separated rights, you can also ask to have the sole separated rights passive payment amount reduced by the amounts paid to other writers entitled to shared separated rights to a floor of one-half the passive payment for sole separated rights. That way, if the other writers' payments are considerably less than yours, you might not be reduced to your floor.

Studios that award passive payments for sole "written by" or "screenplay by" credit will not usually reduce the payment by one-half for shared "screenplay by" credit. Ideally, you want to provide for payment one way or another if you receive sole or shared separated rights or sole or shared screenplay credit. Try to get it.

If you sell a script, try to get passive payments without hitches. After all, you do have some leverage if you are selling your script. Remember: You do not have to sell it and it is fair to say that if your script is turned into a feature and a sequel and maybe another sequel and/or a television series, then you should get something, regardless of credit and regardless of whether the script is changed. If you are being hired to write, you have less leverage, so undoubtedly you will have to live with whatever conditions the studio imposes. All studios have different policies and these policies are sometimes changed (usually not in your favor, but sometimes so).

Most important, you want passive payments for sequels and re-makes. The general rule is that you get 50 percent of what you were paid for the first picture for each sequel produced and 33 percent for a remake. Make sure that it is 50 percent and 33 percent, respectively, of the *entire* compensation you were paid for the first picture, including the *bonuses*. Usually, the initial contract presented by the studio does not refer to the bonus. The moral here is: *Ask and you shall receive.* The accepted standard is that your passive payment is based on *all* of your compensation, including the screenplay bonus, budget bonus, and the like. As an example, if you received $180,000, including bonuses, for the first picture, you will receive $90,000 for a sequel and $60,000 for a remake. Again, you should not have to do anything. Payment should be automatic when the applicable produc-tion is produced.

You should also receive 50 percent and 33⅓ percent (for sequels and remakes, as applicable) of the contingent participation you were entitled to receive on the first picture. Thus, if you were entitled to 5 percent of 100 percent of the net profits on the first picture, you will be entitled to 2.5 percent of 100 percent of the net profits for a sequel.

Television Series

You should also negotiate passive payments for a television series. In television, these are commonly called "episodic royalties" (they are paid for each original episode produced). There are usually three different figures: one for a thirty-minute series, one for an hour-long series and one for a ninety-minute series. There are no ninety-minute series today and this is a holdover from days gone by, but it is still negotiated. Low-end writers will receive in the realm of $1,775–$2,000 per episode for a thirty-minute series, $2,700–$3,000 per episode for a sixty-minute series, and $3,600+ per episode for a ninety-minute series. These num-bers are based on guild minimums. At the higher end, the figures may increase to $5,000 (although anything over $5,000 is high, even for top writers). The range is not that large.

The series royalty payment is generally for a network show (ABC, CBS, NBC) broadcast in prime time in the United States. Fox should be included as a network. Nowadays it usually is. Try also to get 50 percent of the respective payments for non-network or non–prime time shows. Most studios will accept this. In other words, if the royalty is $3,000 per episode for a network prime time show, the royalty would be $1,500 per episode for a non-network or non–prime time show, but in no event less than the WGA minimum.

Additionally, you should also be entitled to a royalty for reruns of a series. The norm is to receive again the same amount that you received for the first series episode as payment for the first five reruns. This is called "100 over 5." It is payable in installments, in other words, 20 percent of the royalty for each rerun.

Royalties are also paid for spin-offs. There are two types of spin-offs: "generic" and "planted." A generic spin-off is a television production that is primarily based on another television production and is itself a remake of or a sequel to the first series. A generic spin-off also features characters that appeared as primary characters in the first production. A planted spin-off is one based on a previous series that presents as its essential continuing character one who either did not appear in the first series or served as a continuing character in the previous series. Royalties for generic spin-offs are usually 50 percent of the applicable royalties that you negotiate for the first television series; royalties for planted spin-offs are 25 percent of the applicable royalties. Thus, if your royalty for a thirty-minute network prime time broadcast is $3,500 for the first television series produced based on your work, then the royalty for a thirty-minute network prime time generic spin-off episode is $1,750 and $875 for a comparable planted spin-off.

You can also negotiate passive payments for a television movie-of-the-week or a miniseries that is produced after the first feature film. Figures start at around $7,000 an hour and go up to $20,000 per hour for top writers. There is usually a cap of six hours. (In other words, if the miniseries is ten hours long, you only get paid for six hours. Using $7,000 per hour as an example, you would be paid $42,000 if the cap is six hours.) Some studios accept a cap of eight hours, and it is rare that a miniseries would be longer than that. You could also try for the

"100 over 5" rerun formula for reruns of a movie-of-the-week or a miniseries. Generally, the studio will not accept an additional rerun payment for these productions. Your payment, in other words, is a buyout of all reruns. If you are a member of the WGA, the WGA does provide for payment for reruns, however.

Usually, even though you are entitled to profits from the first picture and especially if you are a writer for hire, you will not be entitled to receive profits from a series or a subsequent movie-of-the-week or miniseries, but it doesn't hurt to ask. If the buyer is an independent producer and you have leverage, you may succeed. And if you have a lot of leverage at a studio, you may succeed.

Sample Passive Payment Provision

Here is a sample of a passive payment section from a contract:

ADDITIONAL CONSIDERATION: In addition to the basic consideration provided for above, (a) If Owner is not in material default of this Agreement, and (b) Owner is entitled to sole separation of rights under the WGA Agreement with respect to the Picture, and (c) Owner is not engaged to render writing services in connection with the applicable production, then Purchaser agrees to make contingent and supplemental payments to Owner based upon certain events and certain uses of the Work as follows:

(a)   In the event Purchaser shall produce a feature-length motion picture intended for initial theatrical release based upon the Work pursuant to the rights granted (or agreed to be granted) to Purchaser pursuant to this Agreement, and shall thereafter produce a "remake" of such motion picture (i.e., a feature-length motion picture intended for initial theatrical release, which contains substantially the same story and the same leading characters as contained in the Work and used in said motion picture), and Writer is not engaged to render writing or other services in connection therewith, Purchaser shall pay to Owner the additional sum of one-third (⅓) of the Purchase Price not later than commencement of principal photography of such remake.

(b) In the event Purchaser shall produce a feature-length motion picture intended for initial theatrical release based upon the Work pursuant to the Agreement, and shall thereafter produce a "sequel" of such motion picture (i.e., a feature-length motion picture intended for initial theatrical release, which contains substantially the same leading characters, but a substantially different story than contained in the Work), and Writer is not engaged to render writing or other services in connection therewith, Purchaser shall pay to Owner the additional sum of one-half (½) of the Purchase Price not later than commencement of principal photography of such sequel.

(c) In the event Purchaser shall produce a feature-length motion picture intended for initial theatrical release based upon the Work pursuant to the rights granted (or agreed to be granted) to Purchaser pursuant to this Agreement or a television motion picture, and shall thereafter produce a feature-length motion picture based upon the Work intended for initial exhibition on U.S. free network television, Purchaser shall pay Owner the sum of $7,500 pursuant to the rights granted (or agreed to be granted) to Purchaser pursuant to this Agreement in respect of each such motion picture having a running time of one hour or less, and $7,500 per hour for each hour in excess of the first hour; provided, however, that in no event shall the maximum aggregate amount payable under this paragraph (c) exceed $60,000. Purchaser and Owner acknowledge that the amount payable hereunder is separate from any compensation payable pursuant to paragraph (b) above.

(d) In the event a television series (excluding a "miniseries," "movie-of-the-week," or the Picture itself) is produced by Producer based on the Picture for initial prime time network

(U.S.) exhibition and Owner is not engaged to render writing or other services in connection therewith, Owner will receive the following royalties for each original episode produced and broadcast (within ten [10] days after completion of each episode).

(i) For each program of up to and thirty (30) minutes in length, Two Thousand Dollars ($2,000); or

(ii) For each program in excess of thirty (30) minutes and up to and including sixty (60) minutes in length, Three Thousand Dollars ($3,000); or

(iii) For each program in excess of sixty (60) and up to and including ninety (90) minutes in length, Four Thousand Dollars ($4,000).

Twenty percent of the applicable series royalty will be payable for each of the first five U.S. reruns of each episode. No further sums will be payable for any other runs of such episode. Initial run royalty payments shall be made upon commencement of production of the program involved. Rerun payments shall be paid within sixty (60) days after the broadcast triggering payment. If such episodic television series is broadcast more frequently than one program per week (e.g., a daytime serial), the applicable per program royalty set forth above shall constitute payment for each full week of programming.

(e) In the event a spin-off of the television series referenced above (excluding a "miniseries," "movie-of-the-week," or the Picture itself) is produced by Producer based on said series and Owner is not engaged to render writing or other services in connection therewith, Owner will receive fifty percent (50%) of the applicable network royalties specified above for "generic" spin-off series and twenty-five percent (25%) of the applicable network royalties specified above for "planted" spin-off series.

(f) In the event any television production referenced in subparagraphs (c), (d), or (e) above is initially produced for

U.S. non–prime time or U.S. non-network broadcast, Owner shall be entitled to an amount equal to fifty percent (50%) of the applicable royalty set forth in said paragraph.

In the event Purchaser shall fail to make any of the aforesaid payments within the time and in the manner hereinabove set forth, Owner acknowledges and agrees that Owner's sole remedy shall be an action at law to recover such payments, and in no event shall any of said rights revert to Owner, nor shall Owner have or be deemed to have any lien, charge, or other encumbrance upon said rights to secure payment of said sums.

Note that usually you will not be entitled to receive a passive payment if you happen to *write* the particular production for which you would otherwise receive a passive payment. The reason: You will probably receive a lot more money to write a sequel or other subsequent production than the amount of the passive payments (as a rule, sequels and other subsequent productions are only produced if the first picture was a hit) and the studio does not want to pay you twice.

FIRST NEGOTIATION TO WRITE A SEQUEL OR OTHER SUBSEQUENT PRODUCTION

Odds are that if the first picture is a huge hit and you wrote it, the studio will want you back to write a sequel at a much higher price. Still, studios do have their pet writers and you may be aced out if you do not negotiate some protection for yourself in this arena. It is quite common to negotiate a right of first negotiation to write a sequel, remake, or other subsequent production. And if the first production was a feature, for example, the studio will agree that your price on a sequel picture will not be lower than the salary you received on the first picture.

Whether you sell a script or you are commissioned to write one, your right to write a sequel will most certainly be based on your having received sole "screenplay by" or sole "written by" credit on the first picture *and* sole separated rights. (The Writers Guild awards "written by" credit if no other writer wrote the story and screenplay, "screenplay by" credit if there is a separate storywriter or another screenwriter entitled to credit.) The studio's argument is that if other writers have to be brought in on the first picture, the picture consists of material that is no longer just your material (in the studio's view, your material was not good enough to make a picture), and, thus, studio negotiators insist on these conditions. Remember: If a picture is produced based on your original story and characters—unless a subsequent writer changes the essential elements dramatically—you will probably be awarded sole separated rights. Given Hollywood's tradition of using many writers on a project, you may not receive sole "screenplay by" credit. Unfortunately, therefore, you may easily lose your right to write subsequent productions. This is usually not negotiable.

What if your screenplay is based on a book or other source material? Let's say that you do receive sole "screenplay by" credit on the first picture. You will not receive sole separated rights, unless you also wrote the book, and, thus, you may not get the opportunity to write a sequel. In such cases, I try to negotiate for the writer the right to write a sequel if he gets sole "screenplay by" credit. Separated rights should not be an issue, because the book writer will not be asked to write a sequel screenplay to the movie. So why should the studio care? While some studios accept this argument, most do not, which I think is unfair. Keep in mind that if the first picture is a big hit and you did receive sole "screenplay by" credit, you will probably get the right to write the sequel anyway, so it is not worth breaking a deal over.

What if the first picture is a big hit and then becomes a television series? You should also try to get the right to write the pilot script (the prototype episode for the series). If you do, though, your right will always be subject to network approval, and, unless you have written for television before and, in particular, have written a pilot script, you may not get the shot. Networks tend to favor, and hire, experienced writers of television series to write their pilot scripts. It is a barrier that is extremely difficult to overcome.

GUARANTEED REWRITES AND WRITING ASSIGNMENTS: WHEN YOU SELL A SPEC SCREENPLAY OR A BOOK

Your philosophy, of course, is to stay with the project as long as you can. If you have optioned or sold an original script to a producer, you want the opportunity to do at least one rewrite and, moreover, the opportunity to do that rewrite before any other writer is hired. Under the current WGA Guild rules, the producer must offer the writer the first rewrite. This was a major breakthrough in negotiation between the producers and the Writers Guild. It was a long time coming.

Article 16.A.3.c of the WGA Basic Agreement provides that: . . . "with respect to a screenplay sold or licensed to Company (i.e., the studio or producer) by a "professional writer" [*see discussion in chapter 15 as to the meaning of this term*] who is awarded separated rights, the Company shall offer the first writer the opportunity to perform the first rewrite services at not less than the applicable minimum compensation for a rewrite. If such writer is unable to perform such services or waives his/her right, the Company may engage another writer.

In addition, the Company shall offer such writer the opportunity to perform one (1) additional set of revisions, if they are required by the Company, because of a changed or new element (e.g., director or principal performer) assigned to the development or production of the writer's screenplay. The Company's obligation to make such an offer shall exist for a period of two years after delivery of the writer's first or final set of revisions, whichever occurs later. *However,* this obligation does not arise if the Company engaged another writer to make revisions to the screenplay before the first changed or new element was assigned to the project. If the first writer is unable to perform such services or waives his/her right, the Company may engage another writer."

Even if you are not a WGA member, you should still insist on the guaranteed opportunity to write the first rewrite. After all, it is your script that someone else is tinkering with. You should have the first crack at rewriting it. This is crucial. Once you have optioned or sold your script to a studio or production company, decision makers at that company own it. They control it. In their minds and in accordance with Hollywood tradition, they can do whatever they want with it.

Luckily, today, few producers will object to giving you the first crack at a rewrite. Since this provision was added to the WGA Agreement, it has become an accepted norm of the business. If a producer does object, then you should suspect his intentions—obviously, the producer intends to kick you off the project as soon as he gains control of the material. Confront him. If the producer doesn't back down, think twice about that deal.

Note that under the Guild rule, you are only guaranteed WGA minimum for a rewrite, which as of May 2004 is $17,047 for a low-budget picture (under $5,000,000) and $25,989 for a high-budget picture (over $5,000,000). You should try to negotiate a higher fee. If you have been paid $100,000 for a first draft, it is ridiculous to accept a mere $25,989 for a rewrite. Between $30,000 and $40,000 would be more appropriate. Depending on your leverage and how much you may have been paid in the past for a rewrite (studios always ask for previous quotes), you will be able to increase the guaranty above the minimum compensation dictated by the Guild.

Most agreements that combine the option/purchase of a spec screenplay with writing services also provide that the payment for writing services be applicable against the purchase of the screenplay. Thus, if your script is optioned to a third-party producer and you are asked to render writing services, your writing compensation (not including pension, health, and welfare payments made on your behalf to the Writers Guild) will be deducted from the purchase price when the option is exercised. As an example, your script is under option. You are asked to write a rewrite and a polish and are paid for such. You receive $35,000 for your writing services. The purchase price is $300,000. There were two $5,000 option payments, one nonapplicable. At the time of purchase, you will receive $300,000, less $5,000 for the applicable option payment, less $35,000 for the writing services, or a total of $260,000. When a script is purchased outright, the buyer might also require writing services as part of the compensation. A young client of mine recently sold his screenplay for $300,000. The Agreement provided that the buyer could require him to render unlimited writing services. We tried to negotiate for a limit on such services (for example, three rewrites tops). The studio would not budge, and, ultimately, the writer accepted the deal. The studio maintains that the script is close to a shooting script. We'll see. (Note that the Writers Guild imposes certain limitations on unlimited rewriting. As a rule of thumb, if the compensation on a weekly basis doesn't at least add up to $4,228 per week, the studio can't ask for more writing. That is, if you are getting $40,000 for ten weeks of work, the studio can't ask you to write for eleven weeks.)

"Dead Screenplay" Problem

There is one downside to your obtaining the right to do rewrites on scripts that you option to a studio or a producer that is not a WGA signatory. It is a critical problem that you need to be aware of. The reality in Hollywood is that very few screenplays that are optioned actually get purchased and/or made. I don't know if anyone could give you an exact percentage, but it is fairly low. Given that reality, the question you should be asking yourself is: "What happens to my rewrite if my script is only optioned and not purchased?" Remember that writing services fall under the category of a "work-made-for-hire" (see chapter 2). In other words, the person who pays for it owns it. Thus, if your script is optioned but it is not purchased (that is, the option expires), you get your original script back, but the person who commissioned the rewrite owns the rewrite!

Suppose this happens to you. An option expires and now you want to option your screenplay to someone else. You can only option the original screenplay without the rewrite and all the good work that you put into that rewrite. Remember: Someone else owns the rewrite and you cannot touch it—any of it—except those portions that existed in the original screenplay. If you do use any of the rewritten material, you or whoever uses the rewrite can be sued for copyright infringement by the owner of the rewrite. The studio owns that material and the copyright in that material. You will also be sued by the second buyer of your script if you do not disclose the fact that someone else owns a rewrite. As you will note later in this book (under Representations and Warranties in chapter 8), one of the warranties that a writer must make to the buyer of his material is that he owns that material. If not, the writer has breached that provision of the contract and could be denied certain entitlements (that is, monies) under that contract.

Reversions

As discussed in chapter 4 above, the WGA now provides a mechanism for getting your rewrite back, but you can't do it for at least a year after the option expires and you lose your right to buy it back six years after the option expires. There is one solution to this problem for non-guild writers. You can ask for a *reversion* of your rewrite(s) if your script is optioned, but not purchased. In other words, when the option expires, the rights to your rewrite are then assigned to you. You will control it and may sell it again. If you are lucky enough to get a reversion clause included in your option contract, you may have to— and you probably *will* have to—agree to pay back the cost of the rewrite when and if the picture gets made. More likely, you will probably be asked to (1) pay back all costs that the initial buyer has incurred in connection with the project instead of just rewrite costs (in this case, try to limit it to actual costs—without overhead or interest) and (2) to pay back the costs *when you set up the project* with someone else. Keep in mind that you will not actually pay these costs. The subsequent buyer of your material will have to pay. It may be a deterrent for the buyer, but if he wants it badly enough, then at least you have the opportunity to make a deal.

What if the payback cost is too high? Will that prevent you from ever selling or optioning your script again? It shouldn't. If the costs are too high, then the next buyer may try to renegotiate with the owner of the rewrite(s) at the time the next buyer comes on board. At least if you get a reversion, you will have *control* of your rewrites and will be able to sell them, which may be essential depending on how much material you added.

Luckily, most of the major studios and companies in Hollywood are WGA signatories, and assuming you are a "professional writer" (see chapter 15) under the WGA you have the ability to get your rewrites back and your screenplay if it's actually been sold and there is no activity.

A Guaranty to Write

The goal of most writers is to stay with the project as long as possible. Contractually, this is called a guaranty. You are guaranteed the right to write a certain number of drafts. (The guarantee is discussed in more detail in chapter 9.)

The WGA provision that guarantees the writer of a spec screenplay one rewrite under certain circumstances (discussed above) also guarantees the writer the opportunity to write that rewrite *before* the company can engage the services of another writer. Even if you are not a Guild member, you should try to get this same right. In other words, the contract should explicitly stipulate that the studio/producer may not engage the services of another writer until you have turned in your rewrite.

You should also ask to be guaranteed more than one writing step, such as a rewrite and a polish. Most studios will not guaranty that they will keep you on until you've completed two drafts. With the guaranty though, even if they don't want you to write the second draft, you will be paid for it. Note that many studios agree to hire the writer for the first rewrite with the right to "cut off" any further writing steps after that point. Invariably, the studio will want an option for further writing steps. Remember that any such provision is an option only, for the studio's purpose. It guarantees you nothing.

BOOK OPTIONS

Agreements for the option and sale of books are similar to those for screenplays. I have already discussed some of these above. Recall that, with books, it is essential and customary for the author to reserve all publication rights. It is also easier to negotiate a reversion should a picture not be produced within a certain period of time. There are several other differences.

For one, if the book is optioned prior to publication, you may want to provide for a bonus should the book be a success. Such bonuses are normally payable only if the option is exercised and are generally tied to the *New York Times* bestseller list. The norm is that you will receive a payment for each week that the book is #1 on the list, a lower payment for each week that the book is #2 through #4 on the list and a still lower payment for each week that the book is #5 through #10 on the list.

Second, you will be required to have the publisher of your book sign a "publisher's release." This is a statement by the publisher that it does not own any motion picture, television, or other allied rights in the book. Publishers are accustomed to signing such releases. Here is a sample of such a release:

Publisher's Release

For good and valuable consideration, receipt of which is hereby acknowledged, the undersigned hereby acknowledges and agrees for the express benefit of Big Studio Films ("Purchaser"), and Purchaser's successors, licensees, and assigns, in perpetuity throughout the universe, that the undersigned has no claim to or interest in the motion picture, television, and allied and incidentally rights, or any other rights of any other kind whatsoever other than print publication rights which have been heretofore granted to the undersigned in or to that certain literary work (the "Property") published by the undersigned and described as follows:

Title: "The Hot Book"
Written by: [Your Name]
Copyright
Registration:

The undersigned hereby consents insofar as it is concerned to the publication and copyright by and/or in the name of Purchaser, or its successors, licensees, and assigns, in any and all languages; throughout the universe, in any form or media, (i) synopses, dramatizations, abridged, and/or revised versions of, or excerpts from, the Property, not exceeding 10,000 words each and to be serialized, adapted, or extracted from the Property or from any motion picture and/or other version of the Property for the purpose of advertising, publicizing, and/or promotion any such motion picture and/or other version or (ii) screenplays, so-called photonovels consisting of still photographs from any motion picture produced based on the Property with captions or other written material, and/or so-called making-of-the-picture publications. IN WITNESS WHEREOF, the undersigned has executed this instrument this ＿＿＿ day of ＿＿＿＿＿＿, 20＿＿.

By: ＿＿＿＿＿＿＿＿＿＿＿＿

Its: ＿＿＿＿＿＿＿＿＿＿＿＿

If you are a book writer, you are probably aware that even though you have created the characters, the plot, and everything else, in Hollywood's eyes you are probably not qualified to write a screenplay based on your book. Of course, you *do* have leverage. You do not have to sell the rights to your book without being afforded the right to write the screenplay.

If you are given the opportunity to write a screenplay, the question then becomes: How many drafts will you be allowed to write? If you are fortunate, one draft and a rewrite. That is the most usually given. And remember: Even if you get that right, it is not uncommon for producers to start again from scratch. They may throw out all of your material.

If you have never written a screenplay, about all you can expect is minimum compensation to write the screenplay. When we say "minimum" in Hollywood, that usually means WGA minimum, i.e., the minimum payment required by the Writers Guild of America for the particular work you are asked to write. As of May 2004, the minimum for a first draft and a set of revisions based on a book without a treatment for a low-budget film (under $5 million) is $34,096. For a high-budget picture (over $5 million), the minimum is $64,970. Make sure that this payment is over and above the monies you will receive for your book. In other words, the screenwriting monies are not applicable in any way to the book monies.

If the producer you are dealing with agrees to your writing the screenplay, he will almost certainly ask for something in return, such as a low option price on the book for the opportunity they are giving you to be hired to write the screenplay. That is not a bad position to be in.

The question then becomes *when* will you be hired. Commonly, the producer will agree to hire you if anyone is hired to write a screenplay. In such a case, you will be hired before anyone else has a chance. That works in your favor if the producer intends to hire a writer upon commencement of the option. If the producer is looking for a studio to finance the writing services, then you will have to wait until he sets up the project at a studio. Most producers are unwilling to pay for writing services without the backing of a financier, even if you are a seasoned screenwriter. It is a critical reality of the business. In that case, you have no way of knowing when, if ever, your services will commence.

Odds are that the studio will want a script written as soon as the producer makes his deal with the studio. Studios are in the film business and tend not to option books unless they intend to develop them. It is rare today that a studio will option a book just to take it off the market. More important, odds are that the producer is also looking to a studio to finance the option payment for the book and may even have made a deal with the studio to produce a movie based on that book before the producer closes the book deal with the writer. In my opinion, if you are interested in writing the screenplay, and the producer agrees to give you that right, you should take the deal even if the project has not yet been set up. That is, if you believe in the producer's abilities to set up the project with an appropriate financier. If you are unsure and are concerned that you may never get the chance to write the screenplay, ask the producer if he is financing the writing of the screenplay himself or if he has already presented the book to a studio. That way, you will know before signing the deal what your chances are of actually writing the screenplay yourself (and getting paid to do it).

8

Option/Purchase Agreements: Other Provisions to Watch Out For

W hile the monetary terms of your agreement are important, there are other significant provisions that may affect your entitlement to compensation or create liabilities for you. These provisions also need to be reviewed carefully.

CREDITS

The Writers Guild determines credits through formal procedures. Before the credits for a film or television program are placed on the screen, the company that has produced a show must submit its proposed credits to the Guild. This notice is sent to all writers (Guild and non-Guild) who have written any material in connection with that program. If the writer protests the proposed credits, he may object, in which case the Guild will arbitrate a decision.

Note that in the case of a dispute, the Guild, under Theatrical Schedule A.7, allows all participating writers to reach a compromise among themselves. Beware of this provision, however. Most studio contracts that provide bonuses to writers based on screenplay credit *disallow* the bonus if the writers decide among themselves how the credits should be finalized. The reason: One writer may get a very high bonus for a sole credit. He could conceivably make a side deal with the other writers to split his compensation for sole screenplay credit, which, in the end, may earn *all* writers more money than if they had not made such a deal. That is why the following language appears in contracts with respect to screenplay bonuses: "If the writer is awarded sole screenplay credit (other than pursuant to Theatrical Schedule A of the WGA Basic Agreement), then he/she shall receive . . . "

In an arbitration, three arbitrators are mutually selected to read all drafts of a work. The writer who disputes a proposed credit is requested to write a detailed analysis of why he is entitled to screenplay credit. Nonproducer and nondirector writers must contribute at least 33 percent of the final screenplay to receive credit. The requirement for producer/writers or director/writers (called "hyphenates" in Hollywood) is more stringent. Hyphenates must contribute 50 percent to get credit (see discussion in chapter 15 on Credit Arbitrations).

The advantage of the WGA credit arbitration is that it is free for the writers and the producers. It is a service of the Guild and a very valuable one.

REPRESENTATIONS AND WARRANTIES

If you sell or option a spec screenplay or a book, and even when you are commissioned to write, you will be required to make certain representations and warranties concerning your work. These "reps and warranties" as they are commonly referred to are crucial to the studio. Here is an example of a typical reps and warranties provision:

1.   WARRANTIES: Owner represents, warrants, and agrees:
   (a)   That Owner is the sole owner of all rights herein granted and has full power and authority to grant said rights to Purchaser, as more particularly set forth in this

agreement, and to agree to the restrictions upon the exercise of the rights reserved to Owner, as more particularly set forth in this agreement; that none of said rights have been granted, encumbered, or otherwise disposed of in any manner to any person; that no motion picture based in whole or in part upon the Work has been produced or authorized by or with the knowledge or consent of Owner; that neither the Work nor any version thereof nor any play or dramatic adaptation based thereon in whole or in part have been published or presented or authorized on television, radio, or on the spoken stage by or with the knowledge or consent of Owner; that Owner has not done or omitted to do and will not do or omit to do any act or thing, by license, grant, or otherwise, which will or may impair or encumber any of the rights herein granted or interfere with the full enjoyment of said rights; and that there are no claims or litigation pending or threatened which will or might adversely affect any of the rights herein granted to Purchaser.

(b)   That the Work is original with Owner; that neither the Work nor any part thereof is taken from or based upon any other material or any motion picture; and that neither the Work nor any part thereof, or the exercise by Purchaser of any of the rights herein granted, will violate or infringe upon the trademark, trade name, copyright, patent, literary, dramatic, musical, artistic, personal, private, civil or property right, or to the best of Owner's knowledge, right of privacy or publicity, or constitute a libel or slander of any person.

(c)   That the Work is not in the public domain and enjoys, and will enjoy, either statutory or common law copyright protection in the United States and all countries adhering to the Berne and Universal Copyright Conventions; and that the rights granted to Purchaser hereunder are and will be exclusive.

> Owner will defend, indemnify, make good, save, and
> hold harmless Purchaser, its successors and assigns,
> from and against any liability, losses, claims, damages,
> costs, charges, reasonable attorneys' fees, recoveries,
> actions, judgments, penalties, expenses, and other loss
> whatsoever, which may be obtained against, imposed
> upon, or suffered by Purchaser, its successors and
> assigns by reason of the use of the Work by Purchaser,
> its successors or assigns, or the breach of any war-
> ranty, covenant, agreement, or representation herein
> made by Owner. Purchaser shall indemnify and hold
> Owner harmless against any and all liability, losses,
> claims, damages, costs, charges, reasonable attorneys'
> fees, recoveries, actions, judgments, penalties, expens-
> es, and other loss arising out of or in connection with
> any assigned material or material added by Purchaser
> to the Work except to the extent any such liability
> results from a breach of Owner's representations,
> warranties, or agreements hereunder.

Basically, the studio wants to know that it will obtain good title to your material. Just as with the sale of a house or a car, the studio must be assured that you own the rights that you are selling and that no one else is going to claim ownership in that material. The studio also wants to know that your work is yours alone and that you haven't worked with another writer on it or, if you have, that you have disclosed that fact. Studio executives also want to be assured that your material is not based on an actual person's life story, in which case they would need a release from that person.

Article 28 of the WGA

You should know that under Article 28 of the Writers Guild Agreement, the Guild insists that any warranties concerning material that may be based on actual persons be "to the best of the writer's knowledge" only. These warranties are the ones contained in subpara-graph (b) above concerning rights of privacy, publicity, libel, and slander. In other words, you will not be required to say absolutely that your characters do not resemble actual persons. Rather, to the best of your knowledge, your characters are not based on actual persons, and you are not aware of infringing any other person's personal rights. The Writers Guild has recognized that writers are not lawyers and that writers often create material that is based on personal experience and personal relationships. In that sense, you are likely to draw from your own experience and use incidents that have happened between you and other persons. While you will probably not depict those other persons' lives as the core of your material, you may use an event, a meeting, an encounter with that real person in your material and the depiction of your own fictional character.

The other reason that the Writers Guild limits representations concerning libel, slander, rights of privacy, and publicity to the best of the writer's knowledge is that the Writers Guild recognizes that there may be someone in the world who might try to *claim* that one of your characters resembles that person's character and that your plot resembles that person's life story. And, indeed, successful pictures often spawn "nuisance suits," with someone trying to make a buck by filing a lawsuit. Even if you are not a member of the Guild, you should insist that your contract contain the same "to the best of your knowledge" qualification as set forth in Article 28 of the WGA Basic Agreement and that you are covered by the buyer's errors and omissions policy (see discussion below). You should not be blamed for, or be liable for, nuisance suits.

For your reference, Article 28 states:

Article 28: Warranty and Indemnification (General)

1. Company and writer may in any individual contract of employment include provisions for warranties of originality and no violation of rights of third parties, indemnification against judgments, damages, costs and expenses including attorneys' fees in connection with suits relating to the literary material or the use of the literary material supplied by the writer or the use thereof by Company; provided, however, that the writer shall in no event:

(a) be required by contract to waive his/her right to defend himself/herself against a claim by Company for costs, damages, or losses arising out of settlements not consented to by the writer; and Company reserves all of the rights it may otherwise have against the writer;

(b) be required to warrant or indemnify with respect to any claims that his/her literary material defamed or invaded the privacy of any person unless the writer knowingly used the name or personality of such person or should have known, in the exercise of reasonable prudence, that such person would or might claim that his/her personality was used in such material;

(c) be required to warrant or indemnify with respect to any material other than that furnished by the writer;

(d) be required to warrant or indemnify with respect to third party defamation, invasion of privacy, or publicity claims, where the writer is requested by the Company to prepare literary materials which are based in whole or in part on any actual individual, whether living or dead, provided writer accurately provides all information reasonably requested by Company for the purpose of permitting the Company to evaluate the risks involved in the utilization of the material supplied by writer.

Contracts are often drafted in the following manner to reflect the provisions contained in Article 28:

Owner represents and warrants that the Work is original with Owner; that neither the Work nor any part thereof is taken from or based upon any other material or any motion picture; and that neither the Work nor any part thereof, nor the exercise by Purchaser of any of the rights herein granted, will violate or infringe upon the trademark, trade name, copyright, patent, literary, dramatic, musical, artistic, personal, private, civil or property right, or to the best of Owner's knowledge, right of privacy or any other right of any person or constitute a libel or slander of any person.

Assuming that you created your material independently and are not in breach of any of your representations and warranties, what do you do if there is a lawsuit against the studio concerning your material or any additions that may be made to it by the studio? Will you be sued? Odds are you will be named. Does that mean you run the risk of spending thousands of dollars on legal fees by virtue of your being in business with a powerful, rich third party? Is the risk worth it?

Errors and Omissions Insurance

Rest easy: Studios and producers are able to protect themselves against many of these claims by obtaining insurance. This insurance is called "errors and omissions insurance," and is commonly referred to as "E & O insurance." Basically, this insurance covers claims of similarity, such as claims of copyright infringement and similarity. It also covers claims by persons who assert that the material in question is about their own life story—that is, the plot in the story is that person's own life story or a character in the screenplay has the same character traits as that person. Nuisance suits and copyright infringement suits are covered by the insurance company to the extent that the studio and you are not actually guilty of infringement. As an example, the writer of a book about Amistad sued DreamWorks, Steven Spielberg, and the writers of the motion picture *Amistad*, stating that the movie constituted an infringement of her book. As a writer of the screenplay, an errors and omissions insurance policy would protect you and pay for the cost of defending such a suit and settlement, if any, up to the policy limit— unless, of course, the plaintiff proved that you actually stole your material, in which case the insurance company would have a cause of action against you for reimbursement.

The insurance company assumes innocence and unless the company can prove that knowledgeable infringement has occurred, the insuror will cover the damages over and above the deductible. Yes, just like any other insurance policy, there is usually a deductible—$15,000 and up for each claim. While contracts do not state specifically that the studio will cover the deductible, it is an unwritten common policy for the studio or the producer to do so, and I do not know of any instance in which a writer has been asked to contribute. Policy limits are generally $1 million for each occurrence ($3 million aggregate cover-age on any one picture), although in recent years these amounts have increased to $3 million for each occurrence ($5 million aggregate cov-erage on any one picture). Most claims are settled out of court.

What you need is to be certain that you are covered by the insur-ance policy. Indeed, the Writers Guild Basic Agreement requires that "the Company shall name or cover the writer . . . as an *additional insured* on its errors and omissions policies respecting theatrical and television motion pictures."

In addition, the Basic Agreement states that "the Company shall indemnify such writer of all liability in connection with any claim or action respecting material supplied to the writer by the Company for incorporation into the writer's work by employees or officers of the Company other than the writer." This indemnity is often referred to as a "reciprocal indemnity"—reciprocal because the writer also gives an indemnity regarding his own material (as discussed above).

Even though these provisions exist in the Guild Agreement, I always ask that the contract specifically spell out the protections embodied in these two provisions. (Note also that the WGA provisions do not apply to all writers. Animation writers, as an example, are not covered by the WGA Agreement.) It is common practice in the industry to do so and it is also important for the writer making his own representa-tions and warranties to see in the contract that he will be protected. I also try to embellish the provision concerning added material to include changes made to the writer's material (a change, such as a dele-tion, may not necessarily be construed as an addition). Bottom line: What this means is that (1) the studio will cover the costs of any law-suits that the writer is named in resulting from material that is not the writer's and that may be included in the final screenplay or motion pic-ture and (2) the insurance policy will cover material that is the writer's as long as the writer has not knowingly infringed someone else's rights.

Here is an example of the provision:

Except with respect to (i) matters constituting a breach by Writer of any of the representations, warranties, and/or agreements con-tained in this Agreement and/or (ii) gross negligence or willful

misconduct by Writer, Purchaser shall indemnify Writer and his successors in interest, and hold him harmless from and against any
and all Damages and Expenses (other than with respect to any settlement entered into without Producer's written consent). Purchaser
shall indemnify and hold Owner harmless against any and all liability, losses claims, damages, cost, charges, reasonable attorneys'
fees, recoveries, actions, judgments, penalties, expenses, and
other loss arising out of or in connection with any assigned material
or material added by Purchaser to the Work and arising out of any
third party claim against Writer resulting from Purchaser's production, distribution, and/or exploitation of the Picture; provided Writer
adhere to any and all instructions given by Producer consistent with
this Agreement. Purchaser agrees that Owner shall be covered as
an additional insured under the errors and omissions policy in connection with the Picture to the extent Purchaser has obtained errors
and omissions insurance for the Picture.

There is one pitfall that you need to be aware of. The WGA Agreement
refers to the fact that the company must cover the writer under its
policy. Suppose it does not have a policy? The word *its* is ambiguous in
this context, and, arguably, if the company has no policy, it does not
have to list the writer as an additional insured. I therefore ask that the
writer be named on *an* errors and omissions policy. If the company does
not take one out, then it is in breach, and it will have to cover you. The
reciprocal indemnity also ensures the company's obligations to you.

If you are not a member of the Writers Guild, then you must ask for
these provisions and make sure that the company agrees to list you as a
additional insured on its coverage. This involves a minimum incremental
cost for the studio, and it should send you a certificate indicating that
you have been covered. Note that some of the big studios self-insure. If
it's a huge company, the indemnity from the studio is generally accepted.

INDEMNIFICATION: BREACH VS. ALLEGED BREACH

Look carefully at the last paragraph of the reps and warranties provision that I quoted above. Notice that you are requested to indemnify
the studio if you have breached (violated) your reps and warranties.

Your indemnity requires you to pay for the damages incurred by the studio as a result of your failure to live up to your reps and warranties, including lawyers' fees and court costs. On a successful motion picture, needless to say, the damages could be extremely high! The studio holds you accountable in these critical areas.

Most contracts in their initial draft state that the writer must indemnify the studio for a "breach" or "alleged breach" of that writer's representations, warranties, and agreements under that contract. It is important to understand the distinction between these two terms.

If the writer has "breached" his contract, that means that the writer has basically failed to comply with his obligations under that contract. This is also called "default." For instance, the writer may have stated that he wrote his material alone when, in fact, he wrote with a writing partner. The writer may have actually based his material on a true story without disclosing this fact. The writer may have violated any of the other reps and warranties or any other promise contained in the writer's contract. If the writer is rendering services, he may have delivered material past the delivery date. If you do breach—specifically, you take too long to write a draft, you write another project when your services are supposed to be exclusive, you are not available during a reading period, you disregard the studio's instructions regarding a rewrite (when asked to do a rewrite, the contract always provides that you must incorporate the studio's requests), you sell a screenplay that you do not own, you say you are the sole writer and someone else has helped you—your contract automatically terminates certain benefits. Even if you are entitled to a screenplay credit, for instance, you may be denied your bonus. You may be denied your profits, denied the opportunity to write a sequel, and you may be denied your right to receive the passive payments that you negotiated.

An "alleged breach" is a *claim* that the writer has breached. In other words, a studio may claim that you have breached, but you can also say that you have not. Ultimately, if there is a dispute as to which side is right, it is up to a court to decide. That is expensive. And even if you win, remember that lawyers' fees are not automatically awarded to the prevailing party, so you might find yourself having to pay for them yourself.

The main reason to focus on the distinction between "breach" and "alleged breach" is that if you can be denied compensation for an alleged breach, you can be denied compensation if the studio *says* you have not complied. That is enough to deny you your rights—most important, your compensation. Screenwriters' lawyers always ask to have this provision deleted, and, often, the studios will agree to delete it. The contract will then say that you must have breached your contract in order for there to be the right to deny you your rights, which means that the *burden* is on the *studio* to *prove* that you breached. Unfortunately, taking out the "alleged breach" language does not mean that the studio will not try to claim that you breached before it has been proven and will not stop paying you your money. You may have to sue anyway. At the very least, though, the consensus in Hollywood is that by deleting the "alleged breach" language, it means that the studio will not be able to claim breach without having *strong* grounds to do so.

Fortunately, most writers do not breach their contracts, and if they need more time to write a particular draft, for instance, the studio will listen. Make sure that if the studio agrees to give you more time to write a screenplay, you confirm this point in writing. If the studio has agreed to it, then technically it is not a breach, but you will want to make sure that you have a record of it. The consequences of breaching a contract may be costly and you do not want to take any chances.

Finally, in defining what is a breach or default, lawyers always make the point that the breach or default must be a "material" one in order for you to be denied your rights. You will often see language such as "provided writer has not *materially* breached his obligations hereunder . . ." If you deliver the screenplay a half hour late, in most circumstances, that will not be considered "material," so you should not be denied your compensation or other perks.

NAME, LIKENESS, AND BIOGRAPHY

The studio will invariably insist on the right to use your name not only for credit purposes, but also for publicity. That right is generally unlimited. The studio also wants the right to use your likeness—a picture or the right to do interviews with you. You might even be asked to go on the road for promotion. This, of course, should be subject to your availability. No additional compensation is paid, but they should agree to fly you first class and pay for your hotel and per diem.

Finally, the studio also wants to be able to talk about other material you have written and other aspects of your life. The studio will agree, if asked, to use only a biography that has been approved by you, but you must submit your biography upon request or you will lose your approval rights. Here is a name, likeness, and biography excerpt from a writer's agreement:

> **Name and Likeness.** Artist hereby grants to Studio the nonexclusive right, in perpetuity and throughout the universe, to use Artist's name, likeness, activities, attributes, and/or approved biography (it being agreed that Artist's right of approval over Artist's biography is conditioned upon Artist's submission to Studio of a factually accurate biography within five (5) days of Studio's request therefor) in connection with the production, exhibition, advertising, and other exploitation of each Picture, if any, and all subsidiary and ancillary rights therein, in any and all media, including, but not limited to, recordings (in any configuration) containing any material derived from such Picture, including, without limitation, all or any part of the soundtrack of such Picture, publications, merchandising, and commercial tie-ups; provided, however, that in no event shall Artist be depicted as using any product, commodity, or service without such Artist's express prior consent. Notwithstanding the foregoing, it is understood and agreed that Studio's use of Artist's name in a billing block on any item of merchandise or other material shall constitute an acceptable use of such Artist's name which shall not require his consent.

No Injunctive Relief

In all contracts in Hollywood, there is a provision that states that under no circumstances is the writer entitled to injunctive relief. You will see this in your option/purchase agreement. You will also see it in your employment agreement. What this means is that under no circumstances will you be able to *stop* the development or production of any production based on your work. You can sue for damages, but you cannot interfere with the rights once you have signed them away. This point is *nonnegotiable*. Don't even try. Here is a sample of one such provision:

> EXTENT OF RIGHTS; REMEDIES. All the rights, licenses, privileges, and property herein granted to Purchaser are irrevocable and not subject to rescission, restraint, or injunction under any circumstances. Specifically, but without limiting the generality of the foregoing, Owner hereby expressly recognizes that in the event of a breach of Purchaser's obligations hereunder, the damage, if any, caused to Owner thereby is not irreparable or otherwise sufficient to entitle Owner to injunctive or other equitable relief. Consequently, Owner's rights and remedies in the event of a breach hereof by Purchaser shall be limited to Owner's rights, if any, to recover damages in an action of law, and in no event shall Owner be entitled by reason of any such breach to rescind this Option Agreement or any rights granted to Purchaser hereunder, or to enjoin or restrain Purchaser's exercise of any rights granted to Purchaser hereunder.

On the other hand, the studio does have the right to seek injunctive relief against you. For instance, suppose you are contracted to render exclusive writing services, but you are actually working on another project at the same time. The studio will be able to stop you. Again, this provision is nonnegotiable. Here is an excerpt:

> The parties agree that the services agreed to be rendered by Employee hereunder are of a special, unique, unusual, extraordinary, and intellectual character which gives them a peculiar value, the loss of which cannot be reasonably or adequately compensated in damages in an action at law. Therefore, in the event of any breach or threatened breach of this Agreement by Employee, Producer shall be entitled to seek equitable relief, by way of injunction or otherwise.

9

Commissioned Screenplays

Many writers in Hollywood are hired and paid to write. The producer may have an idea for a movie or the writer may pitch an idea to the producer in hopes that he will be hired to write it. Many writers simply cannot afford to take the time to write a "spec" screenplay. They need to be paid. In this chapter I discuss the important provisions of a writer's employment agreement.

EXCLUSIVITY

Almost all writing services' agreements contain a requirement that the writer's services must be exclusive during the period that the writer is writing that particular screenplay. The studio is paying for your services and it wants to ensure that your services are wholly devoted to the material that it is commissioning. Barring extenuating circumstances, the studio expects to receive the material it has commissioned at the time stipulated in your contract. That is not to say that studios will not give you more time. However, if the cause of the delay is that you are working on another project, they may not. The so-called reading periods that follow delivery of each step of the writing process (for example, after delivery of the first draft, rewrite, polish, and so on) require the writer to be nonexclusive. That is the period for the producer to review the material, talk to you about it, and talk to whomever he needs to talk to (for instance, studio brass) before going to the next step.

GUARANTEED STEPS

If you are commissioned to write a screenplay, you will usually be commissioned for a first draft and a rewrite, and, sometimes, a polish (although the polish is usually optional). The nonoptional commitments are called the "guarantee" and you are guaranteed the negotiated compensation for those steps.

Writers usually get ten to twelve weeks to turn in a first draft and another four to six weeks for a rewrite. The polish writing period is two to four weeks. Reading periods are usually four weeks. What this means is that once you have committed to write, you cannot take on any other assignments until you finish the guaranteed steps. Thus, if you are commissioned for a first draft screenplay and rewrite and the writing periods are ten weeks and four weeks respectively, you may not take another writing assignment for ten weeks (first draft) + four weeks (reading period) + four weeks (rewrite) for a total of eighteen weeks. If you are a Writers Guild member, there is a limit to the number of weeks that a producer may employ you, depending on your level of compensation. (See discussion below.)

Almost all studios pay one-half the required compensation on commencement of services for the particular draft and one-half on delivery. Suppose you are paid $80,000 for a first draft and a rewrite, with $50,000 allocated to the first draft and $30,000 allocated to the rewrite. You will be paid $25,000 on commencement of the first draft, $25,000 on delivery of the first draft, $15,000 on commencement of the rewrite and $15,000 on delivery of the rewrite.

POSTPONEMENT

The studio may decide to postpone the second step after the reading period or the third step, and at another point in the process. In that case, you should be able to take other assignments. Studios usually do have the option to postpone the second or third guaranteed step, in which case you will still have to render the applicable services at a later date, but that will be subject to your professional availability. There are two points to be negotiated in this regard. First, if the studio postpones a step you should still get paid for that step *as if* the step had not been postponed. Thus, using the example above, if you were supposed to have started writing the rewrite after fourteen weeks but it is postponed, you would still be paid your commencement money for the rewrite in the fourteenth week and your delivery money in the eighteenth week. (Remember: You were given four weeks to write it.)

The second point you can try to negotiate is a limitation on the amount of time that the studio has to postpone your services. Some studios will give a limitation of one year, some two years. Thus, if a writing step is postponed, the studio cannot ask you to write that step later than one or two years past the date on which that studio decided to postpone the step. Of course, if you are unavailable to write during that entire period, the period will be extended for the span of your unavailability.

MAXIMUM WRITING TIME: WRITERS GUILD LIMITATIONS

The Writers Guild Agreement provides for a minimum weekly writing salary for writers employed by the week. As of May 2003, the amount is $4,228 for writers of feature films. Suppose the studio wants you to write a first draft screenplay for $50,000. The studio must employ you for not more than eleven weeks for $50,000, so contractually you will not be able to write for fourteen weeks if you are a WGA member. Even if you are not a member of the Writers Guild, most studios are signatories to the Guild so they are bound by Guild rules. Since this is a WGA requirement, studios are also loath to give you more than the maximum time allowed by the Guild, even noncontractually. If they knowingly allow you extra time to write, they expose themselves to a claim that you are entitled to extra compensation for the extra weeks worked and they do not want to expose themselves to such claims. That is not to say that extensions are never given. The studio has to trust that you will not raise the issue with the Guild. You might think that if an extension is beneficial to the writer (in other words, the writer needs the extra time and doesn't care about the extra money), the Guild shouldn't care. Believe me, the Guild does. The WGA is a stickler regarding compliance with its rules. If the WGA finds out that you are a member and you have violated WGA policy, the Guild may fine you for noncompliance.

COMPENSATION: GUARANTEED PAYMENT

The most important part of any writer's deal is the up-front guarantee. How many drafts are you guaranteed: one draft; or one draft and one rewrite; or one draft, one rewrite, and one set of revisions? The more you write, the better your chances of getting credit and, probably, a bonus. Most writing deals include a bonus for sole "screenplay by" or sole "written by" credit and even shared "screenplay by" credit.

Ideally, if you are writing a first draft, you want a guaranteed rewrite and another polish. No one expects to deliver a perfect first draft, so studios do not balk at giving you the added steps. They just try to keep the price down. Of course, if you are a Guild writer, there are limitations. The minimum price for a "treatment" (which is a detailed outline of your screenplay—studios like to see this before you begin writing and they will pay extra for it), first draft, and final draft screenplay (meaning revisions on your first draft) based on an original story is $45,463 for a low-budget feature (less than $5,000,000), $84,546 for a high-budget picture, plus pension, health, and welfare payments, which are paid directly to the WGA (prices effective May 2, 2003).

There is one drawback to being guaranteed too many steps. As mentioned above, you are under contract, *exclusive contract*, which means you cannot take other assignments. This could be particularly costly, for instance, if you were guaranteed one draft, one rewrite, and four polishes. You get paid a fraction of the draft price for polishes; $8,528 for polishes for a low-budget feature, $12,992 for a high-budget feature. Compare this to the WGA's allocated amount for a first draft screenplay of $20,460 for a low-budget film, $38,981 for a high-budget first draft screenplay (prices effective May 2, 2003). In other words, during all the time that you are polishing a script, you might have been hired to do a first draft screenplay on another script for almost three times the price of a polish. This is a big difference. Note that this is not a point to get hung up on. Studios usually will not guarantee four polishes anyway (remember that they want you to be disposable).

The more likely scenario is that the studio will require optional steps, meaning that if they like the first draft and the rewrite (Remember: They tend to give you at least one shot to get it right), then they will want to keep you on. They also like to build in options at a set price. Optional services are almost always subject to your availability, unless they are ordered *immediately after* the guaranteed steps, in which case you have to remain available just as with a guaranty, but you are not guaranteed the assignment. This is slightly unfair, but optional steps are almost always postponed, and, anyway, studios tend to be more flexible in this area, working around your availability. In short, it is more than likely that you will be free to take on other assignments, so most writers plan on taking other assignments immediately after the guaranteed period is over. Studios usually need time to think, so odds are they will not ask for the optional steps right away. *Note:* When the studios talk about writing steps being subject to your availability, they mean "professional" availability. Personal unavailability does not count. You must be *contractually* bound to someone else.

Bonus Based on Credit

The other critical aspect of the employment deal is the bonus. Suppose you are the only writer on the project (rare, but it might happen). You get sole "screenplay by" or sole "written by" credit (if it is also your original story). You should be entitled to a bonus. Even if you get shared writing credit, you should get a bonus. Hollywood agrees. As I have mentioned, writers are basically disposable. However, if you stay on the project long enough and/or a sufficient amount of your work ends up as part of the final product, entitling you to a shared credit or maybe a sole credit, the studio will give you a reward. Most writers are able to negotiate a sole "screenplay by" credit bonus and a shared "screenplay by" credit bonus.

Writing deals are structured so that all of your guaranty and any additional monies you have been paid for optional steps are applied against the bonus. Thus, for example, if you negotiate a $175,000 sole "screenplay by" bonus and you have been paid $50,000 to write a draft and a set of revisions, you will receive $125,000 if you are awarded sole "screenplay by" credit.

The shared "screenplay by" bonus is usually one-half of the difference between the amounts you have been paid and the sole "screenplay by" bonus. Thus, using the above example, your shared bonus would be $175,000 minus $50,000 = $125,000/2 or $62,500. Some studios only give a flat fee for a shared bonus. If your deal is structured this way, the flat fee is usually a lower amount than you could make under the one-half sole "screenplay by" bonus formula. The flat rates would usually range between $25,000 and $75,000. Of course, this is negotiable. Top writers will receive more.

It is rare to see a "story by" credit bonus in a writer's employment deal. It does not hurt to ask, but I do not recall having seen one in recent years. In any event, it would probably not be more than $25,000. The studio figures that your guarantee covers this possibility.

Be aware of the terminology in your contract. Sometimes the initial draft of a writer's agreement will say that if you get sole "written by" credit, you will receive the bonus. If you are the sole writer, you will probably get this credit. But, if your material is based on someone else's story, then the storywriter will probably receive a "story by" credit. In that case, you are the only *screenplay* writer to receive credit as distinguished from the story, and you will receive "screenplay by" credit. To cover this possibility, I ask that the language be changed to reflect that if you receive sole "written by" credit *or* sole "screenplay by" credit, you will receive the sole "screenplay by" bonus. The studio usually does intend to give the sole "screenplay by" bonus if you are the sole screenplay writer, even if someone else received "story by" credit, so the contract language should reflect that. Finally, if you think that your work might be used as the basis of a television movie or any other television production, you should also add "teleplay by" credit to the list. The wording should thus be: "If the writer receives sole 'written by,' 'screenplay by,' or 'teleplay by' credit, the writer will receive the sole 'screenplay by' bonus." The same language should be used to describe the shared "screenplay by" bonuses: "If the writer receives shared 'written by,' 'screenplay by,' or 'teleplay by' credit, the writer will receive the shared 'screenplay by' bonus." Most studios will not agree to add this language. As a general rule, television writers receive less and studios do not want to pay more generous feature screenplay prices if they make a television movie. If they do, however, that should not affect your guaranty, as you will have been paid to write a feature and they should not ask you to return monies paid.

The bonus is usually payable when credits are determined. If you are a member of the WGA or your employer is a signatory to the WGA, credit will be determined by arbitration (see discussion below). Even if you are not a member of the WGA, credits are usually determined through arbitration. Most non-WGA companies will agree to use the same procedures and criteria prescribed by the Guild to determine credits, even if they are not signatories to the WGA.

If you are the sole writer on a movie, you may also ask to be paid your bonus earlier than the credit determination. Why should you wait until credits are determined (which will not be until after principal photography of the movie) to get your payment? Most studios agree that if no subsequent writer is hired prior to commencement of principal photography, you will receive your *shared* "screenplay by" bonus on commencement of principal photography of the picture. They will not give you the *sole* "screenplay by" bonus because the director or producer could rewrite the whole script during shooting (not an uncommon occurrence) and directors and producers are entitled to claim writing credit. The criteria for them is different. Note that for directors or producers to receive any credit, they must have contributed at least 50 percent to the screenplay. This requirement is designed to protect writers from losing their credits to people who do not make their living solely by writing. It is an explicit recognition that credits are very important to writers.

Keep in mind that this provision is usually worded in such a way that any screenplay credit bonus monies you receive before credit arbitration (that is, on commencement of principal photography) are considered an *advance* against your bonus. In other words, if, for some reason, you do not get shared credit, you will have to repay the money. This is an unlikely scenario, but the studios protect themselves just the same.

Profits Based on Credit

The employed writer's entitlement to net profit participation is also based on credit. The norm is that the writer will receive 2.5 percent of 100 percent of the net profits for shared "screenplay by" credit, and 5 percent of 100 percent of the net profits for sole "screenplay by" credit. Remember the importance of adding the language "of 100 percent" in your contract.

As discussed in the previous section, you want to be careful with the language that is used to define your entitlement. Be sure to use the words "written by," "screenplay by," and "teleplay by" to describe your credit. In short, you do not want to lose your benefits because of the terminology. The studio intends to reward you if there are no other screenwriters or you share a screenplay credit, so make sure to cover yourself by referring to the various credit possibilities. Remember: Someone else's entitlement to a "story by" credit should not cheat you out of your *bonus* or *points*. It is one of the few norms that is decidedly in favor of the writer.

Passive Payments: Right to Write a Sequel or Other Subsequent Production

The requirements for passive payments are usually the same for writing assignments as they are for spec scripts. At the studios, the writer must receive sole separated rights (and sometimes shared) to receive payments (unlike the credit bonus entitlement, which is usually based on credit, as discussed above). The same criteria are used for writing assignments as for spec scripts when it comes to the writer's right to write a sequel or other subsequent production (refer to the discussion in chapter 3 to refresh your understanding of these provisions). The key to writing assignments is this: Unless you write the first draft, you may never receive separated rights, or for that matter, credit. Thus, if you are asked to do a rewrite of someone else's script, you should focus on the writing compensation. That is not to say that you should not negotiate other provisions for passive payments or the right to write a sequel. You never know: Your script may be the script that is actually shot. There is an expression in Hollywood that refers to an extensive rewrite. It is called a "page one rewrite." It is not uncommon for a writer who is hired to do a rewrite to write a whole new script. It is not what the studio is paying for, but it happens. Thus, always protect yourself, and if you are asked to do a rewrite and you contemplate major changes, try to negotiate the same points that you would have sought, had you been asked to write the first draft screenplay.

REWRITES, POLISHES, AND OTHER WRITING SERVICES

When you are hired to write revisions on a screenplay that has already been written, your deal will look similar to an agreement for your writing services to write a first draft screenplay. The basic difference is the compensation. The initial compensation paragraph of the agreement will usually set forth your compensation for guaranteed services. This would be your "fixed compensation." There may be options for additional services.

Your agent will probably negotiate a sole "screenplay by" bonus and a shared "screenplay by" bonus, similar to those in an agreement for a writer who has been commissioned from the start. Obviously, when you are rewriting, the shared "screenplay by" bonus is more important. You will also be negotiating for passive payments. While it will be difficult for you to obtain sole separated rights for purposes of gaining passive payments, you should still negotiate this point. As noted above, many writers who are hired to do a rewrite end up doing a "page one rewrite" with new characters, new story lines, and so on. Under such circumstances, you might very well be entitled to at least shared separated rights and, depending on the studio, some compensation in this area.

In addition, you should set forth your contingent compensation. Again, this will probably be based on sole and shared "screenplay by" credit. All other provisions would basically be the same as contained in an agreement for a first draft screenplay.

One point to note: With enormous leverage, in some circumstances I have seen writers negotiate that they will receive a sole "screenplay by" bonus if they get shared credit with anyone *other than*, for instance, the first writer (if the studio intends to throw out most of that writer's material). Or, sometimes you can get a bonus if the picture is made *without regard to credit*. Again, it is rare with studio deals, but under certain circumstances, particularly if you are paid very little money for rewriting services, you might insist on some payment if the project gets made.

TERMINATION RIGHTS

All writing contracts provide that the employer may terminate your services if you have breached or are in default of your contract or if you become disabled.

Default or Breach

The default or breach provision exists in all employment agreements. This means that you have not complied with your obligations or you have violated your representations and warranties. The provision regarding representations and warranties, indemnity, and breach are virtually identical in option/purchase and writing agreements.

If the default is "material" (and you should always ask to have this word, meaning "significant," inserted), then the studio has the right to terminate your contract. Usually that right is enforced immediately upon the occurrence of such an event.

Sometimes the studio will allow you time to cure certain defaults. Suppose you hand in a script late or do not include some material that the studio executive asked you to add in your rewrite. The cure period is usually twenty-four hours (in other words, you had better cure fast) and a one-time-only event. If you continually breach your contract, studios will not give you any more rights to cure and you may be terminated. Note that there is no cure for a breach of representations and warranties. For example, say the studio finds that your script is not your own original work. Someone else owns it. You have used your best friend's life story as the basis for your screenplay, but you failed to get a release from her. If it is serious enough, the studio will simply terminate the contract and get out of business with you. Some studio contracts state that in the event of your default, you will have to repay all the money that you have received. Sometimes, I am able to have this provision taken out. The studio can always sue you for damages and the damages might not total the sums that you have been paid. Let a court or arbitrator decide.

Once you are terminated for cause (which is basically what a default is), you will receive no further payments and, essentially, all bets are off. The contract will stipulate that you do not get your bonus (even if you manage somehow to get the requisite credit), you will not get your points (contingent compensation), and you may not get your credit (although the WGA should protect you if your writing entitles you to credit notwithstanding your default). It is not a good situation and you should avoid a breach at all times.

Disability

Your contract allows the producer to suspend or terminate your contract if you are disabled (in layman's terms, sick or incapable of rendering services). The contract provides that the producer may initially suspend your services. The studio's right to suspend in that event is immediate and with a suspension based on disability also comes the studio's right to suspend payments as well. If the disability continues for a certain period of time, the producer may then terminate your contract, meaning that you will not be entitled to any additional compensation (that is, you may lose some of your guarantee). Unlike default, however, you will usually not lose your bonus or credit.

The initial draft of any writer's agreement is usually strict. Some agreements say that the contract may be terminated if you are sick for three consecutive or five aggregate days (meaning you have been sick on and off for five days). Note that studios will usually not terminate you (in fact, I do not know of any instances when this has occurred), but they have the right to. I always try to increase the time period and most studios will agree. First, they will distinguish between exclusive and nonexclusive periods. Second, they will establish different time periods for consecutive sick days and aggregate sick days. Conservatively, you should be able to increase the time period to five or seven consecutive days and ten or fourteen days in the aggregate, during the exclusive period. That means that your agreement cannot be terminated during your exclusive periods unless you are sick, and the studio has suspended your contract during this sick period, for at least five to seven consecutive days, or ten to fourteen days in the aggregate. I ask to increase the time periods to seven or ten consecutive days and fourteen or twenty-one aggregate days of sickness during nonexclusive periods (the nonexclusive periods being the reading periods, as discussed above).

What happens if your services are terminated two days prior to your delivery of a writing step? Does that mean that you will not be entitled to your delivery money? (Remember: Usually half of your compensation is payable on commencement of a particular writing step; the other half on delivery.) Technically, yes. In reality, if you can turn in your material, you will be paid. And if you are a member of the Writers Guild, the Guild will determine what portion of your compensation should be paid if you cannot finish it. Thus, if you wrote three-quarters of the script, odds are you will be paid three-quarters of your compensation if the Guild handles your claim. If you are not a Guild member and the producer is not a signatory, then, unfortunately, you may have to sue to get your compensation and that can be costly.

Force Majeure

As indicated in chapter 3, in the discussion about option/purchase agreements, the occurrence of a force majeure event may toll (extend) the option period. It is generally not a cause for termination. In a writer's employment agreement, it is cause for suspension and, in some instances, termination. The primary reason for this is the occurrence of a writers' strike. In the view of studio executives, if there is a strike, you should not be paid. Their position is not illogical.

Employment agreements generally provide for an automatic suspension of the writer's services if there is a force majeure event. Writers' contracts usually state that such an event is also cause for termination. As with option/purchase agreements, you want to make sure that the force majeure event is one that affects *your* services. A tornado in Mississippi is not necessarily relevant to your circumstances, but it is technically a force majeure event. My basic philosophy is that you never want to leave room for your employer to get rid of you if there is no legitimate reason for the termination. In other words, my goal is to try to eliminate escape clauses such as those that may give your employer an out if he doesn't like you. Thus, with a force majeure event, try to state that a force majeure event must be one that affects the business of your employer and, more particularly, your writing services.

Second, try to ensure that your employer does not single you out in an event of force majeure. Suppose your services are the only services that are suspended during an event of force majeure. All other writers working for that employer continue writing. In other words, try to link the studio's ability to suspend you to its simultaneous suspension of others. The same principle applies to termination. Studio executives should not single you out for termination. If they do, it generally means that your employer is using this clause as a means to get rid of you for other reasons.

Force majeure provisions usually provide that if the force majeure event continues for a certain period of time, then your employer may fire you. That period of time is usually eight consecutive weeks; in some cases, four to six weeks. Each studio or producer has its own policy in that regard. This point is usually not negotiable. However, you also want to make sure that if the event continues for a certain period, you, too, can get out of the contract. You may have other plans, other obligations, and you do not want to be tied up indefinitely. This is called a "reciprocal right of termination." It is not automatic, however. Once you have given notice that you want to terminate, your employer may bring you back by agreeing to lift its suspension; that is, by living up to its contract from the time it lifts the suspension going forward.

Another point to raise is that there should be only one suspension for each event of force majeure. Otherwise, your employer could suspend you during such an event for three weeks, put you back on for one week, suspend you again for three weeks, and so on. This would prevent you from even trying to terminate your agreement. The four-week, six-week, or eight-week consecutive period, as applicable, would never come into play and you could be tied up indefinitely.

Keep in mind that studios rarely implement their force majeure provisions unless it is an event that truly interferes with the development process. And the only event that does categorically interfere with that process is a writers' strike, in which case you can be sure that the studios will enforce these provisions.

If your employer terminates your services and the force majeure event ends (such as the end of a writers' strike), will your employer rehire you? The initial draft of the contract does not provide for this. What you want is a right of *reinstatement*. In other words, if development of the project is resumed after the event of force majeure, then your contract will be reinstated when the force majeure event no longer exists. There are usually several limitations. In general, a studio will only reinstate your services if it decides to continue development within six months (sometimes one year) after the cessation of a force majeure event. Second, you must be available to provide services when the studio resumes development. If these conditions are met, you go back to work. This is a very important right. Remember that if your contract is terminated, you will not receive any additional compensation and you may lose out on guaranteed compensation, bonus, profits, and the like. Make sure to ask for the reinstatement provision.

CERTIFICATE OF AUTHORSHIP

Writers are usually asked to sign a Certificate of Authorship in addition to a writing agreement. Like the short form option and assignment (see chapter 4), the main purpose of the Certificate is to register in the copyright office the fact that the employer of record owns the material that has been commissioned.

The Certificate of Authorship usually contains the writer's representations and warranties. It does not recite the salary.

The significance of the Certificate is that, once signed, it establishes that the employer owns the material. It is like the pink slip for a car. Ownership is absolute. For that reason, I like to have the Certificate make reference to the actual writer's agreement. Some studios will do this; some will not. If there is any ambiguity in the contract or breach by the studio, the studio does not want the contract to affect its ownership of the material.

You should know that, because of the legal significance of this piece of paper, studios will often agree to pay a writer his commencement monies upon the writer's signing of this Certificate. They will pay, that is, even before the long-form contract has been drafted. I do not recommend doing this, no matter how desperate for money you are. I like, at least, to see the long-form contract to make sure that all the financial provisions are described accurately. I also want to make sure there are no major problems with the contract. Remember: Once you sign the Certificate, you have no more leverage! You have signed away your rights. Once the major points are worked out in the long form, then it is up to you if you want to wait until every last "t" is crossed and "i" dotted. Some writers do. Some writers trust that the nonmonetary provisions will get worked out in accordance with custom and practice, and they are usually right. Of course, it depends on who the employer is. If it is not a mainstream company, you are probably better off waiting until the whole contract is finalized.

Here is a sample Certificate of Authorship:

Certificate of Authorship

The undersigned hereby certifies that, pursuant to an agreement between _____ ("Producer") and _____ ("Writer"), for good and valuable consideration, the receipt and sufficiency of which is hereby acknowledged, has rendered and will continue with the terms of said agreement to render services to Producer in connection with a proposed feature-length motion picture currently entitled "_____" (the "Picture"); that all of the results and process of such services are and will be created within the scope of Writer's employment by Producer and are and will be deemed to have been specially ordered or commissioned by Producer to use as part of a motion picture, that such results and proceeds are and will be a work made for hire within the meaning of the United States Copyright Law and that Producer shall be deemed to be the author thereof and the owner of all rights therein, with the right to make such changes therein and such use thereof as Producer may from time to time determine as the author thereof. Writer hereby represents and warrants that, except with respect to material supplied to Writer by Producer, the results and proceeds of Writer's services hereunder are and will be original with Writer, do not and will not, defame, infringe, or violate the rights of privacy, or other rights of any third party and are not the subject of any litigation or claim that might give rise to litigation. Writer hereby agrees to indemnify Producer, its licensees, and assigns against any loss, cost, or damage (including reasonable attorneys' fees) arising out of or in connection with any breach of any of the aforesaid representations, warranties, or certifications, and to execute such documents and do such other acts and deeds as may be required by Producer or its licensees and assigns to further evidence or effectuate Producer's rights hereunder. Producer shall similarly indemnify Writer against any loss, cost, or damage (including reasonable attorneys' fees) arising out of or in connection with any breach of any of Producer's representations to Writer. Producer's rights in and to the results and proceeds of Writer's services hereunder may be freely assigned and licensed and such assignment and/or license shall be binding upon the undersigned and inure to the benefit of such assignee and/or licensee.

IN WITNESS WHEREOF, this document has been executed this this _____ day of _____, 20___.

                                _____

                                  ["Writer"]

10

Commissioned Teleplays: The Television Marketplace

Before I discuss the primary differences between feature and television writer deals, you must first understand the basic economic difference between feature development and television development.

Apart from the differences in salaries, which can be staggering (well-known feature writers are usually paid in the hundreds of thousands of dollars as their up-front fee; movie-of-the-week writers make $75,000–$100,000 tops as their up-front fee), the structure for financing features versus television productions is dramatically different. For features, studios are the major source of all financing. They usually own the material, finance production, and distribute the product. In television, until recently, because of the Financial Interest and Syndication Rules, commonly called "the Fin-Syn Rules," the networks for the most part have been prohibited from owning their own shows, and yet the networks cover much of the financing. The Federal Communications Commission (FCC) instituted these rules in the early days of television. Due to the monopolistic control of all broadcasting by three powerful networks, the theory was that with power in the hands of so few, there was little opportunity to negotiate. Before the rules were implemented, networks tended to negotiate with a take-it-or-leave-it attitude. Thus, the producer of a proposed television program would often be told by the network that the network would take all the profits in the show or the network would not put it on the air. Under the FCC rules, networks were thus prohibited from owning their own programs, with limited exceptions.

As a result of these rules, powerful producers became powerful suppliers of television programming, owning *all* rights in their shows. The networks became licensees looking to advertising dollars for their profits (which are not shared with the producer), and the producers looked to sales of their shows in syndication (basically airing of their product on independent stations after the initial airings on the network) and to foreign sales for their profits. Since networks were not given all the profits, they said they would not put up all the money to produce a show. A logical argument. The practice evolved for the network to put up most of the money for developing the script (actual writing costs), and in some cases a very small development fee for the producer ($5,000–$10,000 maximum), and 75 percent to 80 percent of the cost of the show. The balance (or deficit) is generally provided through advances from foreign sales or syndication sales. For television movies, a network usually gets two free runs for its investment. The network reserves the right to order additional runs for an additional fee, which would bring profit to the producer. Until recently, when the demand for American movies-of-the-week decreased abroad, a supplier producer knew that it would be substantially in profit (sometimes as much as $1 million) before shooting the picture, based on foreign and syndication sales. This windfall was not uncommon for television supplier producers. (They are called supplier producers because they own the show and supply it to the network as distinguished from employee producers who are hired to actually produce the program.)

The cost of producing shows has increased dramatically since the early days of TV. The network license fees have not. Generally the network pays $2.5 to $3 million for a two-hour movie for network television. The cost to produce a TV movie today is in excess of $3 million generally. Foreign sales are down and syndication sales are not as valuable, now that there are so many channels to watch and so much product in the marketplace. Producers are content to cover their deficit, earn handsome producing fees and, in success, to earn a profit. Gone are the guarantees. Today such shows are produced with only the *possibility* that they might earn out their advances from foreign territories or syndication (the advances cover the deficit), with additional revenues required to turn a profit. Keep in mind that this might now take many years.

For a mainstream television series, it might take many, *many* years to recoup the cost of producing it. And keep in mind that, throughout that time, the series is usually running at a deficit (meaning the cost is in excess of income—advances in series television do not usually cover the entire deficit). If and when the series as a whole (all episodes produced) is sold to syndication, there may be a profit. This sale usually occurs after the network run. At the high end, *Seinfeld* was sold for $6 million per episode to syndication. Many series, on the other hand, never see profit.

In short, producers are finding it much more difficult today to turn a profit in the traditional manner. Naturally, this has affected writers' salaries. Gone are the days when top television series writers were given million-dollar annual guarantees. Salaries have come down and for those writers whose salaries were not very high to begin with, salaries have not gone up. It takes a major negotiation today to increase a movie-of-the-week writer's salary by even $5,000!

You should be aware that the FCC in the mid 1990s voted to relax and then, in essence, eliminate the Financial Interest and Syndication rules, and networks are now allowed to own more of their own programming. The FCC rationale: There is a lot of competition out there now and the networks are not as powerful as they used to be. Hollywood supplier producers (today the studios themselves are the supplier producers—they are the only ones who can afford to cover deficits, particularly for series) are outraged, but the decision has been made.

While I agree that there is more competition, I think it is also important to look at the nature of that competition. If you are a television series producer, for instance, with a mainstream, star-driven sitcom, will the competition finance a series of this type? Fox Television might, but the local cable station cannot. In other words, the competitors are not necessarily in the market for your product. So, again, you are down to the "big three" and Fox. The newer Warner Bros. and UPN networks may change things. We shall see.

DIFFERENCES IN TELEVISION WRITING DEALS

There are certain provisions unique to a television writer's agreement that you should be aware of.

Imagine that you have been asked to write a movie-of-the-week for television, for instance. If you are the first writer on the project, generally you will be hired to write more writing steps than with a feature deal and for substantially less money. The typical television movie-of-the-week writer is usually engaged to write a story, a first draft teleplay, two sets of revisions, and a polish. The writing periods are much shorter for a TV writer. TV executives work at a much faster pace. Generally, writers do not take longer than eight weeks to deliver a first draft teleplay.

As indicated above, the salaries for writing television movies are substantially lower than salaries customarily paid for features. They range from $55,000 to $75,000, for all steps mentioned above. Salaries in the $80,000–$100,000 range are rarer, particularly these days. The *top* end tends to be in the $75,000–$100,000-plus range, unless you have incredible leverage. In television, the writer is given payment for the applicable writing step on *delivery*. The reason: Networks only pay on delivery. Since most television writers are employed by supplier producers and since supplier producers look to the network for payment of the writer's fees, supplier producers do not want to advance monies any sooner than the network pays. That is not to say that exceptions are never made. And if they want you badly enough, they just might have to. As a rule, do not expect payment until delivery.

Television writers usually get a bonus based on credit, just as with features. In television, these are called "production bonuses." The range is generally $10,000 to $25,000 for sole "teleplay by" credit and $5,000 to $12,500 for shared "teleplay by" credit. Payment is made upon determination of credits, but the same principle applies regarding payment of the shared bonus on commencement of principal photography if no other writers are hired (see discussion in chapter 9, Bonus Based on Credit).

Finally, television writers tend to protect themselves in case their teleplay is produced as a feature. Remember: For features, salaries are much higher. You should be entitled to more money if the teleplay is made as a feature, and you will be if you ask for it.

A common provision is the so-called 100/50/50 formula, usually referred to as a "theatrical release bonus." If the picture is exhibited as a feature in the United States (sometimes Canada is included) before it is shown on television, you will be entitled to another payment equal to 100 percent of the monies you were paid to write the TV script. (This should include the bonus, a point that must be established early in the negotiations.) As an example, if you received $80,000, including a bonus, for writing a television script and the picture was released theatrically before airing on television in the United States, you would receive another $80,000 upon theatrical release of the picture. If the theatrical exhibition followed the television run, then you would receive a payment equal to 50 percent of your original monies on release of the picture theatrically in the United States, and another payment equal to 50 percent of your original monies on showing of the picture theatrically outside the United States. In no event would your aggregate bonus exceed 100 percent of your original monies. Using the example above, if the picture was only released theatrically outside the United States after its initial run (this may happen, for instance, with a Showtime or HBO movie), then you would receive another $40,000. (Note that if you are an established feature writer, you may sometimes be able to negotiate full feature film compensation if the picture is released theatrically, although this provision is rare.)

WRITING A SERIES: COMPENSATION

If you are hired to write a pilot script for a series, the main points that you want to negotiate are (1) your up-front compensation; (2) a royalty for each episode produced if a series is ordered based on your script; (3) a bonus for a production order for the series; and (4) profit participation.

Credits

Bonuses and profit participations are usually based on credit. For a television series, the writer who is awarded the "created by" credit gets the bonus. (In television, the *creator* of a series is accorded "created by" credit if the characters and plot in the pilot episode are substantially the same as those created by the writer—the pilot episode being the prototype episode for the series.) The criteria used to determine "created by" credit is similar to that used to determine separated rights for features (see discussion in chapter 7). As with features, several different writers may be brought on board. It is not uncommon to see shared "created by" credit. There is usually one bonus amount negotiated for sole "created by" credit and a lesser amount for shared "created by" credit. Top writers may receive as much as $5,000 per episode for sole "created by" credit, reducible down to 50 percent of that amount per episode for shared "created by" credit. Here's a fine point of negotiation with respect to the series royalty: Just as with passive payments based on separated rights, you should ask that the royalty be reducible by amounts *actually* paid to another writer who receives shared "created by" credit to a floor of 50 percent of the sole "created by" credit. That way, if another writer is receiving a much lower royalty, your royalty will not automatically be reduced to your floor. Example: You receive a $5,000 royalty per episode for sole "created by" credit, reducible to $3,000 per episode for shared "created by" credit by royalties paid to another writer entitled to receive shared "created by" credit. You receive shared "created by" credit with another writer. The other writer is only entitled to $1,500 per episode as her royalty. In this example, you would receive $3,500 per episode. Successful writers are sometimes able to negotiate a royalty regardless of credit. This royalty is usually slightly less than the shared "created by" royalty. If the shared royalty is $2,000 per episode, the royalty regardless of credit would probably be $1,500 per episode.

Often a production bonus will be paid if a series is ordered by the network. This is also based on "created by" credit with two amounts negotiated: one for sole "created by" credit—at the top end, $25,000— and one for shared "created by" credit—usually one-half the sole "created by" bonus amount. The payments may be further reduced depending on the number of episodes initially ordered. For instance, the bonuses may be conditioned on twelve episodes being ordered. If fewer are ordered, the bonus would be prorated, usually down to a floor of six episodes. Using the example above, if eight episodes were ordered and you received sole "created by" credit, you would be entitled to $\frac{8}{12}$ × $25,000 or $12,750. Just as with the royalty, successful writers are sometimes able to negotiate a production bonus regardless of credit. Again, it will be somewhat less than the shared credit production bonus.

Profit Participation

The other main area of negotiation with a television series is your profit participation. Successful writers in television usually receive a piece of the adjusted gross (often referred to these days as modified adjusted gross). The reason: Net profits are even more meaningless in television than they are for features (review the discussion regarding net profits participation in chapter 6). The main reason is cash flow. The major portion of the revenues earned on a hit movie are earned early in the picture's release. Theatrical exhibition and home video exhibition generally account for 42 percent to 45 percent of a picture's revenues. Thus, it is possible to recover all expenditures on a feature if there is an enormous infusion of cash at the outset, thereby cutting down on interest charges on the unrecouped production and distribution expenses that continue to accrue until the picture reaches breakeven. In television, by contrast, the major portion of the profit-making revenues are earned way after the series is launched—when the series is sold to syndication (that is, sales to off-network programming, usually after the initial network run). In the meantime, the series has been accumulating substantial deficits and interest is being charged on that deficit over *many* years. The potential for profit is thus much less with a series, unless the syndication revenues are substantial. And if the series syndication sale does not produce big numbers, it may not be profitable at all. The reason: The deficits are too large and the syndication sales disappointing. Studios may brave a deficit, even a huge one, in hopes that syndication sales will be substantial. Sometimes they miscalculate. Sometimes, even though a series may be on the air for many years, it does not generate net profits or even adjusted gross, for that matter. In recent years, hour-long series have not fared well at all in syndication sales, and half-hour series have to be extremely successful (such as *Cheers*) to generate sufficient revenues for profits to be made.

Recall that the key difference between net profits and adjusted gross is the distribution fee charged. In television, a pure adjusted gross definition eliminates distribution fees. With a modified adjusted gross definition, the supplier company often eliminates its distribution fee altogether on the initial network sale and may only charge the actual distribution fee that it is charged by an outside syndication sales company, if any, or a fee of 15 percent if it is itself the syndicator (which is often the case nowadays with TV series).

If you are only able to negotiate a "net profits" participation, you will probably be entitled to 5 percent of 100 percent of the net profits for your sole "created by" credit and 2.5 percent of 100 percent of the net profits for shared "created by" credit (see the section on Producing or Executive Producing a Series below for a further discussion). If you are lucky enough to get adjusted gross (or modified adjusted gross), it will usually be 2.5 percent of 100 percent of the "adjusted gross" (or modified adjusted gross) for sole "created by" credit, reducible to 1.25 percent of the "adjusted gross" (or modified adjusted gross) for shared "created by" credit. One common formula for "adjusted gross" (or modified adjusted gross) participants is to grant the writer the higher of 5 percent of 100 percent of the net profit or 2.5 percent of 100 percent of the adjusted gross (or modified adjusted gross) for sole "created by" credit, and the higher of 2.5 percent of 100 percent of the net profits and 1.25 percent of 100 percent of the adjusted gross (or modified adjusted gross) for shared "created by" credit. That way, the writer is protected if the "net profits" formula is higher.

Many writers in series television are also producers. These writer-producers are referred to as "show runners." As producers, they can increase their net profit and adjusted gross participations for each year that they serve as producers on the series, sometimes by as much as 2.5 percent and 1.25 percent, respectively. Of course, there will also be a cap. A common formula caps the show runner at 10 percent of adjusted gross and 15 percent of net profits.

One way to protect against the possibility that there will be no "net profits" (or even "adjusted gross," for that matter) is to negotiate a guaranteed advance against your participation (your entitlement to a share of net profits or adjusted gross is also referred to as your "participation"), if the series lasts. The first advance would be paid after the 66th episode. It is generally thought that at least 67 original episodes of a series must be ordered by the network (in short, going into the fourth year) in order for a syndication sale to mean anything. Further advances are often awarded at 89 episodes (going into a fifth year) and at 111 episodes (going into a sixth year). The advance provision might look something like this:

> If Company produces at least 67 episodes of the series, provided the writer is entitled to receive his profit participation, Company agrees to advance writer against writer's share of the series' net profits, if any, and solely out of positive cash flow [*in other words, by then the license fee from the network and other revenues are greater than the cost of producing the episode—including payment of Company's 10 percent overhead fee (the norm for overhead is 10 percent, but it is sometimes as high as 15 percent and this fee is negotiable if you have a lot of leverage)*], the following sums:
>
> (a) In connection with the first sixty-seven episodes produced, Company agrees to advance writer the sum of Two Thousand Dollars ($2,000) per episode.
>
> (b) Said advance shall increase retroactively to Three Thousand Dollars ($3,000) per episode if Company produces at least 89 episodes of said series.
>
> (c) Said advance shall increase retroactively to Four Thousand Dollars ($4,000) per episode if Company produces at least 111 episodes of said series.

The advances are usually payable immediately after the 67th, 89th, and 111th episodes, respectively.

If you are hired to write the pilot script, you should decide whether you want to continue as a writer with the show beyond the pilot script. Writers of episodes (generally referred to as staff writers) receive WGA minimum compensation to write episodes. For a story and teleplay (two drafts), the minimum (as of May 2003) is $19,699 for a half-hour network show and $28,974 for a one-hour network show. If you want to continue writing the series, then you should ask to write a minimum number of episodes per broadcast order.

WRITING A SERIES: YEARLY GUARANTY

Most writers who write pilot scripts become story editors and producers of the series. The pay is substantially higher. If you are in that position, you will probably not want to write more than a handful of individual episodes (see section on Producing or Executive Producing a Series below).

Writers who do not write a pilot episode are often employed as staff writers. If you are in this category, again you will want to negotiate a guaranteed number of episodes and the opportunity, at some point, to render additional services, as story editor, coproducer, and even producer and/or director if you stay with the show long enough.

PRODUCING OR EXECUTIVE PRODUCING A SERIES

Aside from the stars, the hot shots in the television series arena are the writers who also produce or executive produce the series—the folks who oversee the staff writers and the production of the show. These dual-capacity persons are generally referred to as "hyphenates" or "show runners." At the lowest level, a hyphenate may be a story editor on the series. If you have created a series (and received sole "created by" credit), odds are you will be able to negotiate to become at least a coproducer or producer. What this means, aside from a lot more work, is that you will earn a lot more money *and* be entitled to a greater share of the profits. You will also have a guarantee that you will be intricately involved with the production of your series. This tradition probably had its roots in the early days of television when entrepreneurial individuals could achieve great success, and often wore many hats.

A successful producer or executive producer may receive $30,000 and up to produce a series *per* episode. These amounts are generally bumped up about 5 percent for each subsequent year, and the bumps are cumulative. Thus, $31,500 in the second year, $33,025 in the third year, and so on. Coproducer salaries today are usually $10,000 to $15,000 per episode. As you can see, it adds up. Consultants may be paid $10,000 to $15,000 per episode. Generally, your position is elevated over time. You may be a coproducer in the first year, and a producer in the second year. Of course, if you have produced or executive produced a series before, you will probably start out as a producer or executive producer.

Unless you have enormous leverage, most companies will not guarantee that you will be locked into a series for the life of the show as an executive producer, a producer, or a coproducer. If the ratings are sluggish, supplier companies want the ability to bring in fresh blood. Executive producers, producers, coproducers, and even story editors are usually attached for two years, after which they are guaranteed employment as consultants on the show for several more years (usually the same number of years that they were employed in their initial capacity), and sometimes for the life of the show, at a reduced salary. This salary is either 50 percent of the salary that was paid before the switch to consultant or a flat fee as set forth above. This amount is usually *not* subject to increases. As an example, if in the second year of a series, you receive a producing or executive producing fee of $30,000 per episode, you will then receive a salary as a consultant of $15,000 per episode for a period of time, maybe even for the life of the show. Of course, if the show is enormously successful, the studio will probably beg you to stay on as a producer and, at that point, you may be able to negotiate the top rate in town.

Producers and executive producers also receive profits. Indeed, one's profit participation as a writer might double or triple as a result of becoming a producer or executive producer. As a writer entitled to sole "created by" credit, your share of the profits would probably be 2.5 percent of 100 percent of the "adjusted gross" against 5 percent of

100 percent of the "net profits." It is not uncommon for a writer/producer to receive 5 percent of 100 percent of the "adjusted gross" against 10 percent of 100 percent of the "net profits."

The producer's or executive producer's profit participation may also be increased for additional years of service as producer or executive producer on the show. In other words, the company may increase your share if you stay with the show longer. But it takes a lot of leverage to get this kind of deal. I just want to make you aware of the possibilities. The producer would also be entitled to a theatrical release bonus (100/50/50) (see Differences in Television Writing deals above) on her salary as a producer/executive producer, if the pilot, for instance, were released as a feature. This would be a rare occurrence, but your contract should account for it just the same.

In short, if you create a series, you will want some guarantee that you will be involved in the production of the series if it takes off. Obviously, you have to learn how to produce if you have never produced before, so start at a lower level as a coproducer, with increased responsibilities in subsequent years of the series. Be sure to get yourself in there somehow. At some point, you will have gained enough experience to be guaranteed the right to produce or executive produce a show that you create, and, with it, the creative and financial rewards.

11

Protecting Your Money

What if the company that options your material is located in another state or another country? How do you ensure that you will be able to sue without flying off to that country and hiring a lawyer whose language you don't understand? What if the company is on the verge of bankruptcy? How do you protect yourself?

FOREIGN CORPORATIONS

Several notable companies in Hollywood have set up offshore companies for tax purposes. The principal office for one such company is in Curacao, the Dutch Antilles. These companies also have U.S. affiliates. If your deal is with an offshore or foreign company, however, this is not necessarily a reason to panic. Rather, you simply have to make sure that the company will submit to jurisdiction in the United States, so that you will not have to retain a foreign lawyer should a problem arise. You should also insist that the contract is governed by some specific American law, such as California law. If you are successful in having the foreign company submit to local jurisdiction (if you are in Los Angeles, have the company submit to jurisdiction in the California courts located in Los Angeles), then you also want to ensure that you will be able to go after that company in its own country so you can tap that company's main resources. In other words, your victory in a Los Angeles court does not necessarily mean that you will not have to follow up that California judgment in a foreign country to actually collect your money (while this is inconvenient, it is a lot easier than trying a whole case in a foreign country). Here's an example of specific wording needed to cover this contingency:

> This agreement shall be governed by the laws of the State of California. The parties hereby irrevocably submit to the jurisdiction of any California State or Federal Court sitting in Los Angeles, California, in any action or proceeding arising out of or relating to this agreement. Each party hereby irrevocably waives to the fullest extent it may effectively do so the defense of any inconvenient forum to the maintenance of such action or proceeding. Each party agrees that a final judgment in any such action or proceeding shall be conclusive and may be enforced in other jurisdictions by suit on the judgment or in any other manner provided by law. Nothing in this paragraph shall affect the right of either or any other party to serve legal process in any other manner permitted by law, or affect the right of either or any other party to bring any action or proceeding against either, or any other, party or its property in the courts of any other jurisdiction.

SHELL CORPORATIONS

If you are entering into an agreement with a corporation, the other issue you need to examine is whether this is a so-called shell corporation with no assets. Sometimes major companies will set up a separate corporation for a particular project. Ask your buyer or employer if the contracting entity is the main company or just a "shell" corporation. If it is not the main company, ask for a guarantee from the main company. That way, if, for some reason, you are not paid, you will be able to go after the company with *assets*. Often, the main company is the parent company of the smaller company, but often it is not, so simply asking to be guaranteed by the parent company would not be enough. If you know there is a major company involved, ask about the relationship between the shell company and the major company, if any, and even if there is no relationship, you can ask for a guarantee.

Here is an example of a guarantee:

Guarantee Agreement

Dated as of _____

Reference is made to that certain Writer Agreement ("Agreement"), dated as of _____, 20__, between _____ ("Producer") and _____ ("Writer") in connection with the motion picture currently entitled "_____" ("Picture"). In order to induce Writer to enter into the Agreement, Studio ("Guarantor") agrees as follows:

1. In consideration of the execution of the Agreement by Writer, Guarantor hereby guarantees the full, timely, and complete payment and performance by Producer of its obligation to pay Writer the fixed compensation ("Fixed Compensation") set forth in Paragraph ___ of the Agreement, contingent compensation set forth in Paragraph ___ of the Agreement, any and all Writers Guild of America ("WGA") residuals which may become due Writer pursuant to the terms of the WGA Basic Agreement, and all other obligations of Producer pursuant to the Agreement and in connection with the exploitation of the Picture, subject to the terms and conditions of the Agreement, including, without limitation, Producer and Guarantor's rights and remedies arising out of Writer's material breach of any of their representations warranties or agreements set forth in the Agreement.

2. Upon material breach or material default by Producer of any of its obligations to Writer, Writer may proceed immediately against Producer and/or Guarantor, provided Writer has first provided Producer and Guarantor with ten (10) days prior written notice of such material breach or material default.

3. In the event that Producer enters into an agreement with a "major" motion picture company, pay or free television network, or other similarly financially responsible party and such party assumes in writing all or a portion of Producer's WGA residuals payment obligation to Writer pursuant to the Agreement, then with respect to that portion of Producer's WGA residuals obligation so assumed, Producer shall be under no further obligation to Writer and the obligations of Guarantor hereunder with respect thereto shall be of no further force or effect.

4. Except as expressly provided above, Guarantor hereby waives (a) notice of any kind including, without limitation, notice of acceptance of this Guarantee, protest, or presentment; (b) any rights to require Writer to first enforce its rights or remedies against Producer under the Agreement or otherwise; and (c) any right of subrogation.

5. Producer and Writer may, without notice to or consent of Guarantor and without in any way releasing, effecting, or impairing Guarantor's obligations or liabilities hereunder, at any time and from time to time, amend the Agreement by written agreement (the term "Agreement" as used herein shall include any such amendment), grant extensions or renewals of the Agreement, assign or otherwise transfer its interest in the Agreement or in this Guarantee Agreement, and consent to any transfer or assignment of Producer's interest in the Agreement.

6. Guarantor (a) hereby irrevocably submits to the jurisdiction of either the Superior Court of California, Los Angeles, or to the jurisdiction of the United States District Court for the

Central District of California for the purposes of any suit, action, or other proceeding arising out of or based upon this Guarantee Agreement or the subject matter hereof brought by Writer and (b) hereby irrevocably waives, and agrees not to assert, by way of motion, as a defense or otherwise, in any such suit, action, or proceeding brought in such courts, any claim that Guarantor is not subject personally to the jurisdiction of the above named courts, that the suit, action, or proceeding is brought in an inconvenient forum, that the venue of the suit, action, or proceeding is improper or that this Guarantee or the subject matter hereof may not be enforced by such court. Guarantor hereby irrevocably consents to service of process of the applicable court in the same manner as any other notice may be served pursuant to the notice provisions of the Agreement, and Guarantor agrees that its submission to jurisdiction and consent to service of process by mail is made for the express benefit of Writer. Guarantor hereby irrevocably agrees that final judgment against Guarantor (including the exhaustion of all rights to appellate review) in any such action, suit, or proceeding shall be conclusive and may be enforced in any other jurisdiction (a) by suit, action, or proceeding on such judgment, a certified and true copy of which shall be conclusive evidence of the fact and of the amount of any indebtedness or liability of Guarantor under or pursuant to such judgment or (b) in any other matter not prevented under applicable law; provided, however, that the plaintiff may at its option bring suit, or institute other judicial proceedings against Guarantor or any of its assets in any country or place where Guarantor or such assets may be found.

7.   This Guarantee shall be governed by and construed in accordance with the laws of the State of California applicable to agreements made and fully performed therein.

GUARANTOR

By: _____

Its: _____

If the company you are contracting with is a WGA signatory company, the WGA may have already investigated the relationship between the contracting entity and a separate, more major corporation. The WGA will try to link related companies so that Guild members have some recourse, even if they sign an agreement with a shell corporation. But the WGA rules are tricky and there are ways to shield a major corporation from a shell, particularly if the major corporation does not own any shares (or specifically, less than 50 percent of the shares of the shell corporation) and there are no common officers or directors. If in doubt, make sure to get the guarantee.

BANKRUPTCY

If you suspect that the company you are contracting with is on the verge of bankruptcy (unfortunately, an all-too-common occurrence in Hollywood today), then there are further protections that could be asked for, such as taking a security interest in your screenplay. This secures your interests ahead of all unsecured creditors at the time bankruptcy is declared. In short, it puts you in a priority position to get your money. Unfortunately, companies are loath to grant security interests for screenplays and unless you have incredible bargaining power, you will not be able to get this kind of protection. However, if you are selling a screenplay that the buyer desperately wants, and other companies are interested in the project, you may succeed. But believe me, it is rare.

ESCROW ACCOUNTS: LETTERS OF CREDIT

As discussed in chapter 4, if you option your script to someone else, the best way to protect payment of the purchase price is to state in the contract that the option may not be exercised (in other words, the grant of rights will not be effective) unless and until the purchase price is paid. That way, the buyer has to pay the purchase price in order to obtain any rights. Keep in mind that this only protects the exercise price, not your bonuses. Your only recourse for nonpayment of a bonus is, alas, a lawsuit for breach of contract.

If you are unsure that the company will be able to pay your bonus(es), then you could also ask to have the bonus(es) placed into an escrow account. As most bonuses are predicated on production of a picture, however, and most producers look to the financier to pay this cost only when the production funding is in place, this request will undoubtedly fall on deaf ears and I do not know if it is ever done. The studios, themselves with deep pockets, are insulted by such requests and the general rule is that if you enter into an agreement with a studio, you should expect them to pay. They would not be in business very long if they proceeded to make pictures based on rights that were not paid for.

The escrow account is more appropriate for writing services agreements, particularly if you are going into business with an independent company or foreign corporation. The studios refuse to place salaries in escrow for the reason stated in the previous paragraph. Once a contract is negotiated and signed, we do trust the studios to make payments when due.

Here is a sample escrow agreement:

Escrow Agreement

"As of _____, 20___

_____ Bank
_____ Branch
_____
_____

Re:Escrow Number _____

Gentlemen:

The following constitutes bilateral escrow instructions to you, as the "Escrow Holder" and also constitutes the Escrow Agreement between Productions, Inc. ("Company") and Writer with respect to the matters set forth herein.

1. Reference is hereby made that certain executed Writer's Agreement (the "Agreement") between Company and Writer dated as of _____, 20___ (a copy of which is attached hereto as Exhibit "A"), pursuant to which company engaged Writer to provide the services of Writer as a writer of the fea-

ture-length, theatrical motion picture presently entitled "Big Picture" (the "Picture"). This escrow is established to carry out the provisions of the Agreement relating to the deposit in an escrow account of the compensation payable to Writer for the rendition of Writer's services thereunder. No provisions hereof are intended to modify or amend, as between Company and Writer, the terms and conditions contained in the Agreement. You, as Escrow Holder, are not to be concerned with the terms, conditions, or contents of the Agreement or with the accuracy of any information contained in any notice from Company or Writer given pursuant to this instrument. It is understood that your only duties are those expressly set forth in these instructions.

2. Not later than five (5) days after execution of the Agreement, Company will deposit with you the sum of _____ ($_____) (the "Escrowed Funds"). You will immediately advise Writer of your receipt of the Escrowed Funds from Company.

3. Upon your receipt of written notice on behalf of Company from producer A, the producer of the Picture, that the events described in paragraph 3(a) and (b) below have occurred, you shall, except as expressly noted below, within five (5) banking days following receipt of such notice that such events have occurred, deliver by cashier's check to Writer at the address set forth below, the applicable installment of the Escrowed Funds in U.S. Dollars payable to Writer:

    (a) _____ Thousand Dollars ($_____) five (5) banking days after receipt of notice by Company that Writer has commenced the Second Draft Screenplay to Company, or in the event Company elects to postpone the writing of the Second Draft Screenplay, then four (4) weeks after Writer delivers the first Draft Screenplay to Company; and

    (b) _____ Thousand Dollars ($_____) five (5) banking days after receipt of notice by Company that Writer has completed the Revisions, or in the event Company elects to postpone the Polish, then ten (10) weeks after the date on which Writer delivers the Second Draft Screenplay to company, or if the Second Draft Screenplay was postponed by Company, then twenty-four (24) weeks after the First Draft Screenplay was delivered by Writer to Company.

4. The parties agree that in the event Company does not give notice as set forth above in Paragraph 3, then Writer may notify Company and Escrow Holder that said notice should be given, and (i) if Company fails to object in writing within five (5) days after Writer's notice is given that a particular event has occurred or (ii) in the alternative, if Company in the interim gives Escrow Holder notice that the particular event has occurred, then the particular event shall be deemed to have occurred and Escrow Holder shall pay the applicable installment set forth above within five (5) days after the event is deemed to have occurred.

5. If Company shall give you written notice at any time instructing you not to disburse any or all of the Escrowed Funds, you will immediately notify Writer of your receipt of such notice from Company. Following your receipt of such notice objection, the undisbursed Escrowed Funds shall be retained in the escrow account and you shall make no further disbursements thereof to either Writer until the occurrence of the first of any of the following events:

   (a) Your receipt of written instructions from Company to resume disbursement of the Escrowed Funds to Writer, in which event you shall resume such disbursement in accordance with Company's instructions; or

   (b) Your receipt of mutual and consistent instructions from Company and Writer to disburse the Escrowed Funds to either Company or Writer (as the case may be) or a portion thereof to either of them, in which event you will make disbursement in accordance with such instructions; or

(c) Your receipt of an order of any court of competent jurisdiction instructing you as to the manner in which to
make disbursement of the Escrowed Funds, in which
event you will comply with said order; or

(d) Your receipt of written instructions from an arbitrator or
arbitrators selected in the manner set forth in Paragraph
6 below advising you to disburse the Escrowed Funds
in accordance with such arbitrator(s)'s final decision, in
which event you will comply with said instructions.

6. In the event Company gives Escrow Holder written notice
instructing Escrow Holder not to disburse any or all of the
Escrowed Funds or if company objects in writing within five
(5) days after Writer's notice to disburse any or all of the
Escrowed Funds, Company or Writer may initiate a proceeding for binding arbitration by giving notice to the other parties as provided herein and each of the parties agrees to
participate in an expedited arbitration as follows: After notice
has been given by one party to the other, the parties hereto
shall attempt mutually to designate a single arbitrator; provided, however, if such arbitrator has not been mutually designated within fifteen (15) days after the foregoing notice is
given, Company and Writer shall within ten (10) days thereafter, designate one arbitrator each. No later than twenty
(20) days after the date the foregoing notice was given, the
two designated arbitrators shall agree upon a third arbitrator
who shall be a neutral disinterested party. If the two arbitrators do not agree upon such third arbitrator within the specified period, such third arbitrator shall, upon request of either
Company or Writer, be named by the American Arbitration
Association. If one of the parties fails to nominate an arbitrator within the period provided above for such nomination,
the arbitration shall be conducted by the sole arbitrator
named by the other party. The arbitrators or arbitrator thus
named shall promptly thereafter receive such evidence and
hold such hearings in Los Angeles, California, as such arbitrators shall decide. All decisions of the arbitrators (if there
are three) shall be by majority vote and all such decisions

shall be final and conclusive. Each party shall pay so much of the total cost and expense of such arbitration, including reasonable attorneys' fees and costs, as is determined in accordance with the award of the arbitrators.

7. Each party hereto hereby agrees to furnish each of the others and their respective legal counsel with a copy of each and every notice sent out by it to any other party concerning the subject matter hereof.

8. You will be entitled to treat as genuine, and as the document it purports to be, any letter, paper, telex, or other documents furnished or caused to be furnished to you by or on behalf of Company or Writer and believed by you to be genuine and to have been transmitted by the proper parties, and you shall have no liability with respect to any action taken by you in good faith and in accordance therewith.

9. The escrow account shall be closed at such time as all the Escrowed Funds have been disbursed as provided for herein.

10. All notices hereunder shall be in writing. Any notices hereunder shall be given by personal delivery or by mail prepaid (certified or registered), or by telexing the same to the appropriate parties at the addresses listed below, and the date of such personal delivery and one (1) day after the date of mailing or telexing, shall be the date of the giving of such notice.

WRITER   c/o Bloom, Hergott, and Diemer, LLP
                    150 South Rodeo Drive—Third Floor
                    Beverly Hills, California 90212
                    Attention: _____

ESCROW HOLDER
c/o   _____

                 _____

                 _____

                 _____

COMPANY   _____

                 _____

                 _____

11. Company agrees to pay for all costs of the Escrow, which are $_____ .

12. All of the terms and conditions of this Escrow Agreement and its instructions shall be binding upon and inure to the benefit of Company, Writer, and their respective heirs, successors and assigns.

13. This Escrow Agreement may be amended, modified, superseded, or canceled, and any of the terms and conditions hereof may be waived, only by a written instrument executed by Company and Writer, or in the case of a waiver, by the party waiving compliance. No waiver by any party of any condition or of the breach of any term of this Escrow Agreement, whether by conduct or otherwise, in any one or more instances, shall be deemed to be or construed as a further or continuing waiver of any such condition or breach or waiver of any other condition or a breach of any other term of this Escrow Agreement.

14. Company shall be entitled to the benefit of any interest accruing between the date the Escrowed Funds are received by you and the payment dates referred to in Paragraph 3 above.

15. You will not be held liable for the efficacy or correctness as to form, manner, or execution or validity of any instrument deposited in this escrow, nor as to the identity, authority, or rights of any person executing the same, nor for the failure to comply with any of the provisions of any agreement, contract or other instrument filed herein or referred to herein, and your duties hereunder shall be limited to the safekeeping of such monies, instruments or of the documents received by you as Escrow Holder and for the disposition of same in accordance with the written instructions accepted by you in this escrow.

16. This Escrow Agreement may be executed in counterparts, each of which shall constitute an original, but, when taken together, shall constitute one agreement.

17. As Escrow Holder, you shall not be required to give security for your conduct, and, provided that you have acted in good faith and without gross negligence, you shall not be responsible for acts, omissions, defaults, errors, failure, or misconduct nor for those of any agent you may reasonably employ in carrying out your obligations hereunder. However, you shall, upon the joint written request of Company and Writer and without expense to you, take all such action as may be open to you, Company, Writer, or any of them in respect of any loss sustained by any act or omission of you or any of your agents. Notwithstanding the foregoing, in the event of any dispute initiated either by Company or Writer, you, in such circumstances, shall be entitled to retain the Escrowed Funds until the dispute is resolved in furtherance of the provisions contained in Paragraphs 5 and 6 herein, and failing such resolution of the dispute within a reasonable period of time, you shall be entitled to interplead and cause the Escrowed Funds to be deposited with a court of competent jurisdiction in Los Angeles, California, and/or to submit the matter for arbitration in Los Angeles pursuant to the rules and regulations of the American Arbitration Association. Company and Writer hereby jointly and severally agree to indemnify and hold you harmless from and against any loss, claim, charge, or expense including, without limitation, reasonable attorneys' fees arising out of the resolution of any dispute arising out of this Escrow Agreement.

Kindly indicate your agreement to act in accordance with your acceptance of these Escrow Instructions by signing in the space below.

Very truly yours,
PRODUCTIONS, INC.

By: _____
Its: _____

AGREED AND ACCEPTED:
WRITER

By: _____
Its: _____

AGREED AND ACCEPTED:
_____ BANK
By: _____
Its: _____

An alternative to an escrow account is an irrevocable letter of credit issued by a creditworthy bank. The letter of credit from the bank states that under certain conditions (such as exercise of the option or completion of certain services), the bank will issue a certain payment that is contained in your contract.

If you are engaged to write a screenplay and you have any doubt about the viability of the company you are doing business with, you should ask to protect your payments.

Assumption of Obligations

If you are simply entering into an agreement with a producer, as opposed to a studio or other major financier, then you must ensure that when that producer enters into an agreement with a studio, the studio will be bound by the agreement that you and the producer signed. That is, the studio must agree to assume the obligations of the producer. This will not be a problem. The producer does not want to be held liable for your obligations. He is going to be an employee, just like you, so he certainly does not want to be stuck with *any* financial obligation to you. But you should beware. In this case, what is to prevent the producer from assigning all of his rights in your screenplay to a shell corporation instead of to the big studio directly? There is one provision you can put in your contract that will help alleviate this concern. This provision provides that the producer is still on the hook unless he assigns his rights to a major studio or mini-major studio. Since he wants to be off the hook, he will ensure that the assignment is to the right entity.

Note that nowadays you must be careful to specifically define what a mini-major studio is. Many have gone bankrupt. Rather than leaving the term general, it is better to name the few healthy mini-majors— such as New Line Cinema and Miramax.

12

Copyright, Ideas, and Titles

U.S. copyright law derives from our Constitution:

> The Congress shall have power . . . to promote the progress of science
> and useful arts, by securing for limited times to authors and inventors
> the exclusive right to their respective writings and discoveries.
>
> [U.S. Constitution, Article I, Section 8]

If your work is an original creation, then it is automatically protected under copyright law. "Copyright protection subsists . . . in original works of authorship fixed in the tangible medium of expression, now known or later developed, from which they can be perceived, reproduced or otherwise communicated, either directly or with the aid of a machine or device." Works of authorship include literary works;

musical works; dramatic works; pantomimes and choreographic works; pictorial, graphic, and sculptural works; and motion picture and sound recordings. A writing is a work of authorship in a fixed form.

BENEFITS

Copyright is a property right. Like the house or car you own, copyright can be transferred, passed on by will, mortgaged, and so on. Copyright is established by the single act of original creation and embodiment of that creation in a fixed, tangible form, as listed above. Under the old copyright act (1909), certain formalities were required to obtain copyright protection in the first place. For instance, under the 1909 act, registration was a prerequisite for copyright protection and had to be made within twenty-eight years of publication. Under the new act (1976), effective January 1, 1978, no formalities are required: You own a copyright in your work *when you write it;* nothing more.

What if your work is based on other material, such as a true story or a book? You still own the copyright in your work. In that case, you do not own the copyright in the underlying material—the material that existed before you put pen to paper and created your *own* work—but you do own copyright in your additions and creations.

There is one major exception to this rule: the "work-for-hire." As discussed in chapter 1, when you are hired to write, your material is owned by the employer and the employer holds the copyright. Remember: The employer is called the author!

The duration of copyright protection depends on the nature of the work and when it was created. It was extended by the Sonny Bono Copyright Term Extension Act, signed into law on October 27, 1998. If the work was created after January 1, 1978, the term of copyright lasts from the time of creation until seventy years after the author's death. In the case of a "work-for-hire," the duration of copyright protection is ninety-five years from the year of first "publication" or one-hundred-twenty years from the year of creation, whichever occurs first. "Publication," in this context, means that the work is first distributed to the public, not necessarily that it is published by a book company.

Aside from establishing ownership in a literary work, copyright provides the owner with the right to sue in the case of any unauthorized use of the copyright owner's material. Just as a homeowner can sue for property damage in an action for trespass or encroachment, the copyright owner can bring an action for infringement when his rights are violated. "Anyone who violates any of the exclusive rights of the copyright owner . . . is an infringer of the copyright" (17 U.S.C. 501(a) [1976]). Examples of infringement are unauthorized copying and adaptation of someone else's work. The key element of any such suit is to prove (1) that the infringer actually copied the work, by establishing similarity and (2) that the infringer had access to the similar work.

The defense to any infringement suit, on the other hand, is to prove that one did not copy someone else's work. As long as you can prove your independent creation of your material, you are not an infringer.

REGISTRATION

One way to establish proof of creation is to register your work with the U.S. Copyright Office. The work can be registered at any time during the copyright term. Remember: Registration is not necessary for copyright protection, but it helps to prove when the work was created. If someone claims that you infringed, and you are able to prove that you created your work before the person claiming infringement created his work, he has no case. And if someone copies your work and you can prove that you created your work before the infringer, such proof will be helpful in court. In fact, registration is essential in order to bring a suit for copyright infringement, although registration may be made after the act of infringement has occurred. If you wait until after the infringement occurs, however, in certain instances, you will not be able to recover certain damages and attorneys' fees.

Obviously, the earlier you register your work, the earlier you will establish its creation. Many writers register their material as soon as it is completed. If you plan to take a long time in finishing your work, then you may want to register major portions of it as you go along. This can be time-consuming and you have to pay each time you do it (as you will note below, however, it is not that costly), but if you are concerned about protecting your rights and concerned that someone might rip you off, you should do it. You can also accomplish the same goal by registering your work with the Writers Guild.

The Guild maintains a script registration service for members and nonmembers. This is valuable as a way to establish proof of creation and time of creation. Simply submit your screenplay to the Writers Guild of America Registration Office. There is one in Los Angeles and one in New York. The cost is $10.00 per submission. Nonmembers can take advantage of the system for $20.00 per submission. The Guild will place a copy of your screenplay in its files and give you a record of the time of registration. For more information, contact the Writers Guild of America, west (Telephone: 323-782-4500) or the Writers Guild of America, east (Telephone: 212-767-7800).

The copyright registration process (the better route) is fairly simple. Write to the Copyright Office, Library of Congress, Washington, DC, 20559 and request Form PA. Complete the form and submit a copy of the screenplay or material that you want to protect. The cost is $20.00. The normal process may take in excess of three months, so be patient. But know that the date of *submission* is determinative. You should also know that your work will be examined. Thus, you cannot claim copyright registration in something that the Copyright Office knows has been copied.

Notice is not required to obtain copyright, but it is helpful and puts the world on notice that you own the copyright. Notice consists of three elements: (1) the word "copyright" or ©; (2) your name; and (3) the year of first publication (when the work is offered to the public). Usually, notice on a screenplay is placed on the title page (with books it is usually placed on the following page, known as the copyright page), but that is not a requirement. It must be "affixed" to the copies in such a manner and location as to give reasonable notice of the claim of copyright. For instance:

© 2004 Stephen F. Breimer

Here is a sample Form PA:

Copyright Office fees are subject to change.
For current fees, check the Copyright Office
website at *www.copyright.gov*, write the Copyright Office, or call (202) 707-3000.

Form PA
For a Work of Performing Arts
UNITED STATES COPYRIGHT OFFICE

REGISTRATION NUMBER

PA   PAU

EFFECTIVE DATE OF REGISTRATION

Month   Day   Year

DO NOT WRITE ABOVE THIS LINE. IF YOU NEED MORE SPACE, USE A SEPARATE CONTINUATION SHEET.

1

TITLE OF THIS WORK ▼

PREVIOUS OR ALTERNATIVE TITLES ▼

NATURE OF THIS WORK ▼ See instructions

---

2 a

NAME OF AUTHOR ▼

DATES OF BIRTH AND DEATH
Year Born ▼   Year Died ▼

Was this contribution to the work a "work made for hire"?
☐ Yes
☐ No

AUTHOR'S NATIONALITY OR DOMICILE
Name of Country
OR ⎰ Citizen of _____
   ⎱ Domiciled in _____

WAS THIS AUTHOR'S CONTRIBUTION TO THE WORK
Anonymous?   ☐ Yes ☐ No
Pseudonymous?   ☐ Yes ☐ No
If the answer to either of these questions is "Yes," see detailed instructions.

NATURE OF AUTHORSHIP Briefly describe nature of material created by this author in which copyright is claimed. ▼

NOTE

Under the law, the "author" of a "work made for hire" is generally the employer, not the employee (see instructions). For any part of this work that was "made for hire" check "Yes" in the space provided, give the employer (or other person for whom the work was prepared) as "Author" of that part, and leave the space for dates of birth and death blank.

b

NAME OF AUTHOR ▼

DATES OF BIRTH AND DEATH
Year Born ▼   Year Died ▼

Was this contribution to the work a "work made for hire"?
☐ Yes
☐ No

AUTHOR'S NATIONALITY OR DOMICILE
Name of Country
OR ⎰ Citizen of _____
   ⎱ Domiciled in _____

WAS THIS AUTHOR'S CONTRIBUTION TO THE WORK
Anonymous?   ☐ Yes ☐ No
Pseudonymous?   ☐ Yes ☐ No
If the answer to either of these questions is "Yes," see detailed instructions.

NATURE OF AUTHORSHIP Briefly describe nature of material created by this author in which copyright is claimed. ▼

c

NAME OF AUTHOR ▼

DATES OF BIRTH AND DEATH
Year Born ▼   Year Died ▼

Was this contribution to the work a "work made for hire"?
☐ Yes
☐ No

AUTHOR'S NATIONALITY OR DOMICILE
Name of Country
OR ⎰ Citizen of _____
   ⎱ Domiciled in _____

WAS THIS AUTHOR'S CONTRIBUTION TO THE WORK
Anonymous?   ☐ Yes ☐ No
Pseudonymous?   ☐ Yes ☐ No
If the answer to either of these questions is "Yes," see detailed instructions.

NATURE OF AUTHORSHIP Briefly describe nature of material created by this author in which copyright is claimed. ▼

---

3 a

YEAR IN WHICH CREATION OF THIS WORK WAS COMPLETED This information must be given in all cases.
_____ Year

b DATE AND NATION OF FIRST PUBLICATION OF THIS PARTICULAR WORK
Complete this information ONLY if this work has been published.
Month _____ Day _____ Year _____ Nation

4

See instructions before completing this space.

COPYRIGHT CLAIMANT(S) Name and address must be given even if the claimant is the same as the author given in space 2. ▼

TRANSFER If the claimant(s) named here in space 4 is (are) different from the author(s) named in space 2, give a brief statement of how the claimant(s) obtained ownership of the copyright. ▼

DO NOT WRITE HERE
OFFICE USE ONLY

APPLICATION RECEIVED

ONE DEPOSIT RECEIVED

TWO DEPOSITS RECEIVED

FUNDS RECEIVED

MORE ON BACK ▶ • Complete all applicable spaces (numbers 5-9) on the reverse side of this page.
• See detailed instructions.   • Sign the form at line 8.

DO NOT WRITE HERE
Page 1 of _____ pages

EXAMINED BY	FORM PA
CHECKED BY	FOR COPYRIGHT OFFICE USE ONLY
☐ CORRESPONDENCE Yes	

DO NOT WRITE ABOVE THIS LINE. IF YOU NEED MORE SPACE, USE A SEPARATE CONTINUATION SHEET.

PREVIOUS REGISTRATION Has registration for this work, or for an earlier version of this work, already been made in the Copyright Office?

☐ Yes ☐ No If your answer is "Yes," why is another registration being sought? (Check appropriate box.) ▼ If your answer is No, do **not** check box A, B, or C.

a. ☐ This is the first published edition of a work previously registered in unpublished form.

b. ☐ This is the first application submitted by this author as copyright claimant.

c. ☐ This is a changed version of the work, as shown by space 6 on this application

If your answer is "Yes," give: **Previous Registration Number** ▼   **Year of Registration** ▼

5

DERIVATIVE WORK OR COMPILATION Complete both space 6a and 6b for a derivative work; complete only 6b for a compilation.

Preexisting Material Identify any preexisting work or works that this work is based on or incorporates. ▼

a

Material Added to This Work Give a brief, general statement of the material that has been added to this work and in which copyright is claimed. ▼

b

6

See instructions before completing this space.

DEPOSIT ACCOUNT If the registration fee is to be charged to a Deposit Account established in the Copyright Office, give name and number of Account.

Name ▼   **Account Number** ▼

a

CORRESPONDENCE Give name and address to which correspondence about this application should be sent. Name / Address / Apt / City / State / ZIP ▼

b

7

Area code and daytime telephone number   (   )   Fax number   (   )

Email

CERTIFICATION* I, the undersigned, hereby certify that I am the

Check only one ▶ {
☐ author
☐ other copyright claimant
☐ owner of exclusive right(s)
☐ authorized agent of _____
   Name of author or other copyright claimant, or owner of exclusive right(s) ▲
}

of the work identified in this application and that the statements made by me in this application are correct to the best of my knowledge.

8

Typed or printed name and date ▼ If this application gives a date of publication in space 3, do not sign and submit it before that date.

_____   Date _____

Handwritten signature (X) ▼

☞   x _____

Certificate will be mailed in window envelope to this address:	Name ▼	YOU MUST: • Complete all necessary spaces • Sign your application in space 8
	Number/Street/Apt ▼	SEND ALL 3 ELEMENTS IN THE SAME PACKAGE: 1. Application form 2. Nonrefundable filing fee in check or money order payable to *Register of Copyrights* 3. Deposit material
	City/State/ZIP ▼	MAIL TO: Library of Congress Copyright Office 101 Independence Avenue, S.E. Washington, D.C. 20559-6000

Fees are subject to change. For current fees, check the Copyright Office website at www.copyright.gov, write the Copyright Office, or call (202) 707-3000.

9

Rev: June 2002—20,000   Web Rev: June 2002   ♻ Printed on recycled paper   U.S. Government Printing Office: 2000-461-113/20,021

INFRINGEMENT

In order to win an infringement suit, first you must establish that you own the script. Registration usually establishes necessary proof. Second, the work must be substantially similar—not identical, but bearing a striking resemblance in story, plot, characters, and/or the interaction among the characters or the dialogue. Even if the elements that are substantially similar to the copied work are few in quantity, copying can be found if the copied elements are quantitatively significant. Third, it is not enough that someone else's work is similar to yours. You must actually prove that your work was copied. This can be done by finding a witness who will corroborate that theory. More often, proof is established indirectly by proving that the violator had access to your material. For instance, if you submitted your screenplay to a producer and the producer thereafter commissioned a screenplay similar to yours, this is sometimes sufficient to establish access (such as the writer of the other screenplay had access to your screenplay via the producer). That is why studios are so paranoid about receiving unsolicited screenplays (see Ideas below.)

The components are viewed as a whole. The more similar the works, the less important proof of access becomes. On the other hand, solid proof of access or copying means that the works do not have to be as similar in order to prove infringement. Keep in mind that the whole work does not have to be substantially similar. Someone might have lifted the last half of your screenplay and the courts are willing to focus on that part.

Under certain circumstances, copyright law allows the writer to use a portion of someone else's work. This is called the "Fair Use Doctrine." These uses are very limited, particularly in screenplays. Fair Use usually comes into play for criticism, news, teaching, research, and the like. A key factor is the purpose and character of the use, including whether such use is of a commercial nature or is for nonprofit or educational purposes. Since screenplays are usually written to be sold, they are definitely commercial by nature, so you should not rely on this doctrine.

A writer client of mine made the mistake of using established song lyrics in his script, basically quoting the whole song. The song was an integral part of the script. He then asked my opinion. I told him that, depending on the context, a songwriter might very well be outraged at such use. You should be aware that it is customary to license song rights for movies. It is quite a business, so you should not plan on making use of someone else's song or any other material, for that matter, as a key part of the script or any other material you're planning to copyright. That is not to say that you won't be able to get permission. But if someone else's work is the *basis* for your script, such as "Ode to Billie Joe," and you use only the words from the song in the title, be sure to get permission first. Otherwise, your writing may be for naught. If the lyrics are incidental, on the other hand, then you can always change the song if you run into trouble. For purposes of showing the script (not selling it), you are probably not going to get sued—although, technically, it is infringing. Beware of the problem.

TITLES

Titles are not protected by copyright. The basic rule is that the author has no inherent right in the title to his screenplay, play, or book title (*Jackson v. Universal International Pictures*, 36 Cal.2d 116 [1950]). Only when the title has acquired a "secondary meaning," that is, when the title is established in the public mind, is the author entitled to its exclusive use. *Gone With the Wind*, for instance, is known as the title of a book and a motion picture. The public immediately thinks of a specific movie based on a specific book when the title is mentioned and the association is clear.

How many persons need to have the required association? There is no set number and it does not have to be masses. The "public" need not necessarily consist of people throughout the nation, but it should be a substantial number of people. If you submit your script to twenty producers, do not count on being able to keep the title. On the other end of the spectrum, it is clear that once a picture is made and distributed to the public, the title acquires secondary meaning, at least for as long as the public remembers the title.

Suppose your script is the hottest script in town and everyone is buzzing about it. *The Sixth Sense* was one such script and no one dared to steal the title. "Secondary meaning" had something to do with it. *Everyone* in Hollywood at the time knew about that script. It was written up in the trade papers (the *Hollywood Reporter* and *Variety*). Also, as a practical matter, regardless of secondary meaning, no one wants to be known as a rip-off artist. It would have been an obvious rip-off to have used that title at the time.

What if your title has already been used often in other contexts? If the title is found to have numerous uses, so that the public does not associate it with one particular business, then you may be able to use it. For instance, take the title *Western Is the Way*. There are many businesses with the title *Western*. Just look in the phone book. It is doubtful that any particular Acme business would sue, because the public as a whole does not associate the name "Western" with one particular business. On the other hand, the word "Pepsi®" is specific and trademarked. You should stay away from it.

While there are no black-and-white rules in this area, the real key to using any title is whether the use of your title will result in confusion in the public's mind about the source of the work. It is not necessary for there to be actual confusion on the public's part, and the mere possibility that a consumer may be misled is not enough. There must be a *likelihood* of confusion. Is the similar title used in the same market? Has the other title been used commercially in recent years? Is it a forgotten title? While it might have achieved secondary meaning many years ago, is that secondary meaning still well known? After a certain period of time, secondary meaning may disappear if the title is no longer associated with a particular work.

What if your title uses only some of the words from another title? One case involved the comparison of the title *The Love Bug* (a Disney movie) and "The Love Bug Will Bite You (If You Don't Watch Out)" (a song) (*Tomlin* v. *Walt Disney Productions*, 18 Cal. App. 3d 226 [1971]). In that instance, even though the alleged owner of the song claimed that his song had been nicknamed "The Love Bug," he lost. One title was used for a song; the other for a film. No likelihood of confusion was found.

Some producers will widely publicize a film title prior to production of a picture—with ads in the trades (short for trade papers), articles, posters at film festivals, and the like (such as Cannes and the American Film Market). Such evidence is usually compelling and usually stops another party from using the same title. A producer may thus help you to protect your title in this manner.

MPAA TITLE REGISTRATION

Producers also have another way to protect titles that is not available to the writer. The Motion Picture Association of America (MPAA) has a Title Registration Bureau. All of the studios and many major production companies and producers subscribe to it. The way it works is simply this: Subscribers register the titles they want to use. If someone else has already registered a particular title, the second person to register is put on a waiting list. If the first party to register the title does not use the title (that is, produce a picture) within a certain period of time (with extensions, eighteen months to two years), then that party loses its priority on the title, unless the second registerer on the list gives permission to the first to extend. The second party might give permission if he does not think the first party will produce a picture soon and the second party is not ready to make a picture. (Remember: Once you are first on the list, the clock starts ticking.) If you sell your screenplay to a studio or a producer that is a subscriber to the Motion Picture Association Title Registration Bureau, the buyer will immediately register your title for you, so your title can also be protected that way.

One problem with the MPAA system is that only subscribers are bound by the terms. A nonsubscriber is free to use a subscriber's title, unless the subscriber's title has achieved secondary meaning. Of course, if the nonsubscriber sells the project to a subscriber, that is, an independent producer independently finances a film and then sells it to a major studio, the major studio will have to play by the Title Registration Bureau rules. If another subscriber to the Bureau has already registered the title at that time, then the studio will not be able to use it as long as that other subscriber has priority.

The other problem with the MPAA system for writers, in particular, is that protection is for the subscriber, not for you. That does not mean that the subscriber will be able to use your title if the subscriber's rights in your screenplay lapse. But once that subscriber's right to your material does lapse, so does your protection under this system. Of course, you are still protected by the secondary meaning doctrine and if there is enough buzz about your title and enough people have seen it, odds are it will not be ripped off.

In short, there are many variables. Clearly, simple submission of your script to several producers, absent unusual circumstances such as *The Sixth Sense* example, is not enough to establish secondary meaning. If you have a great title, you might want to save it until you sell your script to a producer or studio and it looks like it is going to be produced. That way, no one will know about it until something can be done to try to protect it.

IDEAS

Ideas are not protected by copyright law. The essence of copyright law is that the protection granted to a copyrighted work extends only to the particular expression of the idea and never to the idea itself (*Mazer v. Stein*, 347 U.S. 201, 217, 218 [1954]; *Baker v. Selden*, 101 U.S. 99 [1879]).

Nevertheless, under certain very limited circumstances, ideas may be protected by express or implied contract. One thing is for sure: If you "blurt out" your idea, such as at a party, you have no protection at all. So be careful what you disclose.

Under the basic principle of copyright law, ideas are not protected by copyright because only independent original creations are protected. On the other hand, an idea, a concept, or a common plot is not protected because certain concepts and plots must be available to all authors. Take the boy-meets-girl plot, for instance: If one author were entitled to copyright this concept, no one else would be able to use it. For that reason, the material must be sufficiently original in order to qualify for copyright protection.

The law also recognizes, however, that under certain circumstances, it is unfair for people to steal ideas, particularly in Hollywood, where unique ideas are often the basis for successful pictures. One famous case (*Blaustein v. Burton*, 9 Cal. App. 3d 161, 88 Cal. Rpts. 319 [1970]) involved a producer who came up with the idea of casting Richard Burton and Elizabeth Taylor in *The Taming of the Shrew*. The producer also came up with the ideas of using Franco Zeffirelli as the director, eliminating the play-within-a-play device in Shakespeare's play, including two key scenes (the wedding scene and the wedding night scene) in the film version that occurred offstage in Shakespeare's original, and the idea of filming in Italy. No question that these were the producer's ideas and they were unique. Still, copyright law does not cover such unique concepts.

However, the court held that a contract may be established if it is clear that the person disclosing the idea will be paid if his idea is used. (The producer in this case, unfortunately, had not established a contract.) Note that a contract right may not be claimed unless there exists an element in addition to the mere acts of reproduction, performance, distribution or display (copyright rights). That additional element is a promise (express or implied) upon the part of the defendant. 4, Melville B. Nimmer and David Nimmer, Nimmer on Copyright S16.04[C] at 16-25 (2002). Note also that implied in fact contracts are not recognized by all states. While California does recognize such a right, many states do not. To best protect yourself, the principle of compensation should be agreed upon *before* the idea is disclosed. Such agreement may be either *implied* or *express*, depending on the circumstances. An "implied in fact" contract would be, for instance, when a professional producer who makes his living by producing films discloses an idea: It is clear that he intends to produce the film and receive a salary for doing so. A contract will be implied in fact when the parties clearly intended payment to the extent of the use of the idea, though they did not set forth that intention in express language (Katy Dochrermann & Epstein, Inc. v. HBO, No. 97 Civ. 7763 [TPG]), (S.D.N.Y. March 31, [1999]). An "express" contract means that, before you disclose an idea, you have the other person actually agree that you will be paid if he uses it. The listener must also have an opportunity to reject the idea on the terms offered.

The law also recognizes a promise to pay immediately after the idea is disclosed (*Desny* v. *Wilder*, 46 Cal. 2d 715, 299 P.2d 257 [1956]; *Donahue* v. *Ziv Television Programs, Inc.*, 245 Cal. App. 2d 593, 54 Cal. Rpts. 130 [1966]), but once you have blurted out your idea, if your listener makes no such promise, you are out of luck. "The idea man who blurts out his idea without having first made his bargain has no one to blame but himself for the loss of his bargaining power." The *Donahue* case involved the similarity between the series *Sea Hunt* and a similar format for an underwater legion series that had previously been submitted to the producer of *Sea Hunt*. There was no other similarity between the two series, other than concept, which ruled out a suit for copyright infringement. Indeed, this is the reason that one often sees movies with common themes, even in the same year. Studios race to be the first to capitalize on a hot new concept (for example, there are numerous thriller movies, outer space/futuristic movies, and so on). As long as the concept is the only similarity, there is no cause of action. Even if there are similar plot points, as long as one party does not actually copy the other, there is also no copyright infringement. To prove infringement, one has to prove that there was actual copying by access *and* similarity.

The *Sea Hunt* case also stated that the amount of the compensation does not have to be specifically agreed upon, although that certainly helps. A court may establish the value, particularly in the entertainment industry, by testimony indicating what writers have been paid under similar circumstances.

While the implied in fact contract law has been questioned by certain courts recently on the basis that copyright law preempts such claims Endemol Entertainment (B.V. v. Twentieth Television, Inc. 48 U.S.P.Q.2d 1524, 1998 Copr.L.Dec P 27,835 [C.D.CAL 1998]), other cases have kept the doctrine alive. See Groubert v. Spyglass Entertainment Group LP, 63 U.S.P.Q.2d 1764, 2002 Copr.L.Dec.P28, 459 (C.D.Cal. 2002). "Plaintiff only disclosed his idea to Defendants in the first place on the condition that he be compensated for its use, and Defendants allegedly accepted this condition. In this regard, the promise in the formation of this implied contract contains an 'additional element' not covered under the copyright law. Since the whole purpose of the contract was to protect Plaintiff's rights to his ideas beyond those already protected by the Copyright Act, such rights are obviously not 'equivalent.' [citation] Therefore, the Court finds that Plaintiff's claim for breach of implied contract is not preempted by the Copyright Act of 1976."

Applying the law in this area, generally and ideally you would handle idea submissions in the following manner: You have a great idea. You want someone to pay you to write a script about it. You manage to set up a meeting with a producer. You should say to the producer, "I have a great idea. If you decide to use it, you must pay me a certain

sum to write the script." If you have already been employed by someone and have a quote (a "quote" is your previous salary to write), you
might say " . . . you must pay me to write at my going rate." If he says
no, then do not disclose the idea. If he says yes and agrees to your
terms, you have a deal. Your safest bet, of course, is to put it in writing. A simple letter of agreement will do. Or write a letter and say,
"Unless I hear back from you to the contrary, this confirms our deal."
While self-serving, the burden is then on the producer to respond that
he does not agree to the terms.

Submission Agreements

To say the least, this is not an easy process, particularly if you are a
beginner. Most producers will probably respond by saying, "I'm not
going to agree to anything until I hear your idea." If you do not have
substantial credentials, or even if you do, most producers will not be
bothered with such formalities and they will pass on the opportunity. It
is just too complicated and leaves them open to lawsuits. Alternatively,
they may ask you to sign a submission agreement. In essence, this
agreement requires you to waive any rights you may have if that producer produces a film with the same or a similar idea to yours.

Here's an example of such a form:

> Gentlemen:
> I desire to submit to you for your consideration material (herein
> called "submitted material") written or controlled by me intended
> to be used by you as the basis for one or more motion pictures.
> The submitted material is as follows:
>
> _____
>
> _____
>
>
> and I have more fully described the same in "Exhibit A," which is
> attached hereto. I recognize the possibility that the submitted
> material may be identical with or similar to material that has or
> may come to you from other sources. Such similarity in the past
> has given rise to litigation so that unless you can obtain ade-

quate protection in advance, you will refuse to consider the submitted material. The protection for you must be sufficiently broad to protect you, your related corporations, and your and their employees, agents, licensees, and assigns, and all parties to whom you submit material. Therefore, all references to you includes each and all of the foregoing.

As an inducement to you to examine the submitted material, and in consideration of your so doing, I represent, warrant, and agree as follows:

1. I acknowledge that the submitted material is as submitted by me voluntarily, on an unsolicited basis, and not in confidence, and that no confidential relationship is intended or created between us by reason of the submission of the submitted material. Nothing in this agreement, nor the submission of the submitted material, shall be deemed to place you in any different position from any other member of the public with respect to the submitted material. Accordingly, any part of the submitted material that could be freely used by any member of the public may be used by you without liability to me.

2. I acknowledge that at this time you have no intent to compensate me in any way and I have no expectation of receiving any compensation. You agree, however, that you *shall not use the submitted material unless you shall first negotiate with me and agree upon compensation to be paid to me for such use,* but I understand and agree that your use of material containing features or elements similar to or identical with those contained in the submitted material shall not obligate you to negotiate with me nor entitle me to any compensation if you determine that you have an independent legal right to use such other material, which is not derived from me (either because such features or elements were not new or novel, or were not originated by me, or were or may hereafter be independently created and submitted by other persons, including your employees).

3. I represent and warrant that I own the submitted material free of all claims or encumbrances and have the exclusive right to offer all rights in the submitted material to you. I grant to you an option for ninety (90) days from the date of my signing and returning this agreement to investigate and negotiate with me for exclusive rights to the submitted material and agree that during such period I will not negotiate with others regarding the submitted material. If any material is based on another published work, I will so indicate in Exhibit A and I agree that you may use fully without negotiating with me (except to the extent I own or have contractual rights to said published materials) any portions of said published materials as the basis for motion pictures.

4. I agree that no obligation of any kind is assumed or may be implied against you by reason of your consideration of the submitted material or any discussions or negotiations we may have with respect thereto, except pursuant to an express written agreement hereafter executed by you and me, which, by its terms, will be the only contract between us.

5. Except as otherwise provided in this agreement, I hereby release you of and from any and all claims, demands, and liabilities of every kind whatsoever, known or unknown, that may arise in relation to the submitted material or by reason of any claim now or hereafter made by me that you have used or appropriated the submitted material, except for fraud or willful injury on your part.

6. I hereby agree expressly for the benefit of your employees, agents, studios, or financiers with which you have an agreement or arrangement that I will not claim that any such party has, has had, or may in the future have, access to the submitted material other than through you; and this agreement applies to all access of the submitted material had by any such party, even if you never submit the submitted material to such party.

While this form does provide that you will be compensated if your unique material is used and that the producer will negotiate with you first before using it, it also bars you from a future suit based on concept. If you have only an idea, do not sign it. If yours is what they call a "high concept" idea and script, you probably shouldn't sign it either. If you've written a script that doesn't fall into that category and you're not concerned about your idea being ripped off (it's your *plot* that is really unique), then it might be the only way to have your script read. At least this form states that the studio will have to negotiate with you first before using it. (Do not sign a form that doesn't at least incorporate this notion!) Some people also add "at no less than WGA Minimum" after the provision about the studio negotiating with you, to ensure that there is some framework to start from.

The best path for you to follow is to flesh out your idea at least to the treatment stage (a "treatment" is a detailed outline of the plot, description of characters, and so on) or, better yet, write a first draft script. That way, you have copyright protection (tangible evidence of your original creation). A record of your submission may make the producer think twice about using your material. Try not to sign a submission agreement, particularly if your idea is unique.

The Pitch

As a practical matter, established writers often pitch story ideas to studios and producers (usually complete with a plot summary and character description) and there is an understanding in the industry that the writer will be hired if the studio likes the pitch. To the extent that the pitch is more than an idea, there is legal protection. There is also relationship protection. Most established writers are represented by established agents. Agents would not submit material or set up meetings if there were a substantial risk that their clients might be ripped off as a result of such pitch meetings. That is not to say that it never happens. As a general rule, the Hollywood system recognizes certain rules in the course of doing business. Studios, as a rule, will not want to proceed to develop a project without using the writer who came up with the idea if evidence of the meeting and the pitch is sufficiently detailed.

DROIT MORALE

All American contracts require the author to waive his right of *droit morale*. Droit morale (it translates as "moral right") is a European concept, seen particularly in France and Italy. In those countries, by law, authors are granted nonwaivable rights, which are personal to them. These laws limit the changes that the buyer of an author's work can make. The moral rights of authors ensure that the writer be named as the author, and, specifically, prevent the buyer of a literary work from making changes that deform or mischaracterize the original intent of the author or reflect poorly on her professional reputation. They also prevent the buyer from falsely attributing written material to an author (for instance, when a famous writer's work has been changed, yet the publisher or studio still wants to exploit the famous writer's name).

This concept is universally despised by U.S. studios and production companies. As indicated above, their basic philosophy is this: They pay for it, they can do whatever they want with it. Therefore, you must agree in your contract not to assert any rights of "droit morale."

U.S. copyright law does not mention moral rights, so there is no such statutory protection. Yet particular cases have held that writers may have certain moral rights under especially egregious circumstances. The most famous case is the "Monty Python" case (*Gilliam v. American Broadcasting Company*, 583 F.2d 14 [1976]).

ABC had broadcast an episode of *Monty Python's Flying Circus* show, which was originally shown on the BBC. ABC cut 27 percent of the show to allow for commercials. The court stated that the cuts constituted an actionable mutilation of Monty Python's work. The court held that ABC compromised the integrity of Monty Python's work and falsely represented the truncated program to the public as a complete Monty Python production; that is, the show aired was not a true rendering of the creators' material and talents.

Under circumstances like those addressed in the Monty Python case, suits involving egregious butchering of a writer's material may, indeed, be pursued successfully. These suits are usually based on theories of misrepresentation and unfair competition, and are designed to prevent behavior that may injure an author's business and personal reputation. But the circumstances have to be outrageous and, even then, such suits are difficult to win and are few and far between.

All studios require you to waive moral rights. You have *no choice*, but you should be aware of what this waiver means. Here is an example of the moral rights clause contained in most contracts:

> Owner hereby waives the benefits of any provision of law known as "droit morale" or any similar laws and agrees not to institute, support, maintain, or authorize any action or lawsuit on the ground that any motion pictures or sound records, or other items produced hereunder in any way constitute an infringement of any of Owner's "droit morale" or a defamation or mutilation of any part thereof, or contain unauthorized variations, alterations, modifications, changes, or translations.

Recently, the European Economic Community (EEC) has hinted that additional payments may be required for a waiver of moral rights in countries where such rights may be waived. Studios have started including language in their agreements to cover themselves in this regard to the effect that your compensation is deemed to include any such future EEC payments. Studios will not delete it. In the first place, American studios are not bound by EEC regulations. More important, the custom in America is to waive all rights of droit morale without exception. It remains to be seen whether the action of the EEC community will have any effect on Hollywood's customary way of doing business. Perhaps the Writer's Guild will try to incorporate such a provision in its Basic Agreement.

13

Works Based
on Source Material

The film business is an extremely lucrative one. Where there is money to be made, there are bound to be lawsuits launched by people seeking to get their share of the pie. Of course, many such suits are justified, and when a writer's material is stolen, someone has to pay. In chapter 12, I discussed the principles used in determining the outcome in legitimate copyright infringement suits. On the other hand, many such lawsuits are without merit and launched by people seeking to gain simply by muddying the waters.

CHAIN OF TITLE

Throughout this book, I have pointed to the specter of nuisance suits and the reality that there are unscrupulous writers and producers who seek to be rewarded by claiming they have rights in a project. The main problem is that studios tend to shy away from projects if there is any doubt about the ownership of a script. Studios want what they call a clean "chain of title." Chain of title establishes that the seller of a screenplay does, in fact, own the screenplay. For instance, if the screenplay is based on a book, the owner of a screenplay should also have the rights to the book or know that they are available.

The studio will examine the written documents that establish ownership in the seller. They will also ask for full disclosure of any claims known to the seller by any persons claiming that they own the screenplay or that the screenplay infringes on such person's rights in any manner whatsoever.

Producers who claim they have rights in a project, notwithstanding the writer's position, create what is called a "cloud" on the chain of title or doubts about ownership. If there is such a cloud, studios will want it removed quickly before they make a deal. Unfortunately, removal of the "cloud" usually requires making a deal with the person clouding the chain of title. This is much quicker and probably less costly than going to court—so the creator of the cloud wins by trying to throw a wrench in the works. Some cases, however, indicate that courts will put a damper on such attempts to muddy the waters. In an unpublished opinion (*Max Baer, Jr.* v. *American Broadcasting Co.*, B.O. 58056 Superior Court Case No. C601592, 2nd District, California, Court of Appeals [1992]), the court examined the following pattern of facts: ABC tried to obtain the rights to the song "Like A Virgin"; the song was to be used as the basis of a motion picture. ABC's representatives negotiated with the songwriter's lawyer and thought they had a deal, even though the lawyer representing the songwriter wrote back numerous times to ABC stating that no such deal existed, because all points had not yet been resolved. The songwriter then entered into negotiations with Max Baer, who wanted to option the rights to the song for the same reason as ABC. Baer worked out a deal on all points. ABC tried to block the deal. The court awarded Max Baer $2 million, holding ABC liable for tortuous interference with Max Baer's rights. One of the main points cited in the case was that a grant of rights may only be effected by a signed agreement. For one, the Copyright Act requires that "A transfer of copyright ownership, other than by operation of law, is not valid unless an instrument of transfer is in writing and signed by the owner of the rights conveyed or such owner's duly authorized agent" (17 U.S.C. 204[a] [1976]). Correspondence between the songwriter's lawyer and ABC might have created a written agreement, but, in this particular instance, the lawyer had insisted from the onset that a deal would not be closed until a contract was signed.

In short, if you insist on a signed contract in order for there to be a valid option or purchase of your material, you eliminate any persons who might claim they have a deal based on a proposal or correspondence that does not necessarily make clear the absence of an agreement. (Indeed, agents or other representatives often "close" a deal based on acceptance of only material points, leaving to good faith the negotiation of other provisions. Sometimes you can rely on good faith to work out the rest of the details to your satisfaction. Sometimes, you can't.) Insistence on a signed agreement eliminates the vagaries of closing a deal or saying you have reached an agreement if there are outstanding points that have not been resolved and you are concerned about them. It also precludes the problem of an oral agreement. Even though copyright law requires a notice in writing for a transfer to take place, if an oral agreement has been reached (generally speaking in contract law, oral agreements are considered binding), a claim may be made based on detrimental reliance, that may scare a studio away, unless the person making the claim agrees to walk away. The main problem with an oral agreement is that until you prove that no such claim exists, a cloud may remain.

Indeed, the *Max Baer* case stands as a good lesson for would-be "cloud" creators. Hopefully, the size of the award will discourage people seeking a quick buck by muddying the copyright waters around a promising project. Because it is an unpublished decision, the case has no precedential value in California. But a court might very well make a similar ruling based on that kind of pattern of facts. (Letter agreement not signed by copyright owner is insufficient to transfer copyright. *Berger* v. *Computer Information Publishing, Inc.*, 1984 copyright L. Dec. (CCH) $25,681 [S.D. N.Y. 1984]. Alleged oral agreements to transfer film's copyrights to producer were unenforceable per section 204 writing requirement. *Time, Inc.* v. *Kastner*, 972 F. Supp. 236 [S.D. N.Y. 1997]). In *Radio Television Espanola S.A., Television Espanola S.A.* v. *New World Entertainment, Ltd.*, Nos. 97-56418, 98-55128, D.C., No. CV 96-02798

WDK, United States Court of Appeals (9th Cir. 1999), the Court pointed to correspondence between the parties that referenced a deal, but did not specify whether that deal was for an exclusive license for a television program or for other broadcast rights. The reference to a deal in the absence of specificity was considered part of a negotiation rather than an instrument of transfer. In this case, New World was awarded its court costs. The parties' intent, as evidenced by a clear writing, must demonstrate a transfer of the copyright. *Valente–Kritzer Video* v. *Pinckney,* 881 F.2d 772, 775 (9th Cir. 1989). The rule is quite simple: If the copyright holder agrees to transfer ownership to another party, that party must get the copyright holder to sign a piece of paper saying so. It doesn't have to be the Magna Carta; a one line pro forma statement will do. *Effects Assocs., Inc.* v. *Cohen,* 908 F.2d 555,556-58 (9th Cir. 1990).

Note that "clouds" are also created by people claiming that a writer's material is similar to their own and other sly insinuations of infringement. That is why producers are so paranoid about accepting unsolicited submissions. Most producers will only accept submissions from known agents. Fortunately, these types of "clouds" are covered by errors and omissions insurance (see chapter 8, Errors and Omission Insurance), and, thus, are not as deadly to a project as the other examples I cite in this chapter.

PROBLEMS

In dealing with the issue of insurance coverage, I have encountered two problem areas: coverage on the sale of a book (if you are the book writer) and coverage in the event that the written material is based on facts or the lives of real persons (see Defamation, below, regarding material based on fact).

If you are the writer of a published book, studios have tried to argue that they do not have to cover your book material, as the publisher of the book has its own E&O policy. While it is true that legitimate publishing houses do take out E&O coverage for a book, that coverage covers the publisher's exploitation of the book; it does not cover suits resulting from the exploitation of a movie. Suppose, for example, that a "nuisance suit" type of person did not read the book. That person sees the movie and decides to sue, claiming that a character portrayed in the movie is based on his own life story. The suit is not against the publisher, but against the company making the picture. If there is no coverage for you in this circumstance, you are vulnerable. Studios or production companies have various reasons for failing to provide E&O coverage for certain projects, including a refusal to pay an increased premium to cover a pattern of facts or a genuine inability by the company to obtain coverage from an E&O insurer for this particular project. (E&O carriers have also gotten tough in recent years.) In this circumstance, it's crucial to make sure the company will cover you for the same types of lawsuits that the E&O carrier would normally cover. In other words, the company should indemnify you. The major studios are rich companies, and I am comfortable with this indemnity.

Unfortunately, some studios are reluctant to do this. I was involved in one very prolonged negotiation regarding the sale of a book. The book had been on the market for some time. No one had sued. The studio refused to add a provision covering the writer of the book on its E&O policy. The studio said that as a matter of policy, it would always cover E&O–type claims on behalf of a writer, even though it did not want to express this policy in the contract. My feeling is that if the studio says it is willing to do something, then it should put that in writing. If there is nothing in writing, the writer is vulnerable. The studio finally agreed to indemnify the writer in the event of a lawsuit (unless of course, the writer knowingly infringed someone else's rights).

In this instance, based on the indemnity and the solid financial condition of the studio, my client decided to take the risk. He figured that anyone who might have sued would have sued by then, given the popularity of the book. That is a business decision with which I cannot argue. You might be in a situation someday when you have to make such a decision. Do you want to break a deal over it or will you rely on the custom and practice in the industry that supports the studio's assurances? The reality is that studios and other major production companies would not stay in business long if they held writers accountable for claims that are not the writer's fault. On the other hand, suppose the company is on the verge of bankruptcy? The company indemnity may be meaningless. I can only point out the risks.

The decision is ultimately up to the client. Always remember: Your lawyer and your agent do not control third parties. We cannot force them to do things that they categorically refuse to do.

MATERIAL BASED ON FACT

On the one hand, when you write a "docudrama"—a dramatization of real events and specific persons' lives—or when you fictionalize a true story (change the names, locations, certain aspects of a real story), you are protected by the First Amendment: "Congress shall make no law . . . abridging the freedom of speech, or of the press" (U.S. Constitution, First Amendment).

Motion pictures are a form of free speech. Like books, they are "a significant medium for the communication of ideas; their importance as an organ of public opinion is not lessened by the fact that they are designed to entertain as well as to inform; and, like books, they are a constitutionally protected form of expression, notwithstanding that their production, distribution and exhibition is a large scale business constructed for private purpose" (*University of Notre Dame, DuLac* v. *20th Century Fox Film Corp.*, 256 N.Y.S. 2d [1965], affirmed upon the opinion of the Appellate Division, 16 N.Y. 2d 940 [1965]).

On the other hand, depending on your depiction of these events, you run the risk of violating other people's rights. These violations fall into four categories: (1) defamation; (2) violations of the right to privacy by public disclosure of private facts; (3) violation of the right to privacy by depiction of an actual person in a false light; and (4) violation of a person's right of publicity.

You need to be aware of certain areas of the law that make your work vulnerable to legal attack. Because these areas cannot be covered thoroughly in the space of this book, I will only provide you with a brief overview. Keep in mind that there are no black-and-white rules with respect to these areas, and the outcome will always depend on the specifics of your writings. If you suspect that your writings may infringe someone's rights, then you should follow the advice I give at the end of this chapter. Most cases are decided by balancing the right of free speech and the public's right to discuss real events against the individual's rights (that is, the subject of the docudrama) in certain instances.

I assume, first, that you have not obtained a release from the actual person you are writing about. (Even if you have, you are not necessarily in the clear. See discussion below regarding the essential elements that must be contained in any such release.)

DEFAMATION

The Restatement of Torts defines defamation in the following manner: "A communication is defamatory if it tends to hurt the reputation of another so as to lower him in the estimation of the community or to deter third persons from associating or dealing with him. Communications are defamatory because they tend to expose another to hatred, ridicule, or contempt. To be defamatory, it is not necessary that the communication actually cause harm to another's reputation or actually deters third persons from associating or dealing with him. Its character depends upon its general tendency to have such an effect. It is enough that the communication tends to prejudice a person in the eyes of a substantial and respectable minority of persons in the community or association" (Restatement [second] of Torts, Section 559).

More specifically, when we talk about defamation with respect to a screenplay, we are talking about libel. The difference between libel and slander is that "libel consists of the *publication* of defamatory matter by written or printed words, while slander consists of the issuance of defamatory statements by spoken words or transitory gestures" (Restatement [second] of Torts, Section 568[1] and [2]). Truth is a defense to any libel claim. If your publication is about an actual person and it is accurate, then you avoid exposing yourself to this particular violation.

In order for the claiming party to win a libel case, the claimant must establish that: (1) the publication caused damage to his/her reputation; (2) his/her reputation was harmed before a group large enough to constitute a substantial minority of the community to which the statement was addressed—the exploitation of a motion picture constitutes dissemination to such a large group; and (3) the claimant could be identified—not necessarily by name, but through something in the picture that points to the identity of the real person, such as that the movie was based on a book in which the real person was identified and thus the identification can be easily made (*Kelly* v. *Loews, Inc.*, 76 F. Supp. 473 [1948]). If your writing may injure someone's reputation, definitely consult a knowledgeable attorney before writing.

When the writing is about public officials, it is even more difficult for a plaintiff to win a libel suit. In the famous *New York Times Co.* v. *Sullivan* case, the Supreme Court allowed a little more leeway concerning writings about public officials based on the doctrine of free speech, which is derived from the First Amendment. In this case, the speech was indeed false, but the Court found that the *New York Times* was not negligent in failing to discover certain misstatements before printing them. Specifically, the Court held that all defamatory speech directed at public officials was within the orbit of First Amendment protection, *except* speech that is *knowingly* false or that is made with *reckless disregard* of its truth or falsity. Mere proof of a failure to investigate does not constitute reckless disregard of the truth (*The New York Times Co.* v. *Sullivan*, 376 U.S. 254 [1964]). Public figures must establish "actual malice" (*Gertz* v. *Robert Welsh, Inc.* 418 U.S. 323 [1974]).

The issue then becomes, who is a public figure? In the case of *Time, Inc.* v. *Firestone* (424 U.S. 448 [1976]), concerning a story in *Time* magazine about the divorce of the wife of a famous industrialist, the Court held that a socialite in a highly publicized divorce trial did not qualify as a public figure. Moreover, she did not "thrust" herself into a particular public controversy or the issues surrounding it. If you are not sure that the person you are writing about is indeed a public figure, again, consult an attorney knowledgeable in this area.

RIGHT OF PRIVACY

Assuming that you have avoided a libel claim, if your writing is based on an actual person's story, you may violate that person's right of privacy by public disclosure of private facts. The principal difference between libel and invasion of privacy concerns the nature of the injury. Libel constitutes injury to one's reputation or character, whereas invasion of privacy concerns the person's injured feelings alone, without regard to the eyes of others.

Public Disclosure of Private Facts

A person who unreasonably and seriously interferes with another's interest in not having his affairs known to others or his likeness exhib-

ited to the public is liable to the other. Further, "one who gives publicity to a matter concerning the private life of another is subject to liability to the other for invasion of his privacy, if the matter publicized is
of a kind that (a) would be highly offensive to a reasonable person and
(b) is not of legitimate concern to the public" (Restatement [Second]
of Torts, Section 652D). This derives from the principle that in order
to constitute invasion of privacy, the facts disclosed to the public must
be private facts, not public ones. The First Amendment includes the
right to be free from the unwarranted attack of others upon one's lib-
erty, property, and reputation (*Melvin* v. *Reid*, 112 Cal. App. 285
[1931]). For example, a chauffeur was shot and seriously injured. As a
result, he became "mentally ill, nervous, and distraught." A broadcast
dramatization of the holdup used the chauffeur's name without his consent. When he heard the broadcast, he suffered mental anguish. The
Court found the chauffeur's right to be left alone had been violated (*Mau*
v. *Rio Grande Oil, Inc.*, 28 F. Supp. 845 [N. D. Cal. 1939]).

An individual has no basis for a claim when a marriage or birth is
disclosed. These events are matters of public record and public figures,
by virtue of their being public figures, give up their rights to privacy
under many circumstances. In *Melvin* v. *Reid*, the court stated that the
right to privacy "does not exist where a person has become so prominent that, by his very prominence, he has dedicated his life to the
public and thereby waived his right of privacy. Thus, the right of
privacy does not exist in the dissemination of news and news events,
nor in the discussion of events of the life of a person in whom the
public has a rightful interest, nor where the information would be of
public benefit, as in the case of a person running for public office."

That is not to say that public figures have no privacy rights at all.
What happens in the bedroom would indeed be considered private
(although, apparently, if what the public figure does in his bedroom
for that matter, has an impact on public policy or is of legitimate public interest, even this sanctuary is not sacred). The key is that the
scope of privacy is narrowed considerably.

The passage of time may protect a *former* public figure. For instance,
in the *Melvin* v. *Reid* case cited above, a former prostitute who was tried
for murder (thus a public figure at the time) was acquitted and reha-

bilitated herself. She filed a claim against a motion picture company for making a movie titled *The Red Kimono*, based on the earlier murder case and using her real name. She won (*Melvin v. Reid*, 112 Cal. App. 285 [1931]). In other cases, on the other hand, the claimant had been convicted of murder (and later pardoned) and the Court decided that republication of the events of a man convicted of murder and paroled twelve to thirteen years later was not a violation of his privacy (*Bernstein v. National Broadcasting Co.*, 129 F. Supp. 817 [1955]) and that criminal records are publishable "no matter how remote in time or place" (*McCall v. Oroville Mercury*, 9 Media 2. Rep. 1701 [Cali. App. 3d Dist 1983]).

As you can see, there are no absolute rules here, and a lot depends on the facts of a particular case. The point of this chapter is to make you aware of the pitfalls in writing about actual persons and real events.

In general, there is considerably less leeway with dramatizations than with newspaper reporting. Newspaper reporting is designed to report news. Dramatizations are designed to entertain. The motion picture docudrama is riskier because no drama consists of only facts. Indeed, to write a decent script, you *must* convey more than just the facts. You have to write a scene based on what you think was said. Therein lies the real problem.

Fictionalizing; False Light; and Invasion of Privacy

Assuming you have avoided defamation and the public disclosure of private facts, are you totally safe in using someone's life story as the basis for your screenplay by fictionalizing? This is a tricky question. It is a *very* gray area, which is the reason I suggest the advice of counsel if you are specifically using someone's life story as the basis for your material.

For one, by fictionalizing, you may place an individual in a *false light* in the public eye. The injury is to feelings, as distinguished from a defamation claim, where the injury is to reputation. In one famous case, the court examined NBC's broadcast of the dramatization of a true story, which depicted a military man on an airplane that was forced to make an emergency landing. He was depicted as praying during the course of the landing, out of uniform in a Hawaiian shirt, smoking a pipe and cigarettes. Further, the teleplay did not depict his assistance in the evacuation. The Court ruled that such depiction, even though not wholly accurate, would not in itself be offensive to a person of ordinary sensibilities (*Strickler* v. *National Broadcasting Co.*, 167 F. Supp. 58 [1958]). Ultimately, the case turned on the specific facts.

In another case, on the other hand, an unauthorized biography of a famous professional baseball player contained so many errors through substantial fictionalization of events *with the writer's knowledge* of such falsification and a reckless disregard for the truth, that its publication was stopped (*Spahn* v. *Julian Messner, Inc.*, 18 N.Y.2d 324, vacated, 387 U.S. 239 [1966], affirmed, 21 N.Y.2d 124 [1967]).

As you can see, by fictionalizing someone's life story and identifying the person you are fictionalizing, you run the risk of being accused of having a reckless disregard for the truth.

What about fictionalizing someone's life and changing the name at the same time? Is that totally safe?

The answer is no. In the case of *Bindrum* v. *Mitchell* (92 Cal. App. 3d 61 155 Cal. Rptr. 29 [1979], cert. denied 444 U.S. 984 [1979], retig denied, 444 U.S. 1040 [1980]), the Court examined a libel claim by a clinical psychologist who had conducted a "nude marathon" in group therapy to help people shed their psychological inhibitions by taking off their clothes. The claim was lodged by the clinical psychologist against the writer of a so-called novel, who had participated in one such session. In her novel, the writer described the character of the psychologist, changing some of his characteristics, but still making the psychologist recognizable to anyone who knew him. She changed the names, locale, and incidents. One incident she made up was that the psychologist had asked a minister to persuade his wife to participate in one such session. In trying to persuade the minister, the psychologist used extremely foul language, which was uncharacteristic. The court held that even though the book was a "novel," the writer had libeled the psychologist. The decision has given every author cause for concern. On the other hand, in *Davis* v. *Costa-Gavras*, 654 F. Supp 653 (S.D. N.Y. 1987), the Court dismissed a libel claim in connection with the film *Missing*, concerning a public figure and recognized that a docudrama necessarily involves an author's "creative interpretation" of facts. That is to say, alterations of facts, composite characters, and telescoping of facts are not done with "serious doubts of truth of essence. They are not grounds for actual malice." False light claims concerning real people who are public figures are generally less successful. As with libel, grounds for suit must include "actual malice."

The point is to be *very* careful. Calling something a novel does not mean you are in the clear. Mixing fact and fiction may indeed invade someone else's rights.

In this context, as you know, at the end of every motion picture, studios include a statement such as:

> The events, characters, and firms depicted in this photoplay are fictitious. Any similarity to actual persons, living or dead, is purely coincidental.

RIGHT OF PUBLICITY

The right of publicity is considered a property right. You need to be aware of the scope of this right. It basically protects the value of one's name and likeness for commercial purposes if that is one's business—as in the case of celebrities. The right of publicity is distinct from invasion of one's right of privacy in that celebrities seek to be known and not private, but they "would feel sorely deprived if they no longer received money for authorizing advertisements, popularizing their countenances displayed in newspapers, magazines, buses, trains and subways" (*Haelen Laboratories, Inc. v. Topps Chewing Gum, Inc.*, 202 F.2d 866 (2d Cir.), cert. denied, 346 U.S. 816 [1953]). California has codified the right of publicity by statute: "Any person who knowingly uses another's name, photograph, likeness in any manner, for purposes of soliciting purchases of products, merchandise, soaps or services, without such person's prior consent, shall be liable for any damages sustained by the person or persons injured as a result thereof" (California Civil Code, Section 3344). There are similar statutes in other states. This right, unlike libel and the right of privacy, survives death for a period of time, depending on the state, but only if the celebrity had exploited his or her name for commercial purposes during his or her lifetime. The right usually does not apply to use of a deceased person's name, voice, signature, or likeness in film or television programs (California Civil Code, Section 990).

The cases mostly deal with the use of the celebrity's name or likeness in advertising a product. The use of a celebrity in an ad for a product would most certainly constitute exploitation of that celebrity's right of publicity. Merchandising using that celebrity's name and/or likeness would definitely constitute use of the celebrity's rights of publicity.

But does a motion picture about a celebrity itself constitute a violation of the right of publicity? Generally not. Note, however, that if the celebrity is alive, depending on the depiction and the nature of the celebrated status, a depiction may be a violation of the celebrity's right of privacy (e.g., dramatizing events that are not of public record) or libel (e.g., the depiction is false).

In *Guglielmi* v. *Spelling Goldberg* (25 Cal.3d 860 [1979]), the Court held that the right of publicity does not attach when a fictionalized account of the life of a public figure is depicted as fictitious. Similarly, in *Elizabeth Taylor* v. *The National Broadcasting Co.*, Case No. BC 110922 (Superior Court of the County of Los Angeles [September 29, 1994]), the Court held that an unauthorized television docudrama about the life of Elizabeth Taylor would not violate California's right of publicity laws. In *Seale* v. *Gramercy Pictures*, 949 F. Supp. 331 (E.D. PA. 1996), former "Black Panther" Bobby Seale brought a right of publicity claim against producers of the motion picture Panther. The Court stated that while it is admittedly a violation to use a person's name, image, or likeness for "purposes of trade," this does not include "entertainment."

While these decisions are clear that the right of publicity generally does not apply to a motion picture, certain other decisions indicate where trouble may lie. In *Eastwood* v. *Superior CT.*, 149 Cal. App.3d 409 [1983], the use of the actor's name and likeness in an article (generally considered news and therefore exempt) was actionable as a right of publicity claim because the story was, in fact, false. A knowingly false bio-pic using a celebrity's name and likeness to sell it—and at the same time leading an audience to believe it is a true story—may incur liability for false advertising. Also, there may be liability if a celebrity's style or performance is duplicated (filming of on-stage performance by Beatles imitators was actionable in *Apple Corps* v. *Leber*, 229 U.S.P.Q. 1015 [Cal.Super, 1986]). In most cases, the courts will examine and weigh the rights of the heirs (as a property right) and the right of the public to enjoy imitative performances (as a form of free speech under the First Amendment). California Civil Code, Section 990, dealing with the right of publicity of a deceased personality (in particular, the exemptions for film and television), is currently being reviewed.

The point is this: In all these cases, some analysis is inevitable and a court may very well look at a specific screenplay or motion picture and rule that it violates certain rights, no matter how carefully you try to follow the rules of these decisions. Again, that is what the insurance carriers insure against and that is why the insurance carrier's lawyers examine the screenplay carefully when the script concerns actual events and persons. Indeed, these lawyers often dictate certain strict guidelines and changes in an effort to follow the law as exemplified by these cases.

While I have tried to give you an overview of the potential problems involved in docudramas, I strongly suggest that you consult with an errors and omissions (E&O) lawyer before writing a full-length screenplay based on factual events. You are not a lawyer, and you cannot be expected to make a professional analysis based on the brief summary of the law contained in this chapter. These specialists make their living by assessing risks and assessing the risks that an insurance carrier is likely to take on.

REPRESENTATIONS AND WARRANTIES REVISITED

As you can see, writings based on fact may result in claims and liability. That is another reason why it is essential that you be protected on an errors and omissions policy. But beware: The representation and warranty language in your contract may put you in breach if it is not tailored to this kind of material. And if you are in breach, that might negate the E&O coverage, at least as far as you are concerned. Remember that you will be asked to represent and warrant "to the best of your knowledge" that you have not violated the rights of any third party. These rights include the right to be free from libel and the right to privacy. The Writers Guild has recognized that writers are not lawyers and that writers often create material that is based on personal experience and personal relationships. In that sense, you are likely to draw from your own experience and use incidents that have happened between you and other persons. While you will probably not depict those other persons' lives as the core of your material, you may use an event, a meeting, an encounter with that real person in the depiction of your own fictional character. In other words, to the best of your knowledge, you have not used another real person as an actual character, although you may use characteristics of that person in your fictional character. But if you have knowingly based your material on fact (that is, to the best of your knowledge, you *have* invaded someone else's rights), then this language actually puts you in breach of your contract. That means that if there is a claim, the E&O insurance carrier can proceed against you. In short, coverage may not apply to you if you have warranted something that is not true and are therefore responsible for the type of claims that the E&O coverage is designed to cover.

Here is an example of a warranty you can make when your material is actually based on fact:

> The parties hereto acknowledge that a third party attorney ("TPA") shall be engaged to supervise the Writer's writing for the Picture. In this regard, Writer shall write pursuant to the instructions of said TPA. Provided that Writer has delivered to Producer and TPA a fully annotated screenplay and has disclosed all relevant information known to Writer with respect to the Picture to Producer and TPA (including, without limitation, all sources of the contents of the screenplay) and, further provided that Writer has followed the instructions of Producer and TPA with respect to the Picture, and TPA has thereby approved the literary material submitted by Writer, *then Writer's representations, warranties, and indemnifications regarding defamation, publicity, rights of privacy, and publicity contained in the Agreement and in the Certificate of Authorship, shall not be applicable with respect to any claims, liabilities, or expenses, which Writer may incur, including reasonable attorneys' fees that may arise from Writer's writing materials hereunder, including, without limitation, the amount of the insurance deductible, if any.* Writer's failure to disclose information (pursuant to the preceding sentence) that is unrelated to a claim, if any, and Producer's production of the Picture based on material disap-

proved by TPA, shall not vitiate the foregoing waiver of Writer's representations, warranties, and indemnifications, or Producer's foregoing indemnification. To the extent that any materials are incorporated into the screenplay by Writer (which have not been approved by TPA), Writer shall not be covered pursuant to the aforesaid indemnification with respect to such material which has not been approved by TPA.

With respect to the arrangement between Writer and TPA, Writer shall submit writing materials to TPA for TPA's review. In this regard, for each submission Writer shall be afforded a one-time only opportunity to cure any portions of the screenplay that are not approved by TPA pursuant to the TPA's instructions (that is, once Writer has been afforded the opportunity to cure a disapproved portion, Writer shall not thereafter have the right to cure the same portion).

In other words, your only obligation under this warranty is to disclose everything you know to the producer and the lawyer who will analyze your material based on the law that I have summarized in this chapter. Beyond that, you are not responsible for lawsuits.

As you can see from the discussion in this chapter, the cases are varied and there are no clear answers. Was the person a public figure? Is he still a public figure? Is the event newsworthy? Is your fictionalization a reckless disregard of the truth? Because there is uncertainty, many studios take out insurance policies (as noted earlier in this book some do elect to self-insure because of the cost). As no one can be sure of the outcome in a privacy or defamation case concerning real events or loosely based on real events, most motion picture companies insure against the risk. The same rationale should apply to you. You should be covered. Assuming that you have disclosed all of the *facts*, you should not take the responsibility for lawsuits or claims if your material is knowingly and admittedly based on fact. Let the motion picture studio cover you under its policy. It is not a big expense. Most important, you must *not* allow the language in your contract to negate your coverage.

Sounds logical, yes. Is this logic universally accepted, *no*. I have been astounded more than once at a studio's position toward writers concerning liability for material based on fact. The warranty cited above, which I worked out for one client, actually took months of negotiation. It is a very difficult provision to get.

Here is one outrageous example of the problems in this area: A client wrote a script based on the life of a real person for Studio #1. Studio #1 thought that it could get a release from the real person and *the rights to that person's life story* at the time it entered into the agreement with the writer. It did not. The script was subsequently sold to Studio #2. Studio #2 asked my client to *fictionalize* the story since the real person would not sign a release. In fact, the real person had sold his life-story rights to a totally different motion picture company. My client agreed to fictionalize the script, and I asked that the studio indemnify him against claims that might be brought by the real person. Furthermore, I asked that the language in the contract specifically state that under no circumstances would the writer be liable for invasion of privacy, publicity, or defamation claims. In view of the false light privacy cases and *Bindrum* decision, where liability has been imposed for fictionalizing, I also asked that the writer be covered by an E&O insurance policy. The studio's negotiators refused, using the argument that the only way they could trust my client to totally fictionalize the story was to leave my client potentially liable for claims. If my client were potentially liable, there was no way he would fail to comply. This attitude was an insult to my client and to me. The studio basically said that it did not trust my client to do what he was told to do, and it failed to recognize the reality that there is no black-and-white rule in this area, which is precisely why producers take out E&O insurance.

For six months, we were at a standstill until the star, under whose banner the project was being developed, demanded that the deal be closed. The studio finally "gave in" and agreed to cover my client for any claims. This whole experience was unproductive and in my mind, unbefitting, coming from the mouths of studio executives who should have known better. It is yet another example of the cavalier treatment of writers in general.

RELEASES

Ideally, you should obtain a release from the actual person you want to depict. Here is an example of a release form commonly used.

Consent and Release Form

To: _____

_____

_____

_____

I understand that you desire to use all or part(s) of the events of my life in order to have one or more screenplays written and to produce, distribute, exhibit, and exploit one or more motion pictures, based upon the life story of _____ ("Life Story"), of any length in any and all media now known or hereafter devised, and sound recordings in any and all media now known or hereafter devised, based upon, derived from or suggested by all or parts of the events of my life in connection therewith. I have agreed to grant you certain rights in that connection. This Consent and Release confirms our agreement as follows:

1.   GRANT OF RIGHTS: Upon your receipt of this Consent and Release signed by me, for good and valuable consideration, receipt of which is hereby acknowledged, with full knowledge I hereby grant you, perpetually and irrevocably, the unconditional and exclusive right throughout the world to use, simulate, and portray, factually or fictionally as set forth below, my name, likeness, voice, personality, personal identification, and personal experiences, and the incidents, situations, and events that heretofore occurred (in whole or in part) based upon or taken from my life [as the same relates to the life story of _____], and surrounding events, in and in connection with motion pictures, sound recordings, publications, and any and all other media of any nature whatsoever, whether now known or hereafter devised. Without limiting the generality of the foregoing, it is understood and agreed that said exclusive right includes theatri-

cal, television, dramatic stage, radio, sound recording, music, publishing, commercial tieup, merchandising, advertising, and publicity rights in all Media of every nature whatsoever whether now known or hereafter devised. I reserve no rights with respect to such uses. (All of said rights are hereinafter referred to as the "Granted Rights.") It is further understood and agreed that the Granted Rights may be used in any manner and by any means, whether now known or unknown, and either factually or with such fictionalization, portrayal, impersonation, simulation, and/or imitation or other modification you, your successors, and assigns, determine in your sole discretion. I acknowledge that you and others are proceeding in reliance upon my grant to you hereunder. Any or all of the Granted Rights shall be freely assignable by you.

2. CONSIDERATION: As full and complete consideration for all of the Granted Rights assigned to you hereunder, you hereby agree to pay me and I agree to accept the sum of One Dollar ($I) and other good and valuable consideration, receipt of which is hereby acknowledged.

3. CONSULTATION: In further consideration for your efforts in connection with the development of a Picture based on the Life Story, I shall consult with you and the writer(s) of any screenplay based on the Life Story. I agree that any and all ideas, suggestions, plots, incidents, situations, and the results and proceeds of any services furnished by me to you shall be considered a *work-for-hire* for you and accordingly shall become the sole, complete, and exclusive property of yours and you shall have the exclusive and perpetual right to use the foregoing in connection with the Life Story or your exploitation thereof.

4. RELEASE: I agree hereby to release and discharge you, your employees, agents, licensees, successors, and assigns from any and all claims, demands, or causes of action that I may now have or may hereafter have libel, defamation, invasion of privacy, or right of publicity, infringement of copyright, or violation of any other right arising out of or relating to any utilization of the Granted Right or based upon any failure or omission to make use thereof.

5. NAME—PSEUDONYM: You have informed me and I agree that in exercising the Granted Rights, you, if you so elect, may refrain from using my real name and may use a pseudonym which will be dissimilar to my real name; however, such agreement does not preclude you from the use of my real name should you in your sole discretion elect, and in connection therewith I shall have no claim arising out of the so-called right of privacy and/or right of publicity.

6. FURTHER DOCUMENTS: I agree to execute such further documents and instruments as you may reasonably request in order to effectuate the terms and intentions of this Consent and Release, and in the event I fail or am unable to execute any such documents or instruments, you shall have the right to execute such documents on my behalf, provided that said documents and instruments shall not be inconsistent with the terms and conditions of this Consent and Release. Your rights under this Paragraph constitute a power coupled with an interest and are irrevocable.

7. REMEDIES: No breach of this Consent and Release shall entitle me to terminate or rescind the rights granted to you herein, and I hereby waive the right, in the event of any such breach, to equitable relief or to enjoin, restrain, or interfere with the production, distribution, exploitation, exhibition, or use of any of the Granted Rights, it being my understanding that my sole remedy shall be the right to recover damages with respect to any such breach.

8. PUBLIC DOMAIN MATERIAL: Nothing in this Consent and Release shall ever be construed to restrict, diminish, or impair the rights of either of you or me to utilize freely, in any work or media, any story, idea, plot, theme, sequence, scene, episode, incident, name, characterization, or dialogue that may be in the public domain, from whatever source derived.

9. ENTIRE UNDERSTANDING: This Consent and Release expresses the entire understanding between you and me and I agree that no oral understandings have been made with regard thereto. This Consent and Release may be amended only by written instrument signed by you and me. I acknowl-

edge that in granting the Granted Rights I have not been induced to do so by any representations or assurances, whether written or oral, by you or your representatives relative to the manner in which the Granted Rights may be exercised; and I agree that you are under no obligation to produce any motion picture based upon my life story or to exercise any of the Granted Rights; and I agree that I have not received any promises or inducements other than as herein set forth. The provisions hereof shall be binding upon me and my heirs, executors, administrators, and successors. I acknowledge that you have explained to me that this Consent and Release has been prepared by your attorney and that you have recommended to me that I consult with my attorney in connection with this Consent and Release. This Consent and Release shall be construed in accordance with the laws of the State of California applicable to agreements that are fully signed and performed within the State of California and I hereby waive any rights I have, known or unknown, pursuant to Section 15.2 of the California Civil Code which provides:

> A general release does not extend to claims which the creditor does not know or suspect to exist in his favor at the time of executing the release, which if known by him must have materially affected his settlement with the debtor.

Note that this release contains the following important provisions: (1) release from claims; (2) the right to use the person's real name or the right to change the name; and (3) the right to fictionalize events.

I have encountered the following problems with such releases. The person signing the release might insist on your changing his name. If you have to live with that limitation, I would do so, as long as the release is signed. The person signing the release might want approval rights. Approval rights are generally unacceptable. Studios need flexibility. Insurance carriers need flexibility. Approval over the screenplay is a handicap and will make it very difficult to sell your screenplay.

Finally, you may not be able to obtain releases from all the other people who need to sign releases because they are also depicted in your material. You should try to get as many releases as you can. The principal characters are key. The absence of a few releases does not necessarily mean the death of your project.

As you can see, the release is a grant of all life-story rights. If your script concerns only certain events in the person's life story, he may ask you to limit the grant to those events. That is acceptable, but you should reserve the nonexclusive right to use other events in that person's life story as such events may relate to your story. You may want to add some of this material to your screenplay later on and studios generally require this flexibility. If the grant is limited, you should also obtain the right of first negotiation/last refusal to buy other events of that person's life story, as the studio will usually require it (see chapter 4 regarding First Negotiation/Last Refusal Rights). Furthermore, you should obtain a holdback of these other rights. Studio bigwigs do not want another film in the marketplace about the person who is the subject of their motion picture, and certainly not before they have a chance to produce their own motion picture (see chapter 4, regarding Holdbacks).

PAYMENT

In order to obtain a release for a motion picture, you may have to pay money to the person giving you a release if the motion picture is produced. Studios generally will accept this, and you should make it part of your deal with the studio that the studio pays the cost. In other words, it should not come out of your monies. But what is an acceptable amount? It depends on the type of movie (such as television or feature) and whether or not the person signing the release is a principal character in the movie and whether he has achieved some celebrity status. For principal characters, studios generally pay $100,000 for life-story rights for a feature; for a TV movie, $50,000. Of course, there are exceptions and if the story is hot, they will pay more. The top end for TV is $75,000–$100,000, although in very unusual cases the network may pay several hundred thousand dollars. For features, the top end is $200,000 plus. Again, if the story is hot, the amount will be higher.

14

Collaboration Agreements

If you decide to write with someone else, you should work out an agreement with that person before you begin writing. That is, unless you don't mind that your writing partner will effectively have rights equal to yours in connection with your joint work.

Sophisticated buyers of collaborative material will require that all writers sign off on any agreement they may enter into. That means that if you want to option and/or sell the collaborative work to a third party, your collaborator will also have to agree not only on the producer or studio with which you want to be in business, but also on the terms. In short, your partner may block a deal unless he is also satisfied with the terms.

The presumption with any joint work is that the collaborators are fifty-fifty owners of the finished product, unless otherwise specified. But suppose you wrote the story and your collaborator helped you with the script? You probably want additional compensation for your story, so you need to work that out. Another problem you might want to work out is the issue of rewrites. Is your partner tied to all rewrites that you might be asked to do? Suppose he is not available at the time. Will you be able to write without him? If you do all the rewriting yourself, will you be able to keep all of the compensation for the rewrite or will your partner expect a piece? Suppose you have a fight after the first draft. What happens if there are irreconcilable differences and you cannot work together? Can you proceed without your partner? As you can see, there are a number of problems that might arise.

To give you an idea of how complicated collaborations may be, I have reprinted below a deal that I made for a director/writer client who collaborated on a script with another writer.

Screenwriter's Collaboration Agreement

As of _____, 20___

Re: "_____"

AGREEMENT made at Los Angeles, California, by and between director/writer ("Director") and writer ("Writer") hereinafter sometimes referred to as the "Parties."

The Parties are writing in collaboration a draft screenplay, hereinafter referred to as the "Work," based on a story idea and derived from previous drafts of screenplays by Director titled "_____," and are desirous of establishing all their rights and obligations in and to said Work.

NOW, THEREFORE, in consideration of the execution of this Agreement, and the undertakings of the parties as hereinafter set forth, it is agreed as follows:

1. The parties are collaborating in the writing of the Work and shall each own fifty percent (50%) of the actual revenues derived from the disposition of the Work itself, subject to the terms contained herein.

2. Upon completion of the Work, it shall be registered with The Writers Guild of America, west, Inc. as a collaborative Work of the parties. The copyright of the Work, however, shall be retained by Director only and shall be registered for copyright in the name of Director only. For said purposes and in connection therewith, Writer hereby assigns all of his right, title, and interest in the Work to Director in perpetuity.

3. (a) Writer agrees that Director shall have the sole right to dispose of the Work and all underlying rights in connection therewith on terms to be negotiated by Director and her representatives in their sole discretion, subject to the following provisions:

   (i)   Director agrees that she shall not sell the Work for less than *$450,000.* It is agreed that the sale price referred to in this paragraph for the Work shall not include revenues received for the story or any subsequent rewrites and drafts (unless otherwise negotiated pursuant to paragraph 9 below). It is further agreed that in the event Director dies prior to the disposition or sale of the Work or prior to the time that any rights in the Work would revert to Director, then at her death, all rights in the Work shall revert to Writer subject to payment to Director's heirs of the same sums that would have been payable to Writer hereunder had Director not died and on the same basis as paid herein (i.e., 50 percent (50%) of the sums payable to Writer on a prospective basis).

   (ii) It is agreed by the Parties that the Work is intended (1) to be directed by Director at a salary no less than DGA minimum for such services and (2) that Director shall be the executive producer of said picture on terms to be negotiated in good faith by her, depending on the budget of the picture. Both engagements shall be on a pay-or-play basis.

   (iii) Director agrees that Writer and his agent shall have the nonexclusive right after one (1) year and after consultation with Director to (A) submit the Work to third parties and solicit offers to purchase the Work, which such offers must include a condition that the budget of the first picture produced based on the Work be no less than $13.5 Million with an "A" list actor, and that the Work shall be purchased for no less than $450,000 or (B) solicit offers to purchase the Work, which such offers must include conditions that, when the Picture is produced, Director shall be engaged to direct the Picture on a pay-or-play basis on terms to be negotiated in good faith by her provided she will receive a salary which is no less than DGA minimum for such services, and that she will executive produce the picture on a pay-or-play basis on terms to be negotiated in good faith by her dependent on the budget of the picture. In the event such an offer is made, Director's agent and Writer's agent shall jointly negotiate the deal; provided that Writer agrees that Director shall have full authority to finalize any agreement. During this period, Writer agrees that he shall advise Director on a weekly basis of his progress with respect to the solicitation of offers and of any submissions to third parties or offers from third parties which have been made. Director shall also have the right during this period to offer the Work for sale and shall advise Writer on a weekly basis if he so requests of any submissions that he makes.

(b) If there shall be two or more agents negotiating jointly pursuant to this agreement, they shall be instructed to notify each other when they have begun negotiations for the sale or other disposition of the Work and of the terms hereof, and no agent shall conclude an agreement for the sale or other disposition of the Work by any of them, the matter shall immediately be referred to the parties, but in the event of any disagreement, Director's decision shall be final with respect to any such negotiations.

4. Any contract for the sale or other disposition of the Work, where the Work has been completed by the Parties in accordance herewith, shall require, subject to the rules of the WGA, that screenplay credit be given to the authors in the following manner:

Screenplay by Director and Writer

Story by Director

5. It is acknowledged and agreed that Writer's agent(s) shall not be entitled to commission any revenues payable to Director in connection with the Work. Similarly, Director's agent(s) shall not be entitled to commission any revenues payable to Writer in connection with the Work.

   The aggregate commission for the sale or other disposition of the Work shall be limited to ten percent (10%) and shall be divided among the respective agents in the same proportion that their respective client's shares bear to each other.

6. It is acknowledged that in connection with any contract entered into with a third party for the option or sale of the Work, that the negotiating party(ies) shall endeavor to include a provision that Director's and Writer's expenses which have been or shall be incurred by either of them in connection with the writing, registration or sale, or other disposition of the Work shall be reimbursed; provided that in no event will Writer be reimbursed for more than *$2500*.

7. All money or other things of value derived from the sale or other disposition of the Work shall be applied as follows:

   (a) In payment of commissions, if any.

   (b) In payment of any bona fide expenses or reimbursement of either Party for expenses paid in connection with the Work as set forth above.

   (c) To the Parties in the proportion of their ownership.

8. It is understood and agreed that for the purposes of this Agreement, the Parties shall share hereunder, unless otherwise herein stated, the proceeds from the sale or any and all

other disposition and exploitation of the Work and the rights and licenses therein and any elements thereof and with respect thereto, including but not limited to the following:

a.   Motion picture rights

b.   Sequel rights

c.   Remake rights

d.   Television film rights

e.   Television live rights

f.   Videocassette rights

g.   Merchandising rights

h.   Soundtrack rights

i.   Stage rights

j.   Radio rights

k.   Book and magazine publication rights

9. Should the Work be optioned and, as an incident thereto, the third party financier agrees to pay Director alone for a paid revision of the Work or Director and Writer together, then in either case Director agrees that if at that time the Screenplay has not been sold, then she shall pay Writer fifty percent (50%) of the monies she receives for such rewrite after first applying the deductions delineated under paragraph 7(a) and 7(b) above, which sum shall be applicable against Writer's share of the Work sales price pursuant to paragraph 1 above. Director agrees that she will consult with Writer regarding changes she will make to the Work in such case.

Writer agrees that until a paid rewrite is requested, Director shall be entitled to rewrite the Work herself and may consult with Writer regarding any changes of said material. After the first rewrite of the Work (which a third party has paid for) has been completed, Director shall have no further obligation to engage or pay Writer in connection with any subsequent rewrites.

10. If, prior to the completion of the Work, Writer shall voluntarily withdraw from the collaboration, the Director shall have the right to complete the Work alone or in conjunction with another collaborator or collaborators, and in such event the

percentage of ownership with respect to all revenues, as provided herein, shall be revised by mutual agreement in writing (provided that in no event will Writer receive less than $_____), or, failing such agreement, by arbitration in accordance with the procedures hereinafter prescribed. Any withdrawal must be documented by written notice to the other party. In the event Writer withdraws prior to commencement of the paid rewrite, then Director shall be entitled to retain all revenues in connection with said rewrite with no obligation to Writer.

11. Each party represents and warrants to the other party that he or she has not done and will not do any act that is inconsistent with or in conflict with this agreement or any of the rights of the Parties hereunder. Each Party represents and warrants to the other Party that all of their respective material is and shall be wholly original with the respective party and will not violate or infringe upon any right of any third party including, without limitation, any trademark, trade name, copyright, or, to the best of said party's knowledge, right of privacy or publicity, or right to be free from libel or slander. Writer further represents and warrants to Director that he has neither exercised any of the rights in the Work and will not do so except as set forth herein. Each Party shall defend, indemnify, and hold harmless the other Party, his or her successors, licensees, and assigns from and against all claims, liabilities, actions, or cause of action, judgments, recoveries, damages, costs, and expenses (including attorneys' fees) arising out of or in connection with any breach of any of his or her representations, warranties, covenants, or agreements herein or any use, exploitation, or dissemination of his/her material.

12. Nothing contained herein shall be construed as obligating Director to use or exploit any results and/or proceeds of Writer's services hereunder, or to continue any use or exploitation if commenced.

13. In the case of a breach by Director of any of Director's obligations hereunder, Writer's sole right and remedy shall be an action at law for damages, and Writer specifically waives

any right to injunctive or other equitable relief to rescind this Agreement or any of the rights granted to Director hereunder or to terminate this Agreement.

14. Director shall have the unencumbered right to assign this Agreement, in whole or in part, to any third party, and all rights granted to Director hereunder and all representations, warranties, and agreements made by Writer hereunder shall inure to the benefit of any such assignee of Director.

15. This Agreement shall be governed by, construed, and enforced under the laws of the State of California, and suit may be brought in connection with this Agreement only in the State or Federal courts located in the State of California. If for any reason any provision of this Agreement is adjudged by a court to be unenforceable, such adjudication shall in no way affect any other provision of this Agreement or the validity or enforcement of the remainder of this Agreement, and the affected provision shall be modified or curtailed only to the extent necessary to bring it into compliance with applicable law. This Agreement expresses the entire understanding between Writer and Director, and supersedes any previous agreement, whether written or oral, between the parties. This Agreement may be modified or amended only by a writing signed by the party to be charged with said modification or amendment. At Director's request, Writer shall execute a more formal long form agreement reflecting such terms and the terms set forth in this Agreement, but until such time, if ever, as the parties execute such an agreement this Agreement shall be binding. Writer also agrees to execute any documents which Director may reasonably require in order to confirm to the Director the rights granted hereunder.

16. All notices, payments, and correspondence that any party hereto is required, or may desire, to serve upon any other party hereto may be served by delivering same to the party personally or by depositing the same in the United States

mail, first class postage prepaid, or by sending the same, toll prepaid by telegraph or cable, addressed as follows:

If to Director:

_____

_____

_____

_____

With a concurrent copy to:

_____

_____

If to Writer:

_____

_____

With a concurrent copy to:

_____

_____

or to such other addresses as the parties may hereafter designate in writing. The date of such personal delivery, mailing, or telegraphing shall be the date of the giving of such notice.

17. This Agreement shall be executed in sufficient number of copies so that one fully executed copy may be, and shall be, delivered to each Party and to the WGA. If any disputes shall arise concerning the interpretation or application of this Agreement, or the rights or liabilities of the Parties arising hereunder, such dispute shall be submitted to the WGA for arbitration in accordance with the arbitration procedures of the Guild, and the determination of the Guild's arbitration committee as to all such matters shall be conclusive and binding upon the Parties.

Very truly yours,

_____

Director

ACCEPTED AND AGREED:

_____

Writer

My director/writer client wanted to ensure that the project would be sold only if she was attached to direct her screenplay or an A-list celebrity was attached to star. If, after a certain period of time, the project could not be sold with her attached as director, then she was willing to step aside. This was fair for the other writer. He had put in the work. At some point, he wanted to know that he was going to be paid for it. My client also wanted the flexibility to make changes.

Her collaborator, on the other hand, was concerned that there would be a minimum price for the script (as discussed above, it is wise to agree on this point up front). Also, in this particular contract, since the director had the right to hire subsequent writers and the salaries paid to any other writer(s) would ultimately reduce the collaborator's share, the collaborator wanted to protect himself by assuring that he got paid for one rewrite. Another issue that was resolved in this particular collaboration agreement was the order of credits.

This particular collaboration agreement also provides that in the event of a dispute, the writers will resolve the dispute by arbitration. It is possible for you and your collaborator to bypass the court system. With an arbitration, you both choose one or three arbitrators (in Hollywood, retired judges can be hired for this purpose) and present your case. The arbitrator(s) will resolve disputes over such issues as each writer's percentage of ownership in the script. If you are a WGA member, the WGA will arbitrate any disputes for you free of charge, even if only one writer is a member of the WGA, but keep in mind that you can always hire independent arbitrators even if you are a member of the WGA. The cost is considerably less than going to court. These independent arbitrators will use procedures similar to those employed by the WGA. You and your partner agree to be bound by the decision. It works for both of you, so I encourage it. Courts are just too expensive for the average person. That is a sad reality of our legal system, so we all have to figure out a way around it.

This collaboration agreement also deals with the likelihood that there may be two agents involved (one for each writer) and ensures that no double commissions will be paid.

Of course, each collaboration agreement will have its own peculiarities. Read these agreements carefully. Should you decide to write a spec script with another writer, show the agreements to your partner and then address the relevant issues before you start writing. Even under the best of circumstances, disputes arise. Arguments are common in the creative environment. If you are going to devote your valuable time to a writing endeavor, then you need to provide for a mechanism for dispute resolution. Put your agreement down on paper, no matter how good a friend your writing partner is. You will not regret it.

Here is the WGA Collaboration Form:

WGA Screenwriter's Branch Standard Form
Full Collaboration Agreement

AGREEMENT made at _____, California, by and between _____ and _____ hereinafter sometimes referred to as the "Parties."

The parties are about to write in collaboration a(n) (original story) (treatment) (screenplay), hereinafter referred to as the "Work," and are desirous of establishing all their rights and obligations in and to said Work.

NOW, THEREFORE, in consideration of the execution of this Agreement, and the undertakings of the parties as hereinafter set forth, it is agreed as follows:

1. The Parties shall collaborate in the writing of the Work and upon completion thereof shall be the joint owners of the Work (or shall own the Work in the following percentages: _____/_____).

2. Upon completion of the Work, it shall be registered with the Writers Guild of America, west, Inc., as the joint Work of the Parties, and ____ copies thereof shall be delivered to the Writers Guild of America, west, Inc. If the Work shall be in form such as to qualify it for copyright, it shall be registered for such copyright in the name of both Parties, and each Party hereby designates the other as his attorney-in-fact to register such Work with the United States Copyright Office

and to procure a renewal of copyright on behalf of the other party when the original copyright period has expired.

3. It is contemplated that the Work will be completed by not later than _____ provided, however, that failure to complete the Work by such date shall not be construed as a breach of this Agreement on the part of either party.

4. If, prior to the completion of the Work, either Party shall voluntarily withdraw from the collaboration, then the other Party shall have the right to complete the Work alone or in conjunction with another collaborator or collaborators, and in such event the percentage of ownership, as hereinbefore provided in paragraph 1, shall be revised by mutual agreement in writing or, failing such agreement, by arbitration in accordance with the procedures hereinafter prescribed.

5. If, prior to the completion of the Work, there shall be a dispute of any kind with respect to the Work, then the parties may terminate this collaboration Agreement by an instrument in writing, which shall be filed with the Writers Guild of America, west, Inc., and should they fail to agree upon the terms of such termination agreement, they shall submit the dispute for arbitration by the Writers Guild of America, west, Inc., in accordance with the procedures hereinafter prescribed; and said arbitration shall determine any and every matter arising out of such dispute, including but not limited to the question of who is to complete the Work and the respective interests of the parties in the completed Work.

6. Any contract for the sale or other disposition of the Work, whether or not the Work has been completed by the Parties in accordance herewith, shall require that the story credit be given to the authors in the following manner: "Screenplay by X and Y."

7. Neither party shall sell, or otherwise voluntarily dispose of the Work, or his share therein, without the written consent of the other, which consent, however, shall not be unreasonably withheld.

8. It is acknowledged and agreed that _____ and _____ shall be the exclusive agents of

the Parties for the purposes of sale or other disposition of the Work or any rights therein. Each such agent shall represent the Parties at the following studios only:

X AGENT STUDIOS:	Y AGENT STUDIOS:

The aforementioned agent, or agents, shall have _____ period in which to sell or otherwise dispose of the Work, and if there shall be more than one agent, the aggregate commission for the sale or other disposition of the Work shall be limited to ten percent (10%) and shall be equally divided among the agents hereinbefore designated.

If there shall be two or more agents, they shall be instructed to notify each other when they have begun negotiations for the sale or other disposition of the Work and of the terms thereof, and no agent shall conclude an agreement for the sale or other disposition of the Work unless he shall have first notified the other agents thereof. If there shall be a dispute among the agents as to the sale or other disposition of the Work by any of them, the matter shall immediately be referred to the Parties, who shall determine the matter for them.

9. Any and all expense of any kind whatsoever which shall be incurred by either or both of Parties in connection with the writing, registration, sale, or other disposition of the Work shall be (shared jointly) prorated in accordance with the percentages hereinbefore mentioned in paragraph 1.

10. All money or other things of value derived from the sale, or other disposition of the Work shall be applied as follows:
    (a) In payment of commissions, if any.
    (b) In payment of any expenses or reimbursement of either party for expenses paid in connection with the Work.
    (c) To the Parties in the proportion of their ownership.

11. It is understood and agreed that for the purposes of this Agreement, the Parties shall share hereunder, unless otherwise herein stated, the proceeds from the sale or any and all

other disposition of the Work and the rights and licenses therein and with respect thereto, including but not limited to the following:

a.   Motion picture rights

b.   Sequel rights

c.   Remake rights

d.   Television film rights

e.   Television live rights

f.   Stage rights

g.   Radio rights

h.   Book and magazine publication rights

12. Should the Work be sold or otherwise disposed of and, as an incident thereto, the Parties be employed to revise the Work or write a screenplay based thereon, the total compensation provided for such employment agreement shall be shared by them as follows:

If either Party shall be unavailable for the purposes of collaborating on such revision or screenplay, then the Party who is available shall be permitted to do such revision or screenplay and shall be entitled to the full amount of compensation in connection therewith; provided, however, that in such a case there shall be a revision in the original selling price, and the Party not available for the revision or screenplay shall receive from the other Party $ _____ or _____ of the total selling price.

13. If either Party hereto shall desire to use the Work, or any right therein or with respect thereto, in any venture in which such Party shall have a financial interest, whether direct or indirect, the Party desiring to do so shall notify the other Party of that fact and shall afford such other Party the opportunity to participate in the venture in the proportion of such other Party's interest in the Work. If such other Party shall be unwilling to participate in such venture, the Party desiring to proceed therein shall be required to pay such other Party an amount equal to that which such other Party would have received if the Work or right, as the case may be, intended

to be so used had been sold to a disinterested person at the price at which the same shall last have been offered, or if it shall not have been offered, at its fair market value which, in the absence of mutual agreement of the Parties, shall be determined by arbitration in accordance with the regulations of the Writers Guild of America, west, Inc.

14. This Agreement shall be executed in sufficient number of copies so that one fully executed copy may be, and shall be, delivered to each Party and to the Writers Guild of America, west, Inc. If any disputes shall arise concerning the interpretation or application of this Agreement, or the rights or liabilities of the Parties arising hereunder, such dispute shall be submitted to the Writers Guild of America, west, Inc. for arbitration in accordance with the arbitration procedures of the Guild, and the determination of the Guild's arbitration committee as to all such matters shall be conclusive and binding upon the Parties.

ACCEPTED AND AGREED

| _____ | _____ |
| Writer | Director |

DATED this _____ day of _____, 20___.

Note that the Writers Guild Collaboration Form assumes that you are 50/50 partners. How much you give your partner is negotiable. The Writers Guild, for purposes of determining residuals only, attributes 25 percent to the story. The norm is that between 20 and 30 percent of the entire screenplay price is allocated to the story. Let us say you agree to 25 percent. The screenplay sells for $100,000. If you wrote the story and collaborated on the screenplay, you would receive $25,000 plus ½ × $75,000 for a total of $62,500. Your partner would receive $37,500.

Of course, the writer who originates the project and comes up with the story has the most leverage. That person picks his partner. The desired partner cannot steal the story or write a screenplay based on that story unless he works out a deal with the originator.

AVOIDING PROBLEMS

Here is an example of what can happen if you do not work out your arrangement in advance:

I was approached by a young writer who had just graduated from college. He had written a first draft screenplay and then met a producer. Together they worked on a final draft without an agreement. The producer called himself the writer's partner and took the position that since he collaborated with the writer, he controlled the screenplay. The writer asked me what his rights were and acknowledged the contribution that the producer had made to the project. I asked him whether he had agreed on a price for the script, should a picture be made by the producer. He told me he had not. As the writer had written the initial screenplay and there was no agreement regarding that screenplay (the one without any contribution from the producer), I told him that I would call the producer and try to work out a minimum price for his script. I proposed a split of the revenues derived from any sale of the script, which was more favorable to the writer, since he had originated the project. I told the producer that it was also essential to work out an outside date for the producer to make the picture, so that the writer would be able to proceed without the producer at some point, if the producer could not get the project off the ground.

The producer took the position that he was involved with the project almost from its inception, that the writer had contributed only an idea, not a story, that the writer could do nothing without him, and that he was unwilling to set a price for the script (stating that the writer would get a share of the profits). Further, the producer would not agree to a time limit.

The producer also took the position that unless the writer could prove that he had written his screenplay without any involvement from the producer (for instance, if the writer had registered his original screenplay with the Writers Guild before meeting the producer, which he had not), the producer would call any other person that the writer tried to sell his screenplay to and tell him that the writer did not wholly control that screenplay and that a deal had to be made with the producer as well, effectively "clouding the chain of title" (see chapter 13). I knew that we had to make a deal, because in cases such as these, until an independent determination is made (that is, through a lawsuit, arbitration, or settlement between the parties, which may cost a lot of money), no one will touch the project.

The moral is: Straighten out your relationship with your partner before you begin working. The first thing you want to determine is how you can proceed if you and your partner do not agree at the time someone offers you a deal. One simple way to solve this is to say that neither writer will hold up a deal if a minimum agreed-upon price is offered for the screenplay. In other words, if you both agree that the screenplay is worth $200,000, and someone offers $200,000, then neither you nor your partner can *block* the deal. Second, if one person has contributed more and deserves more, work out exactly what the split will be in advance. As mentioned above, if you write the story, work out an agreed-upon value for that story either as a percentage of the whole purchase price (perhaps 20 percent) or a set price (say, $50,000). Agree upon the profit participation that you will accept (such as 5 percent of 100 percent of the net profits if you and your partner are awarded sole screenplay credit or 2.5 percent of 100 percent if you and your partner share screenplay credit with someone else). Agree on the floor for passive royalties (say, 50 percent for sequels and 33 percent for remakes; see discussion of passive payment in chapter 15). Agree that nothing out of the ordinary will be asked for on either side. Agree on a rewrite fee. Agree that one partner will be able to write without the other if one partner is unavailable, and agree on who, in that case, keeps the money for the rewrite. Keep in mind that the studio might insist on both partners writing, so the resolution of this issue might become problematic later on. Finally, discuss the issue of irreconcilable differences. If you originated the story and you have a fight with your partner, will you be able to proceed with rewrites without your partner? And in that case, does your partner get a piece of the rewrite money?

The goal is to avoid *deadlocks* at all costs. And avoid surprises. Remember the key benefit to having an agreement is to avoid ending up in a situation in which your collaborator, on hearing that someone is interested in your joint script, says, "I will not sell for less than $ million and I also want to produce and direct it; otherwise, I am no selling." Believe me it has happened in this town. True, even if you have an agreement, you cannot force your partner to put his signature on a piece of paper. But if you have an agreement with your partner that he will accept certain offers, at least you have the right to sue for damages if he does not agree to such terms when offered.

15

The Writers Guild

The Writers Guild of America 2001 Theatrical and Television Basic Agreement, commonly known as the "WGA Minimum Basic Agreement" or the "WGA Agreement" is 398 pages long plus assorted supplements. It is effective through May 1, 2004. One could write a book about it. I am not able in the space of this book to summarize all the points that it covers. Rather, I would like to make you aware of some of the important advantages that it provides to its members. It is definitely worth being a member.

MEMBERSHIP

Employers are called "signatory" companies. Writers are called "members." The current initiation fee for members is $2,500. Employers pay pension, health, and welfare benefits to the Guild with respect to each writing assignment. You are entitled to become a member by accumulating units of credit, and you accumulate credits by entering into agreements with signatory companies to perform services or to sell screenplays.

The Guild requires an aggregate of twelve units of credit to become a member, as set forth on the Schedule of Units of Credit cited below. The units of credit are based on work completed under contract of employment, or on the sale or licensing of previously unpublished and unproduced literary or dramatic material. The twelve units must be accumulated within two years preceding application. The Guild requires proof of such employment or sales by submission of an executed contract, deal memo, or other acceptable written evidence of the performance of writing services.

Schedule of Units of Credit
Writers Guild of America Constitution and Bylaws
Article IV. Section 3, as amended 9/23/86

TWO UNITS
For each complete week of employment within the Guild's jurisdiction on a week-to-week or term basis.

THREE UNITS
Story for radio play or television program of less than 30 minutes in duration shall be prorated in 5-minute increments.

FOUR UNITS
Story for a short subject theatrical motion picture, or for a radio play or television program of not less than 30 minutes or more than 60 minutes in duration.

SIX UNITS
Teleplay or radio play of less than 30 minutes in duration which shall be prorated in 5-minute increments;

Television format or presentation for a new series;

"Created by" credit given pursuant to the separation of rights provision of the WGA Theatrical and Television Basic Agreement.

EIGHT UNITS

Story for a radio or television program of more than one hour but not more than two hours in duration;

Screenplay for a short subject theatrical motion picture, or for a radio play or teleplay of not less than 30 minutes but not more than 60 minutes in duration.

THE FOLLOWING SHALL CONSTITUTE TWELVE (12) UNITS:

Story for a feature length theatrical motion picture, or for a television program or radio play of more than two hours in duration;

Screenplay for a feature-length theatrical motion picture, or for a teleplay for a television program, or a radio play for a radio program of more than one hour in duration;

Bible;

Long-term story projection as used herein shall be defined as a bible, for a specified term, on an existing, five-times-per-week non–prime time serial.

A rewrite is entitled to one-half (½) the number of units allotted to its particular category as set forth on the schedule of units.

A polish is entitled to one-quarter (¼) the number of units allotted to its particular category as set forth on the schedule of units.

Sale or an option earns one-half (½) the number of units allotted to its particular category as set forth on the schedule of units, subject to a maximum entitlement of four (4) such units *per project* in any one (1) year.

Where writers collaborate on the same project, each shall be accorded the appropriate number of units designated on the Schedule of Units.

In all cases, to qualify for membership, if the writer's employment agreement or purchase agreement is with a company owned in whole or in part by the writer or writer's family, there must be an agreement for financing, production, and/or distribution with a third party signatory producing company or, failing such agreement, the script must be produced and the writer must receive writing credit on screen in the form of "Written by," "Teleplay by," "Screenplay by," or "Radio Play by."

An individual who is employed to write or who sells a script to a signatory company while such individual is serving in a managerial capacity with the company or is rendering managerial services relating to the project for a network or studio, or is employed as a player on the project, shall not be able to utilize the aforementioned assignment or sale to qualify for membership in the Writers Guild unless such script is produced and the individual receives writing credit on screen in the form of "Written by," "Teleplay by," "Screenplay by," or "Radio Play by."

In exceptional cases, the Board of Directors, acting upon a recommendation from the membership and finance committee, shall have the power and authority to grant membership based on work done prior to two (2) years before the applicant has filed an application for membership.

For purposes of the credit requirements in the foregoing provisions, audio credit for a writer employed to write radio or a writer who sells literary material for radio programming will suffice.

The main advantages of membership are minimum required payments for various services and the support of a guild that, at no cost to the writer, will enforce compliance with its rules through Guild-mandated arbitration. (Every Guild signatory company agrees to submit to WGA arbitration if there are disputes.) This is basically a free legal system and of enormous benefit to writers who do not get paid for their work.

MINIMUMS

For theatrical motion pictures ("features") and television agreements, the minimum payments for services are set forth in a handy chart prepared by the Guild. (The following minimums do not constitute the entirety of the WGA Basic Agreement. Further questions can be addressed to the Contracts Department at the Writers Guild.)

ARTICLE 13 - COMPENSATION

A.   THEATRICAL

Company agrees that the minimum basic compensation to be paid a writer who is employed for a feature length photoplay on a so-called flat deal basis shall be as herein set forth.

For the purpose of this Article 13.A.1.a., "High Budget" photoplay shall be a photoplay the cost of which equals or exceeds five million dollars ($5,000,000.00); a photoplay the cost of which is less than five million dollars ($5,000,000.00) shall be referred to as a "Low Budget" photoplay.

The Company may option to purchase or license from a professional writer literary material, which would be covered by this Basic Agreement, for a period of eighteen (18) months upon payment of ten percent (10%) of the applicable minimum compensation for such literary material. Company may renew or extend such option for subsequent eighteen (18) month periods upon payment of an additional ten percent (10%) of the applicable minimum compensation for such literary material for each such eighteen (18) month period. Notwithstanding anything in this Basic Agreement to the contrary, the option payment(s) shall be credited against the purchase price or other compensation payable to the writer.

1. a. Minimum Compensation

FLAT DEAL SCREEN MINIMUMS

HIGH BUDGET

		Effective		
		5/2/01- 5/1/02	5/2/02- 5/1/03[1]	5/2/03- 5/1/04[2]
(1)	Screenplay, including treatment	$79,308	$81,687	$84,546
(2)	Screenplay, excluding treatment	54,842	56,487	58,464
(3)	Final Draft Screenplay or Rewrite	24,379	25,110	25,989
(4)	Polish	12,187	12,553	12,992
(5)	First Draft of Screenplay (alone or with option for Final Draft Screenplay):			
	First Draft Screenplay	36,566	37,663	38,981
	Final Draft Screenplay	24,379	25,110	25,989
(6)	Treatment	24,379	25,110	25,989
(7)	Original Treatment	36,566	37,663	38,981
(8)	Story	24,379	25,110	25,989
(9)	Additional Compensation Screenplay - No Assigned Material	12,187	12,553	12,992

---

[1] The Trustees of the Writers Guild - Industry Health Fund have increased the Health Fund contribution rate for this period by one-half percent (0.5%), thereby triggering a corresponding decrease in minimums. Accordingly, the increase in minimums for this period is as set forth in the column marked "5/2/02 - 5/1/03" and represents a three percent (3.0%) increase over the rates for the preceding period

[2] The Trustees of the Writers Guild - Industry Health Fund may determine that an increase in the contribution rate for this period is needed to maintain the level of benefits in existence on May 1, 2001 or they may determine that a reduction in the contribution rate for this period is appropriate. If either of these changes occur, the increases in minimums in the column marked "5/2/03 - 5/1/04" will be increased or reduced by an equivalent percentage.

FLAT DEAL SCREEN MINIMUMS

LOW BUDGET

		Effective		
		5/2/01- 5/1/02	5/2/02- 5/1/03[3]	5/2/03- 5/1/04[4]
(1)	Screenplay, including treatment	$42,647	$43,926	$45,463
(2)	Screenplay, excluding treatment	26,649	27,448	28,409
(3)	Final Draft Screenplay or Rewrite	15,991	16,471	17,047
(4)	Polish	8,000	8,240	8,528
(5)	First Draft of Screenplay (alone or with option for Final Draft Screenplay):			
	First Draft Screenplay	19,192	19,768	20,460
	Final Draft Screenplay	12,791	13,175	13,636
(6)	Treatment	15,991	16,471	17,047
(7)	Original Treatment	22,082	22,744	23,540
(8)	Story	15,991	16,471	17,047
(9)	Additional Compensation Screenplay - No Assigned Material	6,098	6,281	6,501

E: The minimum for a screen writer shall be not less than the "appropriate" television minimum, stent with the particular literary element and the length of the motion picture.

b. Discount - New Writers

Company may employ a writer who has not been previously employed as a writer under any Guild MBA in television or theatrical motion pictures or

See footnote 3 on page 54

See footnote 4 on page 54

radio dramatic programs on a flat deal basis at not less than seventy-five percent (75%) of the applicable minimum compensation set forth in this subparagraph 1. If such writer receives any writing credit on the theatrical motion picture for which he/she was so employed, his/her compensation will be adjusted to one hundred percent (100%) of the applicable minimum compensation. Such payment will be made within ten (10) business days after determination of final writing credit.

c. Additional Payment - No Assigned Material

When Company employs a writer to write a screenplay on a flat deal basis at the minimum basic compensation provided in this Article 13.A., unless Company in good faith furnishes such writer a novel, play, treatment, original treatment, or story upon which the screenplay is to be based or from which it is to be adapted, such writer shall be paid an additional amount as described in subparagraph 1. above. The assigned material shall be specifically identified in the notice of employment and contract; if not then known, the writer and the Guild shall be furnished with such identification when it is available.

Any dispute as to whether or not Company has so furnished such writer a novel, play, treatment, original treatment, or story shall be subject to automatic arbitration by the Guild arbitration committee (referred to in Theatrical Schedule A); provided, however, that in the event Company or the writer does not accept the decision of such Guild arbitration committee such party shall notify the Guild and the other party, in writing, of its position and such dispute shall thereupon be subject to the grievance and arbitration provisions of Articles 10, 11 and 12 of this Basic Agreement.

2.   Narration by a Writer Other Than any Writer of Screenplay or Story and
      Screenplay

      Minimums for narration are based on status of film assembly and nature of
      previously written material as follows:

Nature of Material Written Prior to Employment of Narration Writer	Film Assembled in Story Sequence	Film Footage Not Assembled in Story Sequence
None	Applicable Screenplay excluding Treatment Minimum	Applicable Screenplay including Treatment Minimum
Story Only	Applicable Screenplay excluding Treatment Minimum	Applicable Screenplay excluding Treatment Minimum
Story and Screenplay	Per Rate Schedule A	Per Rate Schedule A

	Effective		
Rate Schedule A	5/2/01- 5/1/02	5/2/02- 5/1/03[5]	5/2/03- 5/1/04[6]
Two minutes or less	$ 746	$ 768	$ 795
Over two minutes through five minutes	2,636	2,715	2,810
Over five minutes	applicable polish minimum		

Aggregate sound track running time in minutes of narration written by writer hired
pursuant hereto.
Narration writer may be hired on a week-to-week basis.
There is no separation of rights for narration.

3.   Initial Payment

---

[5]   See footnote 3 on page 54

[6]   See footnote 4 on page 54

The Company shall use its best efforts to issue to the writer (or his/her designated representative), for the writer's signature, a written document memorializing the agreement reached between the Company and the writer within ten (10) business days after agreement is reached on the major deal points of a writing assignment (*e.g.*, agreement on initial compensation, including bonus, if any, and number of drafts) for a theatrical motion picture (twelve (12) business days in the case of either a term writing agreement or an agreement for both writing and non-writing services), but in no event later than the earlier of: (a) fifteen (15) business days after agreement is reached on the major deal points of the writing assignment, or (b) the time period required by Article 19. Disputes as to whether Company has submitted such document in a timely manner may be submitted to the "Hot Line" dispute resolution procedure in Article 48.

With respect to any employment under this Article 13.A. on a flat deal basis, the Company will pay to the writer, not later than the next regular payday in the week following the day the Company instructs the writer to commence his/her services, a single advance amount (to be applied against the first compensation which otherwise would be due to the writer) at least equal to the greater of (a) ten percent (10%) of the writer's agreed compensation which otherwise would be due to the writer upon deliver of the first required material, or (b) one week's compensation at the weekly rate for term employment for 14 out of 14 weeks.

4.   Maximum Period of Employment

With respect to writers employed at the minimum basic compensation provided for in this Article 13.A. to write a story, treatment, original treatment, first draft screenplay, final draft screenplay, screenplay, or rewrite, the Company shall not require the writer to render services beyond that period of weeks (and fractions thereof) obtained by dividing such applicable minimum basic compensation set forth above in (1) through (9), as the case may be, by the minimum weekly compensation provided for in Article 13.A., subparagraph 15. hereof, for writers employed on a weekly basis.

In the event that the same writer is employed to write any combination of those items set forth above in (1) through (9), such time periods shall be cumulative.

If the writer is required by written notice from the Company to render his/her services beyond such time period, he/she shall be entitled to the specified compensation on delivery and to the minimum weekly compensation to which such writer would be entitled if employed on a weekly basis, as hereinafter in subparagraph 15. of Article 13.A. provided, for services rendered after the expiration of such period.

5.   Computation of Writer's Period of Employment

In computing the duration of a writer's employment under this Article 13.A., there shall be excluded the following:

a. Any time during which the writer's employment agreement was suspended by reason of any breach or default on the part of the writer;

b. Any time during which the writer's employment agreement was suspended by reason of any of the causes specified in the *"force majeure"* clause of such writer's employment agreement;

c. Except as hereinafter provided, waiting time which occurs during or after the writer's employment.

Any excess waiting time shall be included in computing the duration of the writer's employment. However, excess waiting time after the expiration of the duration of the writer's employment shall not be included in computing the duration of the writer's employment unless the writer holds himself/herself available for the Company's further instructions pursuant to the Company's written notice to the writer so to hold himself/herself available after the expiration of the writer's employment.

Any time during which the writer shall make revisions called for by the Company shall be included in computing the duration of the writer's employment.

6. Waiting Time

The waiting time to be excluded in computing the duration of the writer's employment shall not exceed three (3) days following delivery of material, and such waiting time shall not be compensable. In the event that the same writer is employed to write any combination of story, treatment or original treatment, first draft screenplay, final draft screenplay or screenplay, such waiting time shall be cumulative. "Excess waiting time," as used in this Article 13.A., means waiting time in excess of the waiting time to be excluded as provided in this subparagraph 6. If the writer is called into conference on any day or instructed to perform any services on any day, such day may not be included in waiting time. Sundays and holidays generally recognized in the motion picture industry shall be excluded in computing waiting time.

7. Extension of Employment Period

If the employment agreement under this Article 13.A. for a treatment on a flat deal basis contains any option for additional literary material, and the Company wishes the writer to change, revise or complete his/her assignment after the expiration of the maximum allotted employment period under this Article, the Company may postpone the time for exercise of such option by notifying the writer that it elects to continue the employment of the writer on a week-to-week basis commencing upon the expiration of the employment period then expiring at the minimum weekly compensation prescribed in subparagraph 15. hereof, but without any minimum guaranteed period of employment. The Company must notify the writer to this effect promptly upon the expiration of such maximum allotted employment period. Such employment shall continue until further notice from the Company, and the waiting time shall commence upon such termination of the employment. If the Company thereafter exercises any option, and the maximum allotted employment period under this Article 13.A. for which the Company would be entitled to the writer's services under such option shall exceed the period during which the writer performed his/her services (excluding time for which the writer was compensated on a week-to-week basis and excluding waiting time), then the Company shall be entitled to credit against the amount due under such option an amount equal to the minimum weekly compensation specified in subparagraph 15. herein for the period of such excess. Such credit shall not exceed the amount actually paid to the writer for services performed on a week-to-week basis.

8.   Failure to Deliver Material Within Allotted Time Period

If the writer has not completed and delivered to the Company the material within the maximum allotted employment period provided for in this Article 13.A., or any shorter period specified in the individual writer's employment agreement, then the Company may exercise the succeeding option and require the writer to complete such material within the succeeding option period. If the writer has not completed and delivered to the Company the material within such maximum allotted employment period, or such shorter period specified in the individual writer's employment agreement, and if the failure of the writer so to complete and deliver such material was not caused by any instructions or directions on the part of the Company, then and at any time thereafter and prior to the delivery of such material, the Company may terminate the writer's employment agreement, and the Company shall not be obligated to make any further or additional payment thereunder. For the purposes of determining whether to terminate such contract, the Company may require the writer to deliver for inspection any material then written and compliance with such requirement shall not constitute delivery for the purpose above mentioned without the written consent of the Company. The Company shall retain title to and ownership of any material theretofore delivered for which payment was made by the Company, subject to the provisions of Article 16.A.

9.   Teams

Every writer shall receive no less than the applicable minimum, except that if a *bona fide* team of no more than two (2) writers offers, prior to employment on the script in question, to collaborate, the team as a unit shall receive in the aggregate not less than the applicable minimum compensation.

In addition, if a *bona fide* team of no more than three (3) writers offers, prior to employment on the script in question, to collaborate, the team as a unit shall receive in the aggregate not less than two hundred percent (200%) of the applicable minimum compensation, of which each individual writer shall be paid not less than one-third (1/3) of said aggregate compensation.

10.   Week-to-Week, Term, Flat Deal

The Company may employ a writer on a week-to-week or term basis to write a story, treatment, original treatment, first draft screenplay, final screenplay, screenplay, or rewrite. At any time thereafter, Company may employ such writer or any other writer on a flat deal basis to write any such material in accordance with the provisions of this Article 13.A. If Company employs a writer on a flat deal basis to write any such material, at any time thereafter Company may employ such writer or any other writer to write any such material on a week-to-week basis or term basis. If the Company imposes the condition that such material must be completed and delivered by a specified date, and the writer accepts the employment upon such conditions and completes and delivers the material to the Company in compliance with such condition, then such employment shall be deemed to be employment on a flat deal basis and the writer shall be entitled to the applicable flat deal minimums provided in this Article 13.A. for the work involved. If the Company employs two (2) writers as a team on a week-to-week basis to write a story, treatment, original treatment, first draft screenplay, final screenplay, screenplay or rewrite and imposes the condition that such material must be completed and delivered by a specified date, and if the period by which the writers are to complete and deliver the material under their employment agreement is less than one-half of the applicable maximum period of employment for the work involved as provided in this Article 13.A., the Company shall only be obligated to pay to each such writer one-half of the amount payable to one (1) writer employed on a flat deal basis for the work involved, but if the period by which the writers are to complete and deliver the material under their employment agreement is more than one-half of the applicable maximum period of employment for the work involved provided in this Article, the Company shall not be obligated by this Article 13.A. to pay any additional amount to such writers. For example, if a team of writers is employed on a week-to-week basis during the period May 2, 2001 through May 1, 2002 to write a "screenplay, including treatment" for a High Budget photoplay (for which the flat deal minimum is $79,308.00) and a date later than ten (10) weeks after the commencement of such employment is specified in the employment agreement for completion and delivery of such final screenplay, then if such final screenplay is completed and delivered within such time, the Company need only pay each writer the $39,654.00 received as weekly salary. In the event of a dispute as to whether the Company has imposed such a specified date of completion and delivery, such dispute shall be subject to grievance and arbitration pursuant to the provisions of Articles 10, 11 and 12 hereof.

11.   Applicable Deal Minimum Compensation

When Company hereafter employs one (1) or more writers on a flat deal basis for the minimum basic compensation as above provided, then regardless of the exercise of any option, if a motion picture is actually produced by Company from the screenplay so written under such deal basis, the compensation (hereinafter called "applicable minimum deal compensation") paid to the writer or writers who participated in the writing under such flat deal shall be not less than the applicable "Flat Deal Screen Minimums" set forth in Article 13.A., subparagraph 1.a. above. In the event an amount at least equal to such applicable minimum deal compensation has not been paid to such writer or writers by the time screen credits for such motion picture have been finally determined, then Company shall pay to the writer or writers receiving screen credit for such motion picture, within thirty (30) days after such screen credit has been finally determined, the difference between all of the compensation theretofore paid to the writer or writers employed by Company on such flat deal basis in connection with such photoplay, on the one hand, and the applicable minimum deal compensation provided, on the other hand. A writer or writers employed at the minimum week-to-week compensation to write a treatment and also a screenplay for a motion picture which is produced by Company shall be compensated at not less than the applicable minimum basic compensation provided for in this Article 13.A., and shall be considered as employed on a flat deal basis at such minimum compensation for purposes of subparagraph 1.c. of this Article. No writer employed on a term basis shall be entitled to additional compensation by reason of the provisions of this Article 13.A.

When a planned Low Budget theatrical motion picture is produced as a High Budget theatrical motion picture for reasons other than *force majeure* (including but not limited to disability, illness or inclement weather) or labor cost escalations undetermined at commencement of production, the Company shall pay any necessary increase in the applicable minimum deal compensation within thirty (30) days after Company knows that the cost of the motion picture has increased or will increase past the High Budget break figure, and in any event within thirty (30) days after delivery of the answer print of said motion picture.

12.   Inapplicability of Provisions

The provisions of this Article 13.A. shall not apply to writers employed at compensation in excess of the applicable minimum specified in this Article except as hereinafter provided. However, even though the total compensation shall exceed such minimums, the amount payable for the writing of the story, treatment, original treatment, first draft screenplay, final screenplay, screenplay or rewrite shall be not less than the minimum for such individual work as above designated. The provisions of subparagraphs 4., 5. and 6. of this Article 13.A. shall be applicable to writers employed at compensation not exceeding twice the applicable minimum compensation, except that the three (3) day waiting period in subparagraph 6. shall be two (2) weeks for the above-scale writer covered by this sentence. The provisions of subparagraph 8., subparagraph 14. and the last two paragraphs of subparagraph 15. of this Article 13.A. are applicable to all employment agreements regardless of compensation.

The provisions of this Article 13.A. shall not apply to any short or short subject, except that the Company agrees that any such agreement made by the Company with any writer employed on a similar basis with respect to a short or short subject shall guarantee such writer an aggregate compensation for services rendered in the writing and preparation of such material which shall be not less than a sum equal to the minimum weekly compensation to which such writer would be entitled if employed on a weekly compensation basis, as provided in subparagraph 15. hereof, multiplied by the number of weeks (plus any fraction of a week) during which the writer actually and continuously performed such services, it being understood that the Company may terminate the employment of such writer at the time the writer becomes entitled to additional compensation by reason of the provisions of this paragraph or at any time thereafter.

13. Purchases

    a. The applicable minimums for purchases or licenses subject to this Agreement from a professional writer shall be the flat deal minimum for the appropriate budget as determined by the Company in good faith; provided, however, that if a motion picture is produced based upon the story, treatment or screenplay, as the case may be, and if such motion picture is a High Budget photoplay, and if the purchase price or license fee paid for the acquisition or license was less than the applicable minimum for the respective type of work (story, treatment or screenplay, as the case may be) for such class of motion picture, *i.e.*, High Budget, pursuant to Article 13.A.1., an additional payment shall be made to the professional writer in an amount such that such writer shall have received in the aggregate an amount equal to such higher applicable minimum.

    b. [Deleted.]

14. Payment of Compensation Under Deal Contract

Company will use its best efforts to pay writers employed to write on a deal basis not less than the applicable minimum within forty-eight (48) hours after the delivery of a completed story, treatment or original treatment, first draft screenplay or final draft screenplay, as the case may be, but in no event shall any such payment be made later than seven (7) days after delivery of such material. Payment shall not be contingent upon the acceptance or approval by the Company of the material so delivered. Company shall include in writer's deal memorandum or personal service contract:

a. the place where and the name(s) or function of the person(s) to whom delivery of such material is to be made, and

b. the name(s) of the person(s) authorized to request rewrites of said material.

Company shall give writer written notice of any change in the name(s) of the person(s) to whom delivery is to be made and/or the name(s) of the person(s) authorized to request rewrites.

Company will pay interest of one and one-half percent (1.5%) per month when any initial compensation payment is due and not paid as provided. If the Company has failed to make such payment because the executed contract was not delivered by the writer to the Company, then no such interest is due. If the contract is not so delivered by the writer because of a dispute as to the terms of the contract and the Company shall be held to be wrong, the above-described interest payment shall be applicable.

15. Minimum Weekly Compensation

Every writer employed on a week-to-week or term basis shall receive a salary at the rate of not less than the amount per week specified below for the respective period designated:

<u>At the Rate of Per Week</u>

ARTICLE 13 - COMPENSATION
A - THEATRICAL

Term Contracts	5/2/01- 5/1/02	5/2/02- 5/1/03[7]	5/2/03- 5/1/04[8]
40 out of 52 weeks	$ 3,127	$ 3,221	$ 3,334
20 out of 26 weeks	3,401	3,503	3,626
14 out of 14 weeks	3,682	3,792	3,925
Week-to-Week	3,966	4,085	4,228

Every week-to-week or term contract shall specify the exact compensation for each full week of services rendered or to be rendered thereunder.

If any writer under a week-to-week or term contract shall render services after the expiration of the guaranteed period of employment, then, for purposes only of prorating days worked in a partial workweek (*i.e.*, less than six (6) days), at the end of such employment, the writer shall receive one-fifth (1/5) of the weekly rate for each day worked during such partial workweek, after the expiration of the guaranteed period.

Company may employ a writer who has not been previously employed as a writer under any Guild MBA in television or theatrical motion pictures or radio dramatic or comedic programs on a week-to-week or term basis for a period not to exceed fourteen (14) consecutive weeks at seventy-five percent (75%) of the minimum weekly compensation as provided in this subparagraph 15.

16.   Theatrical Motion Picture Released on Free Television

If a theatrical motion picture is released on free television before it has had a *bona fide* theatrical release (determined as provided in Article 15.A.3.j. of this Basic Agreement), the compensation of the writer or writers who have received screen authorship credit for such motion picture shall be adjusted so that it shall be no less than the appropriate television minimum compensation or the appropriate theatrical minimum compensation,

---

[7]   See footnote 3 on page 54

[8]   See footnote 4 on page 54

whichever is higher.

17. Remakes

The Company's right to remake a theatrical film shall be subject to the following:

a. If a credited writer's material is used for a remake and no writer is employed to rewrite, adapt or revise such material for the remake, the Company will pay such writer(s) the applicable minimum compensation for the intended medium of the remake (but this provision shall not be construed as affecting the rule that a *bona fide* team shall be considered a unit). In addition, the writer will be entitled to receive payment in accordance with Article 15.A. with respect to a theatrical remake licensed to free television, Article 15.B. with respect to reruns or foreign telecast of a television remake, and Article 51 with respect to a theatrical or free television remake released in Supplemental Markets.

b. If a writer is employed to rewrite, adapt or revise such literary material for the remake, then the credited writer(s) of the original material shall also be participant(s) in the credit determination and if accorded credit shall accordingly be entitled to the portion of applicable minimum compensation for the intended medium of the remake equal to the proportion of credit awarded pursuant to subparagraph c.(1) below (but this provision shall not be construed as affecting the rule that a *bona fide* team shall be considered a unit). In addition, the writer will be entitled to share in any additional compensation in accordance with Article 15.A. with respect to a theatrical remake licensed to free television, Article 15.B. with respect to reruns or foreign telecast of a television remake, and Article 51 with respect to a theatrical or free television remake released in Supplemental Markets. The writer's portion of such additional compensation shall be equal to the portion of credit awarded pursuant to subparagraph c.(1) below.

c. With respect to a television remake of a theatrical film, the phrase "applicable minimum compensation" in subparagraphs a. and b. of this subparagraph 17. means the applicable rate provided for in Article 13.B.7.a., b. or e. of this Agreement.

In a credit arbitration concerning such remake, the arbiters shall determine the following issues:

(1)   the contribution made by the writer(s) of the original material expressed as a percentage of the whole, and

(2)   the form of credit to be accorded such writer(s), which credit may include a credit in the nature of a source material credit, such as "Based on a Screenplay by ..."

The foregoing provisions shall apply to material written during the term of this Agreement upon which a remake is based.

18.   Script Annotations

If the Company is to require one or more script annotations, it shall so inform the writer at the time of the negotiation of the writing assignment, or option or acquisition of literary material, unless from the nature of the project the Company's need for the annotation(s) is not reasonably known at the outset. In the latter case, the Company shall inform the writer that an annotation is needed when the Company knows, or reasonably should have known, of it.

If the Company uses written guidelines or standards describing the type of information to be included in an annotation for a fact-based project or a project inspired by fact, such guidelines or standards shall be furnished to the writer when the Company first informs the writer that an annotation is needed.

B.   TELEVISION

1.   **Minimum Basic Compensation**

a.   Options

When the Company options to purchase or license from a professional writer literary material, which would be covered under this Basic Agreement, Company shall pay five percent (5%) of the applicable minimum compensation for such literary material for the first period of up to one hundred eighty (180) days, and an additional ten percent (10%) of the applicable minimum compensation for each subsequent period of up to one hundred eighty (180) days.

Notwithstanding anything in this Basic Agreement to the contrary, the option payment(s) shall be credited against the purchase price or other compensation payable to the writer.

The foregoing paragraphs shall not apply to arrangements under which the consideration for the agreement is the Company's good faith effort to effectuate network or other buyer/licensee interest or otherwise obtain a development commitment for the material.

b.   Other Compensation Minimums

Company agrees that the minimum basic compensation to be paid for writing services covered by this Basic Agreement shall be as herein set forth during the periods indicated below. The periods are herein designated:

	From	Through
"1st Period"	May 2, 2001 -	May 1, 2002
"2nd Period"	May 2, 2002 -	May 1, 2003
"3rd Period"	May 2, 2003 -	May 1, 2004

The applicable minimum shall be the minimum for each writer, except when a *bona fide* team of no more than two (2) writers offers, prior to employment on the script in question, to collaborate, in which event such writers shall be considered a unit, which unit shall receive in the aggregate not less than the applicable minimum compensation.

In addition, if a *bona fide* team of no more than three (3) writers offers, prior to employment on the script in question, to collaborate, the team as a unit shall receive in the aggregate not less than two hundred percent (200%) of the applicable minimum compensation, of which each individual writer shall be paid not less than one-third (1/3) of said aggregate compensation. If all three (3) writers are also employed pursuant to Article 14 of this Basic Agreement, the two hundred percent (200%) of minimum compensation may be reduced to not less than one hundred fifty percent (150%).

With respect to the provisions for increased rates during specified periods, the intent is that, as to freelance employment, the rates applicable when the employment is entered into shall apply, except that when an employment is entered into during one period, but is not to start until a subsequent period, the rate applicable during the subsequent period applies.

2.　"High Budget" Films

For the purpose of this schedule, "High Budget" television motion pictures are those for which the negative costs equal or exceed the following amounts:

15 minutes or less	$150,000
30 minutes or less (but more than 15 minutes)	215,000
60 minutes or less (but more than 30 minutes)	300,000
75 minutes or less (but more than 60 minutes)	400,000
90 minutes or less (but more than 75 minutes)	500,000
120 minutes or less (but more than 90 minutes)	900,000
For each additional 30 minutes or less, an additional	300,000

However, in the case of non-prime time network films, "High Budget" films shall be films the negative costs of which equal or exceed the following amounts:

15 minutes or less	$60,000
30 minutes or less (but more than 15 minutes)	100,000
60 minutes or less (but more than 30 minutes)	200,000
75 minutes or less (but more than 60 minutes)	260,000

90 minutes or less (but more than 75 minutes)	340,000
120 minutes or less (but more than 90 minutes)	450,000
For each additional 30 minutes or less, an additional	125,000

3.   "Low Budget" Films

For the purpose of this schedule, "Low Budget" television motion pictures are those for which the negative cost is less than the amounts indicated above.

4.   "Negative Cost"

a.   "Negative cost," for the purposes of this Article 13.B., shall be deemed to include all actual costs and expenses of production, including overhead and, except to the extent hereinafter provided, excluding deferments. If no overhead has been charged, an amount equal to twenty percent (20%) of all direct charges shall be added to represent an overhead charge.

b.   It is agreed that if the Company rents studio facilities and the customary rental includes a charge for overhead, the provisions of the preceding quoted sentence shall be waived, but the Guild shall have the right at all times to have a determination by arbitration as to whether said customary rental charge has in fact included a charge for overhead.

c.   If more than fifty percent (50%) of the cost of any item is deferred, the negative cost of the film shall be revised to include a charge of not less than fifty percent (50%) of the total cost of such item including the amount deferred.

d.   If the compensation of any actor, writer, director or producer shall include a participation in the receipts of a film and the initial salary paid such employee shall be less than one hundred percent (100%) of his/her established television salary, or fifty percent (50%) of his/her established theatrical motion picture salary (if he/she has not established his/her television salary), the negative cost shall be revised to include an amount equal to such established television salary or fifty percent (50%) of such established theatrical motion picture salary, as the case may be. The "established theatrical motion picture salary" for the purposes hereof shall be computed by dividing the total compensation earned by the employee in theatrical motion pictures during the year immediately preceding the assignment in question by the total weeks and fractions thereof worked for such compensation.

e.   Any dispute relating to the determination of the negative cost of a film shall be resolved by a Price Waterhouse audit, the costs of which are to be borne equally by the Company and the Guild.

f.   If a Low Budget minimum shall be paid to a writer prior to the production of a film whose negative cost shall in fact require the payment of a High Budget minimum, the writer shall be paid the difference not later than thirty (30) days after the completion of production of the film.

5.   Story Claim By Production Executive

If Company shall claim that a writer has been assigned to write a teleplay based upon a story composed or created by a production executive, the story and teleplay shall be subject to an automatic arbitration pursuant to the provisions of Television Schedule A hereof, and if the arbitrators shall accord both the story and teleplay credit to the writer, then the combined story and teleplay minimum above provided for shall apply to the material so written, provided that Company may

appeal any such credit determination to arbitration pursuant to Articles 10, 11 and 12 hereof.

6.   Step Outline

The writer may not be compelled to prepare a step outline of the teleplay. For such purpose, the term "step outline" shall mean a development of the story in the form of a condensed scene-by-scene progression indicating action and the substance of essential story dialogue, but without dialogue.

7.   Schedule of Minimum Compensation

a.   **Story** (For all television films except (1) network prime time and Fox Broadcasting Company ("FBC") prime time programs of the types covered by subparagraph d. below and (2) serials which are covered by subparagraph e.(1) or e.(3) below)

High Budget

Program Length in Minutes	5/2/01-5/1/02	5/2/02-5/1/03[9]	5/2/03-5/1/04[10]
15 or less	$2,186	$2,252	$2,331
30 or less (but more than 15)	4,003	4,123	4,267
60 or less (but more than 30)	7,273	7,491	7,753
75 or less (but more than 60)	10,353	10,664	11,037
90 or less (but more than 75)	10,930	11,258	11,652
120 or less (but more than 90)	14,321	14,751	15,267

Low Budget

Program Length in Minutes	5/2/01-5/1/02	5/2/02-5/1/03[11]	5/2/03-5/1/04[12]
15 or less	$1,861	$1,917	$1,984
30 or less (but more than 15)	3,095	3,188	3,300
60 or less (but more than 30)	5,853	6,029	6,240
75 or less (but more than 60)	8,336	8,586	8,887
90 or less (but more than	8,924	9,192	9,514
120 or less (but more than 90)	11,789	12,143	12,568

[9] See footnote 3 on page 54

[10] See footnote 4 on page 54

[11] See footnote 3 on page 54

[12] See footnote 4 on page 54

b. **Teleplay** (For all television films except (1) network prime time and FBC prime time programs of the types covered by subparagraph d. below and (2) serials which are covered by subparagraph e.(1) or e.(3) below)

High Budget

Program Length in Minutes	5/2/01- 5/1/02	5/2/02- 5/1/03[1] 3	5/2/03- 5/1/04[14]
15 or less	$4,003	$4,123	$4,267
30 or less (but more than 15)	6,499	6,694	6,928
60 or less (but more than 30)	12,596	12,974	13,428
75 or less (but more than 60)	18,330	18,880	19,541
90 or less (but more than 75)	19,373	19,954	20,652
120 or less (but more than 90)	25,696	26,467	27,393

---

[13]   See footnote 3 on page 54

[14]   See footnote 4 on page 54

Low Budget

Program Length in Minutes	5/2/01- 5/1/02	5/2/02- 5/1/03[15]	5/2/03- 5/1/04[16]
15 or less	$2,915	$3,002	$3,107
30 or less (but more than 15)	5,010	5,160	5,341
60 or less (but more than 30)	9,552	9,839	10,183
75 or less (but more than 60)	13,784	14,198	14,695
90 or less (but more than 75)	14,626	15,065	15,592
120 or less (but more than 90)	19,354	19,935	20,633

[15]   See footnote 3 on page 54

[16]   See footnote 4 on page 54

c. **Story and Teleplay** when the same writer prepares both ("bargain rates") (For all television films except (1) network prime time and FBC prime time programs of the types covered by subparagraph d. below and (2) serials which are covered by subparagraph e.(1) or e.(3) below)

High Budget

Program Length in Minutes	5/2/01- 5/1/02	5/2/02- 5/1/03[17]	5/2/03- 5/1/04[18]
15 or less	$5,461	$5,625	$5,822
30 or less (but more than 15)	10,003	10,303	10,664
60 or less (but more than 30)	18,182	18,727	19,382
75 or less (but more than 60)	25,914	26,691	27,625
90 or less (but more than 75)	27,324	28,144	29,129
120 or less (but more than 90)	35,809	36,883	38,174

Low Budget

Program Length in Minutes	5/2/01- 5/1/02	5/2/02- 5/1/03[19]	5/2/03- 5/1/04[20]
15 or less	$4,638	$4,777	$4,944
30 or less (but more than	7,730	7,962	8,241

---

[17] See footnote 3 on page 54

[18] See footnote 4 on page 54

[19] See footnote 3 on page 54

[20] See footnote 4 on page 54

60 or less (but more than 30)	14,642	15,081	15,609
75 or less (but more than 60)	21,209	21,845	22,610
90 or less (but more than 75)	22,314	22,983	23,787
120 or less (but more than 90)	29,474	30,358	31,421

For programs in excess of one hundred twenty (120) minutes, compensation is based on the one hundred twenty (120) minute or less minimum (shown above) plus, for each additional thirty (30) minutes or less, the following additional payments:

High Budget	5/2/01- 5/1/02	5/2/02- 5/1/03[21]	5/2/03- 5/1/04[22]
Story	$3,392	$3,494	$3,616
Teleplay	6,323	6,513	6,741
Story and Teleplay	8,483	8,737	9,043
Low Budget			
Story	$2,860	$2,946	$3,049
Teleplay	4,714	4,855	5,025
Story and Teleplay	7,166	7,381	7,639

The minimums set forth in the above schedules constitute the writer's minimum compensation for the purposes of Article 15.B.

The category of minimums provided for in subparagraph c. of this paragraph 7. (the so-called "bargain rate") is applicable only when

---

[21]   See footnote 3 on page 54

[22]   See footnote 4 on page 54

---

the employment is for story and teleplay, not when the employment is for story with option for teleplay.

cc. **Story with Options**

If Company engages a writer to write a story with an option to have the writer write a teleplay, the Company must exercise such option, if at all, within fourteen (14) days after delivery of the final story.

d. **Network Prime Time and Fox Broadcasting Company ("FBC") Prime Time**

(For all network prime time and FBC prime time episodic series, one-time shows, unit series shows, once-per-week network prime time serials, and anthology programs. This subparagraph d. is not applicable to programs covered by Appendix A and other non-dramatic programs (*e.g.*, *Wild Kingdom* and travelogues). The rates set forth in this subparagraph d. are not to be utilized for the purposes of Article 15.B. of this Agreement.)

(1) Story

Program Length in Minutes	Effective		
	5/2/01-5/1/02	5/2/02-5/1/03[23]	5/2/03-5/1/04[24]
15 or less	$3,394	$3,479	$3,583
30 or less (but more than 15)	6,220	6,376	6,567
45 or less (but more than 30)	8,584	8,799	9,063
60 or less (but more than 45)	10,949	11,223	11,560
90 or less (but more than 60)	14,629	14,995	15,445
For Serials and Episodic Programs 120 or less (but more than 90)	19,537	20,025	20,626
For other than Serials and Episodic Programs 120 or less (but more than 90)	21,322	21,855	22,511

(2) Teleplay

Effective

---

[23]   See footnote 3 on page 54

[24]   See footnote 4 on page 54

Program Length in Minutes	5/2/01-5/1/02	5/2/02-5/1/03[25]	5/2/03-5/1/04[26]
15 or less	$8,241	$8,447	$8,700
30 or less (but more than 15)	13,383	13,718	14,130
45 or less (but more than 30)	14,154	14,508	14,943
60 or less (but more than 45)	18,055	18,506	19,061
90 or less (but more than 60)	26,013	26,663	27,463
For Serials and Episodic Programs 120 or less (but more than 90)	33,378	34,212	35,238
For other than Serials and Episodic Programs 120 or less (but more than 90)	36,423	37,334	38,454

[25]   See footnote 3 on page 54

[26]   See footnote 4 on page 54

(3) Story and Teleplay when the same writer prepares both ("bargain rates")

| | Effective | | |
Program Length in Minutes	5/2/01- 5/1/02	5/2/02- 5/1/03[27]	5/2/03- 5/1/04[28]
15 or less	$10,196	$10,451	$10,765
30 or less (but more than 15)	18,659	19,125	19,699
45 or less (but more than 30)	21,511	22,049	22,710
60 or less (but more than 45)	27,444	28,130	28,974
90 or less (but more than 60)	38,613	39,578	40,765
For Serials and Episodic Programs 120 or less (but more than 90)	50,803	52,073	53,635
For other than Serials and Episodic Programs 120 or less (but more than 90)	55,529	56,917	58,625

For programs in excess of one hundred twenty (120) minutes, compensation is based on the one hundred twenty (120) minute or less minimum (shown herein) plus, for each additional thirty (30) minutes or less, the following additional payments:

Story	$3,278	$3,360	$3,461
Teleplay	6,112	6,265	6,453
Story and Teleplay	8,201	8,406	8,658

---

[27]   See footnote 3 on page 54

[28]   See footnote 4 on page 54

---

dd. Segment Rate

Writers who are employed to write segments for use on programs meeting the requirements of this section may, at the option of the Company, be paid in accordance with this section rather than in accordance with the otherwise applicable provisions of this Agreement. In order to utilize this section, the Company (1) must apply this section to all writers employed on the program or, in the case of a program series, the individual episode; and (2) must inform such writers no later than the time of assignment to the program that this section is being utilized. As to any single dramatic program or any program of a dramatic television series thirty (30) minutes or more in length which consists of self-contained segments of various lengths (whether or not such segments are intercut within each program), the aggregate minimum compensation shall be one hundred seventy-five percent (175%) of the applicable minimum compensation for story and teleplay set forth in subparagraphs c. and d. Writers employed to write segments for use in such programs shall be compensated at the following rates:

Total Length of Program in Minutes	Length of Segment in Minutes	Segment Compensation as Percentage of Aggregate Minimum Compensation
30 or less	3 or less	10%
	5 or less (over 3)	15%
	10 or less (over 5)	30%
	15 or less (over 10)	40%
60 or less (but more than 30)	8 or less	16-2/3%
	15 or less (over 8)	20%
	20 or less (over 15)	25%
	30 or less (over 20)	40%
90 or less (but more than 60)	8 or less	10%
	15 or less (over 8)	12-1/2%
	20 or less (over 15)	16-2/3%
	30 or less (over 20)	27-1/2%
	60 or less (over 30)	40%
120 or less (but more than 90)	8 or less	8-1/3%
	15 or less (over 8)	10%
	20 or less (over 15)	12-1/2%
	30 or less (over 20)	20%
	60 or less (over 30)	30%

Should the total minimum compensation payable to the writers of the segments pursuant to the schedule immediately above be less than the aggregate minimum compensation specified above, the difference shall be distributed among the segment writers in proportion to the segment compensation set forth above. In said distribution, the Company may credit to an individual writer any overscale payment paid to such writer.

With respect to such programs, the following provisions will be incorporated into appropriate sections of the MBA:

(1)   The applicable minimums for rewrites shall be twenty-five percent (25%) of the segment minimum as determined in accordance with the above formula.

(2)   Separation of rights shall apply to each segment, excluding only those elements (continuing characters, etc.) which are part of the continuing series format.

(3)   Any story for which no teleplay is written during the same production season will revert to the writer.

(4)   The minimum compensation as computed above for each writer shall be the basis for calculation of all rerun, foreign telecast and theatrical exhibition payments required under the Basic Agreement.

(5)   Writing credits are to be given for each individual segment, identified by segment title, with a single card devoted to each segment.

e.   Serials

(1)   Employment and purchase of literary material for serials produced for broadcast three (3), four (4), five (5), six (6) or seven (7) times per week other than prime time is treated in Appendix A. (See Appendix A, Article 13.)

(2)   The minimum compensation for stories and/or teleplays, rewrites and polishes for episodes of a once-a-week network prime time serial shall be the corresponding minimums or stories and/or teleplays, rewrites and polishes for episodes of

network prime time episodic series.

(3) As to serials other than those described in subparagraphs e.(1) and (2) above, there is to be no differentiation between stories and teleplays for compensation purposes and minimum compensation for writing such material for such serials shall be as follows:

Program Length in Minutes	5/2/01- 5/1/02	5/2/02- 5/1/03[29]	5/2/03- 5/1/04[30]
15 or less	$3,766	$3,879	$4,015
30 or less (but more than 15)	6,270	6,458	6,684
60 or less (but more than 30)	11,913	12,270	12,699
90 or less (but more than 60)	17,023	17,534	18,148

For programs in excess of ninety (90) minutes, compensation is based on the ninety (90) minute or less minimum shown herein, plus, for each additional thirty (30) minutes or less, the difference between the appropriate ninety (90) minute compensation and the sixty (60) minute compensation.

f. **Installment Payments**

Payment of the writer's agreed upon compensation shall be made in installments as follows:

(1) If employment is for Story and Teleplay, not less than

(a) Thirty percent (30%) of agreed compensation on delivery of story.

(b) Forty percent (40%) of agreed compensation on delivery o

---

[29] See footnote 3 on page 54

[30] See footnote 4 on page 54

first draft teleplay. In no event shall the total of installments (a) and (b) be less than ninety percent (90%) of the applicable minimum compensation for story and teleplay.

    (c)   Balance of agreed compensation on delivery of final draft teleplay.

(2)   If employment is for Teleplay, not less than

    (a)   Sixty percent (60%) of agreed compensation or ninety percent (90%) of applicable minimum compensation, whichever is greater, on delivery of first draft teleplay.

    (b)   Balance of agreed compensation on delivery of final draft teleplay.

With respect to any employment under Article 13.B.7.a., b., c. or d. above relating to pilots and one-time programs ninety (90) minutes or more in length, the Company will pay to the writer, not later than the next regular payday in the week following the day the Company instructs the writer to commence his/her services, a single advance amount (to be applied against the first compensation which otherwise would be due to the writer) at least equal to ten percent (10%) of the monies which otherwise would be due to the writer upon delivery of the first required material.

If the writer of a television motion picture ninety (90) minutes or longer has negotiated a salary sufficient to allow for three (3) revisions of the teleplay as follows, and the writer's contract provides for such revisions, the first draft teleplay shall be delivered to the producer (or other executive) designated in the writer's deal memorandum or contract and such producer shall be authorized to give notes to the writer and the writer shall utilize such notes in the first revision. The producer shall notify the network or other licensee when it has received the first draft teleplay.

Payment for such writing steps would be as follows:

(1)   commencement (10% of agreed compensation);
(2)   delivery of story (20% of agreed compensation);
(3)   delivery of first draft teleplay to producer (40% of agreed compensation);

(4)[31] (a) delivery of first set of revisions to producer, based on
              producer's notes, if any (10% of agreed compensation); or
      (b) if producer has not requested a revision, delivery of first set
           of revisions to network or licensee (10% of agreed
           compensation);
(5) delivery of second set of revisions (10% of agreed
     compensation); and
(6) delivery of polish (10% of agreed compensation).

g. **Plot Outline - Narrative Synopsis of Story**

Company may request writer to prepare a narrative synopsis of
reasonable length (herein designated as an "outline") of a story
owned by writer in order to determine its suitability for television
purposes. The minimum compensation for the preparation of such
outline shall be:

Program Length in Minutes	5/2/01- 5/1/02	5/2/02- 5/1/03[32]	5/2/03- 5/1/04[33]
15 or less	$1,094	$1,127	$1,166
30 or less (but more than 15)	1,823	1,878	1,944
60 or less (but more than 30)	3,455	3,559	3,684
75 or less (but more than 60)	4,506	4,641	4,803
90 or less (but more than 75)	5,107	5,260	5,444
120 or less (but more than 90)	6,733	6,935	7,178

Company shall, within fourteen (14) days from time of delivery of
such outline, notify writer of its election to acquire such outline and
employ writer to prepare a teleplay based thereon. If Company shall
so elect, the agreed compensation paid for the outline shall be
deemed an advance against the applicable minimum compensation
for such story with an option for teleplay, which option shall be
deemed exercised, and writer shall receive the difference, if any. If
Company shall elect not to proceed, it shall return the outline to the
writer not later than the end of such fourteen (14) day period and
writer shall be entitled to retain the above applicable minimum for the
outline and shall own all right, title and interest in the literary material
contained in such outline, except to the extent that the outline was
prepared for an episodic series or serial-type film and program format
and/or characters belonging to the Company were incorporated in the
material written by the writer.

Company shall sign and deliver to writer, on the date of hiring, a slip
stating it has employed the writer to prepare an outline of such
material and that the conditions of such employment are upon terms
not less favorable than those provided by this subparagraph g.

---

[31] See Sideletter to Article 13.B.7.f. at page 415, 417 of this Agreement ("Letter of Understanding Between the Guild and Licensees of Television Motion Pictures (90 Minutes or Longer)".)

[32] See footnote 3 on page 54

[33] See footnote 4 on page 54

h. **Compensation for Rewrites and Polishes**

Company shall pay not less than the following minimum compensation with respect to rewrites and polishes:

(1) Rewrites

High Budget - Non-serial pictures and serials described in 13.B.7.e.(2)

Program Length in Minutes	5/2/01-5/1/02	5/2/02-5/1/03[34]	5/2/03-5/1/04[35]
15 or less	$2,358	$2,429	$2,514
30 or less (but more than 15)	3,938	4,056	4,198
45 or less (but more than 30)	5,694	5,865	6,070
60 or less (but more than 45)	7,449	7,672	7,941
75 or less (but more than 60)	10,455	10,769	11,146
90 or less (but more than 75)	10,973	11,302	11,698
120 or less (but more than 90)	14,495	14,930	15,453

Low Budget - Non-serial pictures and serials described in 13.B.7.e.(2)

---

[34] See footnote 3 on page 54

[35] See footnote 4 on page 54

Program Length in Minutes	5/2/01- 5/1/02	5/2/02- 5/1/03[36]	5/2/03- 5/1/04[37]
15 or less	$1,727	$1,779	$1,841
30 or less (but more than 15)	2,957	3,046	3,153
60 or less (but more than 30)	5,638	5,807	6,010
75 or less (but more than 60)	7,835	8,010	8,352
90 or less (but more than 75)	8,323	8,573	8,873
120 or less (but more than 90)	10,998	11,328	11,724

---

[36]   See footnote 3 on page 54

[37]   See footnote 4 on page 54

ARTICLE 13 - COMPENSATION
B - TELEVISION

Teleplays for serials described in 13.B.7.e.(3)

Program Length in Minutes	5/2/01- 5/1/02	5/2/02- 5/1/03[38]	5/2/03- 5/1/04[39]
15 or less	$1,877	$1,933	$2,001
30 or less (but more than 15)	3,138	3,232	3,345
60 or less (but more than 30)	5,948	6,126	6,340

(2)   Polishes

High Budget - Non-serial pictures and serials described in

13.B.7.e.(2)

Program Length in Minutes	5/2/01- 5/1/02	5/2/02- 5/1/03[40]	5/2/03- 5/1/04[41]
15 or less	$1,180	$1,215	$1,258
30 or less (but more than 15)	1,965	2,024	2,095
45 or less (but more than 30)	2,843	2,928	3,030
60 or less (but more than 45)	3,730	3,842	3,976
75 or less (but more than 60)	5,221	5,378	5,566
90 or less (but more than 75)	5,482	5,646	5,844
120 or less (but more than	7,246	7,463	7,724

---

[38]   See footnote 3 on page 54

[39]   See footnote 4 on page 54

[40]   See footnote 3 on page 54

[41]   See footnote 4 on page 54

Low Budget - Non-serial pictures and serials described in
13.B.7.e.(2)

Program Length in Minutes	5/2/01-5/1/02	5/2/02-5/1/03[42]	5/2/03-5/1/04[43]
15 or less	$859	$885	$916
30 or less (but more than 15)	1,474	1,518	1,571
60 or less (but more than 30)	2,816	2,900	3,002
75 or less (but more than 60)	3,916	4,033	4,174
90 or less (but more than 75)	4,164	4,289	4,439
120 or less (but more than 90)	5,503	5,668	5,866

Teleplays for serials described in 13.B.7.e.(3)

Program Length in Minutes	5/2/01-5/1/02	5/2/02-5/1/03[44]	5/2/03-5/1/04[45]
15 or less	$944	$972	$1,006
30 or less (but more than 15)	1,577	1,624	1,681
60 or less (but more than 30)	2,980	3,069	3,176

i., j., k. and l. [deleted]

m.   **(1)   Format**

---

[42]   See footnote 3 on page 54

[43]   See footnote 4 on page 54

[44]   See footnote 3 on page 54

[45]   See footnote 4 on page 54

Minimum basic compensation for a format shall be:

5/2/01-5/1/02	$7,567
5/2/02-5/1/03[46]	7,794
5/2/03-5/1/04[47]	8,067

If a story, or stories, are included in a purchased format and the story is used, the applicable minimum for such story or stories shall apply. If such story or stories are not used, no story minimum would apply.

If a writer is employed to write a format and a story or stories are included, at the direction of Company, the applicable story minimum shall apply.

At the time of purchase or hire, Company shall submit to writer any formats in control of the Company relating to the project for which writer has been engaged. The writer shall be obligated to read, initial and date such format.

(2) Bible

Minimum basic compensation for a network prime time bible shall be:

5/2/01-5/1/02	$38,259
5/2/02-5/1/03[48]	39,407
5/2/03-5/1/04[49]	40,786

---

[46] See footnote 3 on page 54

[47] See footnote 4 on page 54

[48] See footnote 3 on page 54

[49] See footnote 4 on page 54

---

plus ten percent (10%) thereof for each detailed storyline in excess of six (6) ordered by the Company in connection therewith. With respect to a non-network and/or non-prime time bible for a multi-part closed end series, the minimum basic compensation shall be twenty percent (20%) less than set forth above. The writer of the bible shall be entitled to the applicable story payment (including the additional compensation set forth in Article 13.B.7.d.(1), if applicable) for each segment or episode of the multi-part program or prime-time serial for which he/she receives story credit. Ten percent (10%) of the applicable minimum for a bible may be credited against such payment for each story. Notwithstanding the foregoing, should the Company separately pay the full story and teleplay minimum to the bible writer or any other writer, the story payment (including the additional compensation set forth in Article 13.B.7.d.(1), if applicable) otherwise due to the bible writer under this subparagraph shall not be required.

(3) **Rewrite or Polish of Format or Bible**

Minimum basic compensation for a rewrite of a format shall be fifty percent (50%) of the applicable minimum set forth above. Minimum basic compensation for a polish of a format shall be twenty-five percent (25%) of the applicable minimum set forth above.

Minimum basic compensation for a rewrite or polish of a bible shall be:

	Rewrite	Polish
5/2/01-5/1/02	$19,130	$9,565
5/2/02-5/1/03[50]	19,704	9,852
5/2/03-5/1/04[51]	20,394	10,197

provided, however, that when the writer rewrites or polishes more than six (6) story lines in the bible, the minimum basic compensation shall be increased as follows (for rewrite or polish, as the case may be) for each such story line in excess of six (6):

	Rewrite	Polish
5/2/01-5/1/02	$1,911	$957
5/2/02-5/1/03[52]	1,968	986
5/2/03-5/1/04[53]	2,037	1,021

With respect to rewriting or polishing a non-network and/or non-prime time bible, the minimum basic compensation shall be twenty percent (20%) less than set forth above.

[50] See footnote 3 on page 54 [52] See footnote 3 on page 54
[51] See footnote 4 on page 54 [53] See footnote 4 on page 54

n.   Narration

Minimum basic compensation for a narration shall be as follows:

NARRATION
(by writer other than writer of teleplay or story and teleplay)

FILM ASSEMBLED IN STORY SEQUENCE

Nature of Material Already Written under MBA when Narration Writer Hired	Credit to Narration Writer[54]	Freelance Minimum	Residuals to Narration Writer
1. No Material	"Narration Written by"	See Rate Schedule A	Yes, based on % of applicable freelance minimum in Rate Schedule A
2. Story only	"Narration Written by" (If story credit, then on same card)	See Rate Schedule A	Yes, based on % of applicable freelance minimum in Rate Schedule A
3. Story and Teleplay	None, but if over 8 minutes of narration (aggregate), only receive "Narration by" credit (same card) **Automatic arbitration**	See Rate Schedule C	If "Narration by" credit, then only shared residuals, as determined in WGA credit arbitration (aggregate of no more than story & teleplay residuals)

---

[54]   Credit not to affect rates - There is no separation of rights for narration.

NARRATION
(by writer other than writer of teleplay or story and teleplay)

FILM FOOTAGE NOT ASSEMBLED IN STORY SEQUENCE

Nature of Material Already Written under MBA when Narration Writer Hired	Credit to Narration Writer[55]	Freelance Minimum	Residuals to Narration Writer
1. No Material	"Written by"	See Rate Schedule B	Yes, based on % of applicable freelance minimum in Rate Schedule B
2. Story only	"Narration Written by" (If story credit, then on same card)	See Rate Schedule A	Yes, based on % of applicable freelance minimum in Rate Schedule A
3. Story and Teleplay	None, but if over 8 minutes of narration (aggregate), only receive "Narration by" credit (same card) **Automatic arbitration**	See Rate Schedule C	If "Narration by" credit, then only shared residuals, as determined in WGA credit arbitration

NOTE: Excluded from these provisions is material described in Article 13.B.7.p.

Two writers collaborating equal one unit, to receive in the aggregate not less than applicable minimum.

Narration writer may be hired on a week-to-week basis, subject to Article 13.B.7.s.

---

[55] Credit not to affect rates - There is no separation of rights for narration.

ARTICLE 13 - COMPENSATION

The following rates are for High Budget:[56]

RATE SCHEDULE A

Program Length in Minutes*	5/2/01- 5/1/02	5/2/02- 5/1/03[57]	5/2/03- 5/1/04[58]
15 or less	$4,730	$4,872	$5,043
30 or less (but more than 15)	7,864	8,100	8,384
60 or less (but more than 30)	14,914	15,361	15,899
75 or less (but more than 60)	20,908	21,535	22,289
90 or less (but more than 75)	21,971	22,630	23,422
120 or less (but more than 90)	29,018	29,889	30,935
plus, for each additional ½ hour or fraction thereof	7,050	7,262	7,516

RATE SCHEDULE B

Program Length in Minutes*	5/2/01- 5/1/02	5/2/02- 5/1/03[59]	5/2/03- 5/1/04[60]
15 or less	$5,461	$5,625	$5,822
30 or less (but more than 15)	9,994	10,294	10,654
60 or less (but more than 30)	18,182	18,727	19,382

---

[56] If Low Budget, then applicable rates are equal to corresponding rates for Low Budget teleplay (under "A" above) and Low Budget story and teleplay (under "B" above).

[57] See footnote 3 on page 54

[58] See footnote 4 on page 54

[59] See footnote 3 on page 54

[60] See footnote 4 on page 54

ARTICLE 13 - COMPENSATION
B - TELEVISION

75 or less (but more than 60)	25,001	25,751	26,652
90 or less (but more than 75)	26,360	27,151	28,101
120 or less (but more than 90)	34,538	35,574	36,819
plus, for each additional ½ hour or fraction thereof	8,192	8,438	8,733

* Running time is in terms of soundtrack.

RATE SCHEDULE C

	5/2/01-5/1/02	5/2/02-5/1/03[61]	5/2/03-5/1/04[62]
Aggregate sound track running time in minutes of narration written by writer hired pursuant to this chart			
2 minutes or less of narration	$758	$781	$808
Over 2 minutes through 5 minutes of narration	2,653	2,733	2,829
Over 5 minutes of narration	Teleplay rewrite minimum for applicable program length		

o.   **Remakes**

The Company's right to remake a television motion picture shall be subject to the following:[63]

(1)   If the credited writer's material is used for the remake and no writer is employed to rewrite, adapt or revise such material for the remake, the Company will pay such writer a sum equal to the applicable minimum compensation for the intended medium of the remake appropriate to the writer's initial employment to

---

[61]   See footnote 3 on page 54

[62]   See footnote 4 on page 54

[63]   But as to any series in production prior to March 6, 1973, this paragraph B.7.o. shall remain as in the 1970 WGA Agreement and as to any series in production prior to March 2, 1977, which was not in production prior to March 6, 1973, this paragraph B.7.o. shall remain as in the 1977 WGA Agreement.

write such material. Said minimum compensation shall not be diminished by virtue of any sharing of credit by said writer for the remake (but this provision shall not be construed as affecting the rule that a *bona fide* team shall be considered a unit as provided in subparagraph B.1. of this Article). In addition, the writer will be entitled to receive payments in accordance with Article 15.A. with respect to a theatrical remake licensed to free television, Article 15.B. with respect to reruns or foreign telecast of a television remake, and Article 51 with respect to a theatrical or free television remake released in Supplemental Markets.

(2)   If a writer is employed to rewrite, adapt or revise such literary material for the remake, then the credited writer of the original material also shall be a participant in the credit determination and if accorded credit shall be paid the applicable minimum compensation for the intended medium of the remake appropriate to such credit. In the event of a television remake, the writer of the original material, if accorded credit, will be entitled to share, in accordance with such credit, in any additional compensation for television reruns or theatrical exhibition which may become due. Said minimum compensation shall not be diminished by virtue of any sharing of credit by said writer for the remake, (but this provision shall not be construed as affecting the rule that a *bona fide* team shall be considered a unit as provided in subparagraph B.1. of this Article). In addition, such writer of the original material will be entitled to share in any additional compensation in accordance with Article 15.A. with respect to a theatrical remake licensed to free television, Article 15.B. with respect to foreign telecast of a television remake, and Article 51 with respect to a theatrical or free television remake released in Supplemental Markets. The portion of additional compensation referred to in this subparagraph (2) which is payable to the original writer shall be equal to the portion of credit awarded pursuant to subparagraph (a) below.

(3)   With respect to a television remake, the "applicable minimum compensation" in subparagraphs (I) and (2) of this paragraph o. means the applicable rates provided for in Article 13.B.7.a., b. or e. of this Agreement.

In a credit arbitration concerning such remake, the arbitrators shall determine the following issues:

(a) the contribution made by the writer(s) of the original material expressed as a percentage of the whole; and

(b) the form of credit to be accorded such writer(s), which credit may include a credit in the nature of a source material credit, such as "Based on a Teleplay by ..."

p. **Non-Commercial Openings and Closings**

When a writer other than the writer of the teleplay for a television film writes literary material for self-contained units of entertainment which are used as opening, closing and/or bridging material in such film, the total minimum compensation for all such self-contained units in such film will be:

Aggregate Running Time of Material	5/2/01-5/1/02	5/2/02-5/1/03[64]	5/2/03-5/1/04[65]
3 minutes or less	$1,965	$2,024	$2,095
More than 3 minutes	2,760	2,843	2,943

It is further expressly understood that the foregoing rates are not intended to apply to customary or routine introductions, bridges or conclusions. An example of the material intended to be covered is the material delivered by Alfred Hitchcock on the series "*Alfred Hitchcock Presents*." In addition, if such units are rerun, as the term "rerun" is used in Article 15.B.1.b., Company shall pay the writer additional payments expressed in percentages of said total minimum compensation at the rates specified in said Article 15.B.1.b. It is expressly understood that, except as specifically provided herein, this paragraph is not intended to extend the coverage of this Basic Agreement to, nor provide payment for, any matter in any television film not elsewhere covered by this Basic Agreement.

---

[64] See footnote 3 on page 54

[65] See footnote 4 on page 54

The Guild Agreement also provides that the same minimums apply to purchases of literary material from a professional writer (see discussion below) and that the company may option feature literary material from a "professional writer" for a period of eighteen months upon payment of 10 percent of the applicable minimum.

Using the table for 5/2/03 through 5/1/04, you will find that the minimum compensation for a single-draft high-budget picture is found in category "5"—First Draft Screenplay With or Without Option for Final Draft Screenplay. If you are selling a single draft screenplay— that is a first draft screenplay without an option for a final draft—the price is $38,981. Since your screenplay qualifies as an original screenplay, you also add category "9"—additional compensation for story included in screenplay or $12,992, for a total of $51,973 ($38,981 + $12,992). The minimum option price for eighteen months is $5,197 (10 percent of $51,973).

As noted above, in order to qualify for the minimum payment benefits set forth in the WGA Basic Agreement, the writer must be a "professional writer." A "professional writer" is defined as any person who (a) has received employment for a total of thirteen weeks as a television, motion picture, or radio writer, or (b) has received credit on the screen as a writer for a television or theatrical motion picture, or (c) has received credit for three original stories or one teleplay for a program one half hour or more in length in live television, or (d) has received credit for three radio scripts for radio programs one half hour or more in length, or (e) has received credit for one professionally produced play on the legitimate stage or one published novel.

If you have qualified to become a member, meaning you have accumulated the necessary units of credit and fall into one of the other categories listed above, you would qualify as a "professional writer." Even if you are entering into your first agreement with a Guild company and do not accumulate the requisite points to join the Guild, you should ask, nevertheless, that all the terms of the WGA Agreement apply to you as if you *were* a professional writer. The reason: If you are not a professional writer, the Guild allows a discount in rates. For a writer who is employed for the first time by the Guild, the employer can pay 75 percent of the minimum. (Note that if the company hiring you is a signatory to the Guild, that company has to comply with the Guild rules.) Writers who are not yet "professional writers" are also denied other benefits.

SUPPLEMENTAL MARKET PAYMENTS

The Guild Agreement not only provides for up-front minimum payments, it also requires payments for continued exploitation of a feature motion picture or television program. For features, the signatory company must make additional payments for exhibition of the motion picture in "supplemental markets," which are defined as the exhibition of motion pictures by means of cassettes, DVDs, pay-type CATV or pay television, and the exhibition of television motion pictures on any commercial carrier such as commercial airlines, trains, ships, and buses.

Pay television is specifically defined to include only those exhibitions of motion pictures for which a fee is actually charged to the subscriber (which may be a hotel, motel, or other accommodation) for the program, or where the subscriber or viewer has the option, for a fee, to receive special programming over one or more special channels.

The term "supplemental markets" specifically does not include the exhibition of a motion picture over free television, in the educational market, or on commercial carriers such as airlines, trains, ships, and buses.

All writers who receive credit on a picture for the writing of the story or screenplay are entitled to share on a pro rata basis in 1.2 percent of the company's receipts from the distribution of the picture in the pay TV market. The participating writers are also entitled to share in 1.5 percent of the gross derived from the distribution of the picture on videodiscs or videocassettes until the gross equals $1 million. Thereafter, the writers collectively are entitled to share 1.8 percent of the gross in excess of $1 million derived from such exploitation. If the company is the distributor or the distributor is owned or affiliated with the company, then the gross is deemed to equal 20 percent of the wholesale worldwide receipts derived by the distributor. This is the same formula commonly used by the studios in the calculation of net profits (see chapter 6). Note that in the Guild Agreement, the studios were able to impose the same inequitable formula as is used in studio net profit definitions. The difference here, though, is significant. In this formula, the video receipts are not cross-collateralized with other revenues, so the writer actually receives a piece of the separate revenue stream. The royalty must be paid regardless of whether the picture has generated so-called net profits under the studio definition and the studio is not allowed to deduct *all* other costs of making the picture, so there is a real opportunity to make some money if you receive story credit and/or screenplay credit. Storywriters collectively receive 25 percent of these revenues (with all storywriters sharing equally) and the screenwriters receive 75 percent of these revenues (with the screenwriters all sharing equally).

With respect to theatrical motion pictures exhibited on television, the principal photography of which was commenced on or after August 8, 1988, writers are entitled to 2 percent of the company's accountable receipts from the distribution of such picture on free television. This is computed as 2 percent of the worldwide gross receipts derived by the distributor of such picture from licensing the rights to exhibit the picture on free television (again, if there is more than one writer, they share, as noted above).

RERUNS AND RESIDUALS

The minimum payments for a television writer set forth in Exhibit "A" are for one run (telecast not more than once in any city in the United States and Canada). A television motion picture that has been telecast more than once, but not more than twice, in any city in the United States and Canada, is in its second run. A similar test applies in determining when a television motion picture is in its third and subsequent runs for reruns in the United States and Canada. Payments for subsequent runs are commonly called "residuals." The following formula is used for U.S. reruns:

WGA 2001 THEATRICAL AND TELEVISION BASIC AGREEMENT
RESIDUAL COMPENSATION

PRIME TIME RERUNS ON ABC, CBS, NBC and FBC
All reruns on ABC, CBS, NBC (and FBC as of 5/2/03) in prime time are payable at 100% of the applicable minimums. However, the applicable minimum for the purpose of calculating all rerun compensation is the minimum applicable to "Other Than Network Prime Time" television films.

PRIME TIME RERUNS ON FOX BROADCASTING COMPANY (FBC)

	Effective 5/2/01– 5/1/02	Effective 5/2/02– 5/1/03	Effective 5/2/03– 5/1/04
	Percentage of Applicable Minimum		
2nd run	80.0%	90.0%	100% for all reruns on FBC in prime time*
3rd run	59.9%	67.4%	
4th–6th run	50.0% each	56.3% each	
7th–10th run	30.0% each	33.8% each	
11th–12th run	19.9% each	22.4% each	
13th run and each run thereafter	10.1%	11.4%	

*For programs written for the FBC 2002-2003 prime time season, please contact the Guild.

OTHER RERUN COMPENSATION⁺*
The minimum compensation payable with respect to reruns in the United States and Canada (other than in prime time on ABC, CBS, NBC or FBC as of 5/2/03) is computed as a percentage of applicable minimum as follows:

2nd run	40%; 50% if on ABC, CBS, NBC (or FBC as of 5/2/03)
3rd run	30%; 40% if on ABC, CBS, NBC (or FBC as of 5/2/03)
4th–6th run	25% each run
7th–10th run	15% each run
11th–12th run	10% each run
13th run and each run thereafter	5%

⁺There is a limited waiver based on a ratio of "revenues contracted for" covering syndication reruns of one-hour network (ABC, CBS, NBC) (and FBC as of 5/2/02) prime time dramatic series which were not broadcast in syndication before March 1, 1988. For details, contact the Guild Residuals Department.
*For 30 minute series which have not been syndicated before May 2, 2001, and are sold into syndication in markets representing 50% or fewer US television households, the rerun payment for each run will be 20% of applicable minimum. This additional residual stream will not apply against or otherwise affect the above "Other Rerun Compensation" residuals.

TIMING OF RESIDUAL PAYMENTS

Network residuals are payable within 30 days of the rerun. "Other rerun compensation" residuals are payable with 120 days of the rerun. As of 5/2/03, residuals for reruns on FBC, the WB and UPN will be payable within 30 days of the rerun, like network residuals.

PRIME TIME VARIETY RERUN COMPENSATION, ONCE PER WEEK OR LESS

Compensation for reruns is allocated among the credited writers and shall be computed as follows:

2nd run	100% of applicable aggregate minimum
3rd run	
Prime Time	100% of applicable aggregate minimum
Other Than Prime Time	75% of applicable aggregate minimum
4th run	50% of applicable aggregate minimum for
5th run	each such run
6th run	25% of applicable aggregate minimum
7th run	10% of applicable aggregate minimum

Each subsequent run—5% of applicable aggregate minimum for each such run.

FOREIGN TELECAST COMPENSATION

Initial Foreign Telecast	15%* of applicable minimum

When foreign gross exceeds:
$ 7,000 on 30 minute film
13,000 on 60 minute film   Additional 10% of applicable minimum
18,000 on longer film
When foreign gross exceeds:
$10,000 on 30 minute film
18,000 on 60 minute film   Additional 10% of applicable minimum
24,000 on longer film

In addition, 1.2% of Distributor's Foreign Gross, including both foreign basic cable and foreign free television receipts, in perpetuity, after the following thresholds:

30 minute:	$350,000 ($357,500 as of 5/2/03)
60 minute:	$700,000 ($715,000 as of 5/2/03)
Over 60 minute but not more than 120 minute:	$1,800,000 ($1,830,000 as of 5/2/03)

The above thresholds are reduced by 50% for Appendix A programs such as Comedy/Variety, Daytime Serials and Documentaries.

COMEDY/VARIETY FOREIGN TELECAST COMPENSATION

When calculating foreign telecast compensation for prime time variety programs originally broadcast once per week or less, the applicable story and teleplay minimums are to be substituted for the applicable comedy/variety minimums.

---

*For one-hour network (ABC, CBS, NBC and FBC as of 5/2/02) prime time series covered by the limited waiver (details in footnote on page 28), the 15%, 10% and 10% payments are to be collapsed into a single payment of 35% payable upon initial foreign telecast. Contact the Guild Residuals Department for details.

RERUN COMPENSATION FOR MADE-FOR BASIC CABLE PROGRAMS ON BASIC CABLE "SANCHEZ" FORMULA

The minimum compensation payable with respect to reruns on basic cable of made-for basic cable programs is as follows:

	Effective 5/2/01– 5/1/02		Effective 5/2/02– 5/1/04	
	Percentage of Applicable Minimum			
2nd run	14.4%		17.0%	
3rd run	10.8%		12.0%	
		43.2%*		50%*
4th run	9.0%		11.0%	
5th run	9.0%		10.0%	
6th run	5.0%		6.0%	
7th & 8th run	3.0% each		4.0%	
9th & 10th run	3.0% each		3.5%	
11th run	2.0%		3.0%	
12th run	2.0%		2.5%	
13th run & each run thereafter	1.0%		1.5%	

*Payments for the second through fifth runs shall be made when the residual payment is due for the second run.

RERUN COMPENSATION FOR MADE-FOR-BASIC CABLE PROGRAMS ON BASIC CABLE—"HITCHCOCK" FORMULA

For dramatic programs, the difference (effective May 2, 2002, 120% of such difference) between the corresponding Network Prime Time minimum and the applicable minimum for the program is payable as a reuse fee—covering 12 runs over 5 years on the basic cable service. For other types of programs, the reuse fee is 70% (84% as of May 2, 2002) of the applicable minimum. The reuse fee is payable upon the initial exhibition of the program, but no earlier than the final determination of writing credits.

MADE-FOR-PAY TELEVISION, VIDEOCASSETTE/VIDEODISC RESIDUALS

Generally, for dramatic programs, after the first exhibition year or the first 10 runs (whichever occurs first) on the same pay TV service, residuals are payable for subsequent exhibition years as follows:

30 minute	$2,500 in each of the next 3 years; $750 each year thereafter.
60 minute	$4,333 in each of the next 3 years; $1,000 each year thereafter.
120 minutes or more	$8,333 in each of the next 3 years; $1,250 each year thereafter.

For other types of programs, a 2% residual is payable after certain thresholds are met. For details, contact the Guild Residuals Department.

WGA THEATRICAL AND TELEVISION
RESIDUAL & OTHER COMPENSATION

FREE TELEVISION PRODUCT RELEASED ON BASIC CABLE
A 2.5% residual is payable for free television product produced prior to July 1, 1984, released on Basic Cable. For free television product produced after July 1, 1984, a 2% residual is payable. For details, contact the Guild Residuals Department.

INTERACTIVE REUSE COMPENSATION
The MBA contains provisions governing additional compensation for reuse of MBA-covered writing in interactive programs. Contact the Guild Contracts Department for information.

USE OF EXCERPTS
The use of excerpts (clips) from a theatrical motion picture or television program in another theatrical motion picture or television program requires payment to the Guild for distribution to the credited writers. For details, contact the Guild.

SERIES SEQUEL PAYMENTS
If a Company commences exploitation of the television series sequel rights in connection with material to which separation of rights applies, the writer or writers entitled to separation of rights must be paid not less than the following series sequel payments for each sequel episode:

Series of:	Effective 5/2/01– 5/1/02	Effective 5/2/02– 5/1/03	Effective 5/2/03– 5/1/04
15-minute episodes	$ 851	$ 881	$ 912
30-minute episodes	1,419	1,469	1,520
60-minute episodes	2,696	2,791	2,888
90-minute episodes or longer	3,548	3,672	3,800

MOVIE-OF-THE-WEEK (MOW) SEQUEL PAYMENTS
The writers entitled to separation of rights in the first MOW must be paid not less than the following MOW sequel payment for each MOW sequel:

Effective	
5/2/01–5/1/02	$14,192
5/2/02–5/1/03	14,688
5/2/03–5/1/04	15,200

Under certain circumstances, twice the above payment applies. Contact the Guild Contracts Department for details.

CHARACTER "SPIN-OFF" PAYMENTS
Character "Spin-off" payments equal to the above sequel payments are payable to the writer who introduces a new character in a serial, episodic, anthology, or one-time show if such character becomes the central character in a new serial or episodic series.

WGA 2001 THEATRICAL AND TELEVISION BASIC AGREEMENT
OTHER TELEVISION COMPENSATION & COMMISSIONS

RECURRING CHARACTER PAYMENTS
Recurring character payments are payable to the writer who introduces a new character in an episodic series for each episode in which such character appears in the following amounts:

Effective
5/2/01–5/1/02 $405
5/2/02–5/1/03   419
5/2/03–5/1/04   434

AGENT COMMISSIONS—THEATRICAL AND TELEVISION
Initial compensation*, whether or not at minimum, for writing services and for an option or purchase is subject to a 10% commission.

Otherwise, minimums, including residuals and other payments such as program fees and sequel payments, are not commissionable.

Other overscale compensation (minimum plus overscale) is commissionable but only to the extent the commission does not reduce the writer's compensation to below minimum.

If you have any questions, contact the Guild Agency Department.

---

*Except minimum comedy-variety pre-production payments.

RADIO COMPENSATION
For minimum terms and conditions of the Radio Agreement, please contact the Guild Contracts Department.

Note that unlike supplemental market payments for ancillary exhibitions of feature films, which are allocated 25 percent to the storywriter and 75 percent to the screenplay writer, in television, all writers who receive story and/or teleplay credit share equally in the applicable residuals.

PASSIVE PAYMENTS

The Guild Agreement also requires separate payments for sequels, remakes, and television series. These are known as subsequent production payments. These payments are similar to the passive payments that are usually negotiated as part of a purchase agreement (see discussion of Passive Payments in chapter 7). The major difference between these payments and the passive payments discussed earlier in this book is that the WGA-mandated payments are lower than the commonly negotiated sums. For instance, the Guild-mandated sequel payment is 25 percent of the fixed compensation paid to the writer under employment for her writing services. The norm for negotiated passive payments is 50 percent for sequels and 33 percent for remakes. If you are able to, you should negotiate separate passive payments. Invariably, the Guild-mandated payments are applied against any separate passive payments you are able to negotiate. In other words, you will not be paid twice.

You will see the following language in your writing agreement:

> To the extent Producer becomes obligated to make any additional payments to Writer pursuant to the provisions of the WGA Agreement, said obligations shall be satisfied by payment to Writer of the minimum amounts provided for therein. To the extent that any amounts payable to Writer hereunder may be credited against any amounts required to be paid under the WGA Agreement, or to the extent any amounts required to be paid under the WGA Agreement may be credited against amounts which may become due hereunder, Producer shall be entitled to credit all sums payable pursuant to this Agreement to Writer against any corresponding payments required by the WGA Basic Agreement.

Guild-mandated television series payments are $1,513 for thirty-minute programs and $2,893 for sixty-minute programs. Negotiated passive payments are usually $2,000–$2,500 for thirty minutes, $3,000–$3,500 for sixty minutes. There is not that much difference in this area, but if the show is a hit, the differences may add up over one hundred programs.

The Guild also provides for extra monies for reruns of these subsequent productions. These payments are calculated using the rerun formula discussed above.

The subsequent production payments are made to writers who are entitled to "separation of rights" under the Guild Agreement. Separation of rights is determined by establishing "separable material," which is, in essence, underlying story and character material that is original and not based on any assigned material or source material. The writer must be employed to write original story material (or sell an original screenplay) in order to qualify for separation of rights. All writers who ultimately qualify for separated rights share in the subsequent production payments referred to above.

As noted in chapter 7, studios award passive payments only if the writer is entitled to separated rights. Some studios do not award any payment if the writer shares separated rights. If you are a Guild member, however, you will receive a subsequent production payment depending on your share in separated rights. Thus, do not despair if you are not able to negotiate a passive payment for shared separated rights. Under the Guild rules, you will be entitled to something.

Note that under certain circumstances, the Guild also provides payments to writers entitled to separated rights for stage productions and merchandising. The Guild provides, under Article 1.B., separate merchandising payments for theatrical features. "Merchandising" means the right to manufacture and sell, or otherwise dispose of, any object or thing first described in literary material written by the writer pursuant to an employment agreement required from a professional writer, provided such object or thing is fully described in the original work. Merchandising rights include the right of publication and publications of the generic type described as "photo novels" or "photo albums." The writer shall have no separate merchandising rights. However, if the company exploits the merchandising rights in any such literary material, the company shall pay the writer an amount equal to 5 percent of absolute gross; that is, monies remitted by the manufacturer on account of the exploitation of the subject merchandising rights. The same provisions are also applicable to a writer who is not entitled to separation of rights.

The Guild also provides for separate merchandising payments for material written for television. With respect to television programs, the description for qualification is similar, but writers not entitled to separated rights receive 5 percent of the company's net receipts derived from the merchandising rights. "Net receipts shall be computed by deducting from gross amounts paid to company or its licensing agent, whether affiliated or otherwise, all costs, expenses and charges incident thereto, including a distribution of service fee by the company, which will include any and all subdistributor fees, which fee shall be reasonably in accordance with customary distribution or servicing fees charged in the industry" (Article 15.B.14.m). With respect to writers entitled to separation of rights, these writers are entitled to 6 percent of absolute gross; that is, monies remitted by the manufacturer as derived from licensing for the publication and merchandising rights Comic books, magazine publications, comic strips, cut-outs, and other activity books shall be deemed to be included as merchandising rights (Article 16.B.3.3[2]). Note that in television, under certain circumstances when the writer is earning in excess of a certain amount as defined in the Guild Agreement, the company may negotiate to buy out these rights altogether, but it must negotiate first.

ARBITRATION

Aside from being protected with minimum payment formulas, the other main advantage to being a Guild member is the virtually free litigation service that it offers. The Guild employs several full-time lawyers to direct grievance procedures. Signatory companies are forced to comply with the determination of any arbitration. If they do not they may be blacklisted—meaning they will not be able to hire another WGA member—a severe blow to any mainstream company.

Guild lawyers also carefully scrutinize any signatory company. They want to make sure that the writer will be paid. If there is a link between the membership company and a bigger entity that is producing many pictures, under certain circumstances the bigger entity will also be on the hook as far as the Guild is concerned (that is, the Guild rule states that any entity or person who holds at least a 50 percent interest in a Guild company must also comply with the rules of the Guild). If no link can be established and the Guild is concerned about a signatory's ability to pay, the Guild might require a bond from the smaller company. Or it might require a personal guaranty from the owner of the company.

In order to find such links, the Guild plays detective. The Guild actually searches the corporate public records of any member company to see who the directors and officers are (a matter of public record). If Guild investigators see a potential link to a larger company, they might try to implicate the larger company.

A number of signatory companies in recent years have gone bankrupt. In such cases, Writers Guild payments, particularly residuals and supplemental market payments, got caught up in bankruptcy proceedings and the writers were not paid. The Guild started taking stringent measures with former owners of such companies who wished to start new companies with a clean slate. When the former CEO of one such company subsequently applied to make his new company a signatory in the Guild, the Guild required him to place in escrow all up-front writing monies required to be paid by him under any writer's deal that he wished to enter into. Thus, for example, if a writer was guaranteed $60,000 to write a draft and set of revisions, $60,000 had to be placed into a WGA escrow account before the writer was allowed to perform services. Otherwise, the writer could not be hired.

OTHER BENEFITS

Aside from establishing minimum payment requirements and providing free legal services, the Guild offers other useful benefits for its members.

Credits

The Guild determines credits through formal procedures. Before the credits for a film or television program are placed on the screen, the company producing a show must submit its proposed credits to the Guild. This notice is sent to all writers (Guild and non-Guild) who have written any material in connection with that program. If the writer protests the proposed credits, he may object, in which case the Guild will arbitrate a decision.

Note that in the case of a dispute, the Guild allows all participating writers to reach a compromise among themselves. Beware of this provision, however. As noted in chapter 8, most studio contracts that provide bonuses to writers based on screenplay credit disallow the bonus if the writers decide among themselves how the credits should be finalized. In the end all writers may earn more money than if they had not made such a deal. That is why the following language appears in contracts with respect to screenplay bonuses: "If the writer is awarded sole screenplay credit "other than pursuant to Paragraph 7 of Theatrical Schedule A of the WGA Basic Agreement, then he/she shall receive. . . ."

In an arbitration, three arbitrators are mutually selected to read all drafts of a work. The writer who disputes a proposed credit is requested to write a detailed analysis of why she is entitled to screenplay credit. Nonproducer and nondirector writers must contribute at least 33 percent of the final screenplay to receive credit. The requirement for producer/writers or director/writers (called "hyphenates" in Hollywood) is more stringent. Hyphenates must contribute more than 50 percent to get credit.

To give you an idea of how credit arbitration works, here is an example. A producer optioned a screenplay, including a story by one writer and a first draft screenplay by another writer. The screenplay writer wrote one rewrite. The director insisted on another rewrite, but did not want to use the original screenplay writer. The producer wrote the next rewrite. In the credit arbitration, the producer's name was submitted as the screenplay writer and the name of the story writer was submitted as the story writer (remember that this writer had not written the original screenplay, only the story). The first screenplay writer protested (his material, after all, was based on original story material). Because the producer was a hyphenate, he needed to contribute 50 percent of the screenplay material. The first arbitration awarded the producer sole screenplay credit, with story by the original story writer. The first screenwriter (who had based his screenplay on the story) protested again. Under certain very limited circumstances, one may reexamine an arbitration. In this case, the screenwriter stated to the Guild that the Guild had not examined all the facts. Indeed, it had not, and final screenplay credits were awarded to the producer and the original story writers as having written the screenplay, with story by the original story writers. In this case, the original story was so extensive that it was deemed, in part, to be original screenplay material. Virtually none of the first screenwriter's dialogue or contributions remained, so that writer did not receive any credit. The producer did rely heavily on the story and the original story writer's contribution (which upon examination was closer to a screenplay than just a story), so the story writer was entitled to screenplay credit as well.

The advantage of the WGA credit arbitration is that it is free for the writers and the producers. It is a service of the Guild and a very valuable one.

Pension Fund and Health Benefits

The Guild also has a pension fund and provides health insurance to its members—an extremely valuable perk in this day and age of high medical insurance costs. Members must earn a minimum of $28,833 per year for *writing services* to be eligible for continued benefits. (This is the minimum payment for a half-hour episode.) If they do not earn that much, they can self-pay (cost: $370.87 per month for the same individual coverage the Writers Guild provides) for 18 months to 24 months, depending on how long the individual had already been covered, to keep the insurance in effect until they earn the requisite minimum again.

Signatory companies are required to pay 7.5 percent of the writer's compensation and an additional 6 percent for pension benefits. One must be a member in good standing in order for the pension benefits to vest; otherwise, the contributions are forfeited to the Guild. Once they have vested, they are like any other pension fund (or IRA). You cannot touch it until you reach the age of 59.

THE RIGHT TO WRITE THE FIRST REWRITE

The Guild requires that the writer of an original screenplay must be afforded the right to write the first rewrite.

Article 16.A.c of the WGA Basic Agreement provides that:

> With respect to a screenplay sold or licensed to Company by a professional writer (as defined in Article 1.B.1.b.) to which separation of rights applies, Company shall offer the first writer the opportunity to perform the first rewrite services at not less than the applicable minimum compensation for a rewrite. If such writer is unable to perform such services or waives his/her right, Company may engage another writer.
>
> In addition, Company shall offer such writer the opportunity to perform one (1) additional set of revisions, if any are required by Company, because of a changed or new element (e.g., director or principal performer) assigned to the development or production of the writer's screenplay. Company's obligation to make such an offer shall exist for a period of two (2) years after delivery of the writer's first or final set of revisions, whichever occurs later. However, this obligation does not arise if Company engaged another writer to make revisions to the screenplay before the first changed or new element was assigned to the project. If the first writer is unable to perform such services or waives his/her right, Company may engage another writer.
>
> With respect to a screenplay written under employment by a writer who has separation of rights therein, if Company desires to engage another writer to rewrite such screenplay, it will discuss with the first writer its reason(s) for not continuing that writer on the project after his or her first draft.
>
> With respect to an option of a screenplay written by a professional writer (as defined in Article 1.B.1.b.) to which separation of rights applies, the writer of the optioned material shall be entitled, during the option period, to perform the first rewrite of such material, unless such writer is unavailable or waives this require-

ment in writing in a separate document or in the writer's deal letter/memorandum. If such writer performs such rewrite, the provisions of Article 16.A.3.c. shall be deemed satisfied.

The Producer or a creative executive will consult with the writer regarding each set of revisions requested of the writer by Company.

The payment required is the applicable minimum compensation for the applicable medium, length, and budget.

TURNAROUND/REVERSION

Finally, the Guild and the producer signatory companies have agreed to include a provision in the WGA Basic Agreement allowing a writer to get back his material if a project is not made after a certain period of time and rewrites if an option is not exercised. (If you are entitled to get your screenplay back, you can also get back any rewrite you wrote, but you can't get back *just* a rewrite.)

Writer's Right to Reacquire Literary Material

The provisions of this paragraph apply only to literary material (i) which is original, i.e., not based on any pre-existing material, and (ii) which has not been exploited in any medium.

Reacquisition under the 1998 Basic Agreement.
With respect only to literary material acquired by Company on or after August 8, 1988, the writer may reacquire such literary material pursuant to the terms set forth below upon expiration of the five (5) year period following the later of (i) the Company's purchase or license of the covered literary material or (ii) completion of the writer's services rendered in connection with the literary material, if such literary material is not in active development.

If the writer does reacquire such literary material, such reacquisition is subject to existing commitments, such as security interests, participations, turnaround rights, and employment rights.

Procedures for Reacquisition:

(i)   At any time during the two (2) year period immediately following expiration of the Company's five (5) year period within which to actively develop the material, the writer may notify the Company in writing of the writer's intent to reacquire the material. The writer shall include in such notice the address(es) where further correspondence and notices relating to reacquisition of the material shall be sent.

(ii)   If the material is not in active development at the time Company receives writer's notice of intent to reacquire, then, within sixty (60) days following receipt of such notice, Company shall have the right to place the material into active development. However, during such sixty (60) day period, the material will be deemed to be placed into active development only if, during such period, Company employs a writer to rewrite the literary material or Company employs a director or major actor on a pay-or-play basis for a motion picture based upon the literary material.

(iii) Within sixty (60) days following receipt of writer's notice of intent to reacquire, Company shall give the writer and the Guild written notice of the terms and conditions (which shall not include a "changed elements" clause, i.e., a right of first and/or last refusal or provisions which have the same effect upon which it will sell its right, title, and interest in the literary material), and the price of the material as set forth in this subparagraph, and the encumbrances and/or commitments, if any (such as security interests, participations, employment rights, future options, and/or future turnaround rights) that were attached to the literary material at the time the Company received the writer's notice of intent to reacquire the literary material.

(iv)   In the alternative, the Company may notify the writer
and the Guild that the literary material does not meet
one or more of the conditions precedent specified in
the second paragraph above, or that the literary material
is in active development at the time of the Company's
notification to the writer, or that the literary material has
been sold or is under option or is in turnaround to a
third party. If the Company advises the writer that the
literary material has been sold to a third party, the
Company shall include in its written notice the identity
of the third party and the date of such sale. If the
Company advises the writer that the literary material is
in active development, or is under option, or is in turnaround, at the time of the Company's notification to the
writer, the two (2) year period for reacquisition, or any
time remaining on it, shall be tolled during the period
of such active development, option, or turnaround and
until the writer receives notice from the Company that
the script is no longer in active development, or under
option, or in turnaround. In such event, the Company
shall include in its written notice the expiration date
of any option or turnaround right. Should any such
option or turnaround right be exercised by a third
party, the Company shall promptly notify the writer
and the Guild.

(v)   In the event the literary material is in active development at the time of the Company's receipt of the
writer's notice of intent to reacquire and the Company
later ceases to actively develop the material, and/or if
the Company places the material into active development within the sixty (60) day period following writer's
notice of intent to reacquire the material, and the
Company later ceases to actively develop the material, Company shall notify the writer and the Guild
promptly in writing that the material is no longer in
active development. If, within thirty (30) days after

receipt of such written notice from the Company, the writer advises the Company in writing that he/she desires to reacquire the material in accordance with his/her earlier notice, then the Company shall give the writer and the Guild the written notice of the terms and conditions, purchase price, encumbrances, and/or commitments as described above within sixty (60) days after receipt of the writer's most recent notice to reacquire. In such event, Company shall have no right to place the material into active development during this latter sixty (60) day period, or thereafter during the writer's period for reacquisition. If the writer provides written notice of intent to reacquire more than thirty (30) days after writer's receipt of Company's notice that active development of the material has ceased, then the procedures contained within the first four subparagraphs of this "Procedures for Reacquisition" section shall apply for the remainder of the writer's period for reacquisition.

(vi) If the Company proceeds in accordance with subparagraph (iv) of this "Procedures for Reacquisition" section and the Guild or the writer disputes the factual basis upon which the Company relies for so proceeding, such dispute shall be subject to the grievance and arbitration provisions of Articles 10, 11, and 12 of this Agreement. However, the Company's decision regarding the terms and conditions of the sale, as distinguished from the purchase price, shall not be subject to challenge by the Guild or the writer on any grounds whatsoever, whether in arbitration or otherwise. Notwithstanding the preceding sentence, disputes as to whether the terms and conditions of the reacquisition sale conform to the express provisions of this Article 16.A.B.d. shall be subject to the grievance and arbitration provisions of Articles 10, 11, and 12 of this Agreement.

(vii) The writer shall reacquire such literary material if writer tenders the purchase price within six (6) months after writer's receipt of the Company's notice. The Company shall not further encumber the literary material during such six (6) month period by entering into new agreements or commitments, such as options, turnarounds, security interests, participations, and employment rights, or actively develop or sell the literary material. In the event the writer fails to make the payment within such six (6) month period, the writer may reinstitute the procedure for reacquisition at any time within the time remaining in the two (2) year period referred to above, it being understood that such procedures need only be commenced, and not completed, within the two (2) year period.

Payment:

(i)   The writer shall reacquire the literary material pursuant to this section upon payment to the Company (or the buyer if applicable) of all compensation actually paid by the Company (or the buyer, if applicable) to the writer for services in connection with the literary material and/or for the purchase or license of the literary material from the writer or company. It is understood that the purchase price, as set forth in the preceding sentence, is the sole monetary consideration due from the writer to the Company to reacquire the literary material; in no event will the writer be obligated to pay more than the amount specified in the preceding sentence (e.g., in the form of profit participations to the Company).

(ii) If the writer reacquires the literary material from the Company (or buyer if applicable) and the writer thereafter sells or licenses the literary material to a third party, the writer shall obligate such third party to reimburse the Company (or buyer if applicable), upon the commencement of principal photography, for any other direct cost previously incurred by the Company (or buyer, if applicable) in relation to such literary material (as described below) plus interest thereon. The document by which the writer reacquires the literary material shall contain a provision setting forth the obligations referred to in the preceding sentence.

The purchase price designated by Company shall not be in excess of the total direct costs previously incurred by Company in relation only to such literary material, including payments for the acquisition of the literary material and for writing services connected therewith (including writing services in relation to treatments and screenplays based thereon), and fringe benefit costs in relation thereto, such as pension and health fund payments and social security payments, but exclusive of overhead and exclusive of costs of any other kind (e.g., costs relating to proposed production other than writing costs).

DISADVANTAGES IF YOU ARE A MEMBER

The only real disadvantage to being a member of the Writers Guild is that you cannot work for non-Guild companies. In fact, you can be fined and even thrown out of the Guild for doing so. If you are a Guild member and are tempted with an offer from a non-Guild company, my advice is not to do it. The guild can be belligerent toward their own members and have little or no sympathy for noncompliance with their rules.

As an example of the Guild mentality, I have a client who failed to pay his pension, health, and welfare contributions on time. The Guild requires both the employer and the writer to make contributions. While the employee contribution is relatively small, bottom line, the guild operates based on contributions and they need the money. In this particular instance, my client relied on his accountant to make the proper contributions and to file the appropriate report. Note that both the employer and the employee submit separate reports. At that time, the accountant's wife was dying of cancer and he missed making the payment. The Guild fined my client $4,000! (In this case, it was the Directors Guild, not the Writers Guild, but the same situation could occur.) My client went before the Guild to explain the extenuating circumstances. The Guild refused to give any relief, and he had to pay the fine.

SELLING TO OUTSIDERS: PROS AND CONS

I have a number of clients who have made a living without becoming members of the Guild. It is difficult and the opportunities are limited. All major companies and most producers are signatories to the guilds. The reason: Producers like to work with writers who have experience, and, at a certain point, it is inevitable that writers who continue to work will join the Guild. Writers want to work for mainstream companies: The budgets are bigger, the opportunities are greater. Virtually all studio pictures are governed by the Guild (other than animated pictures, which are not covered by the Guild Agreement, and in this category, Guild writers can work for non-Guild companies). Virtually all network programming is written by Guild writers. Producers who have deals with the studios and those who are the major suppliers for the networks are all Guild signatories.

The only opportunities for the non-Guild writer are in animation, low, low budget pictures, and in some cable programming. But the opportunity for the non-Guild producer to make low-budget pictures today is very limited. The low-budget independent film market is smaller today because the studios are no longer interested in distributing small pictures. Ever since studios started advertising theatrical pictures on television, the cost of releasing a picture has gone sky high. Major studios may spend $12 million and more to open a picture. Odds are, they are not going to spend $12 million to advertise a $500,000 picture.

Recently, the studios have each started their own lower budget division for nonblockbuster, more arthouse-type fare. These "low-budgets" still tend to be in the $5-million-plus range and are usually Guild-governed pictures. Producers who hire non-Guild writers tend to be on the fringes of the Hollywood community, although there are exceptions. While occasionally a very small picture is picked up for theatrical release by some distributor (such as *sex, lies and videotape*), this is very rare.

If you are serious about a career as a screenwriter, your goal should be to become a member of the Guild by either selling a script to a Guild company and getting hired to do rewrites, or by writing for a Guild company. From a business perspective, it is the only way to survive.

SCRIPT REGISTRATION

As noted before, the Guild maintains a script registration service for members and nonmembers. This is valuable as a way to establish proof of creation and time of creation. Simply submit your screenplay to the Writers Guild of America Registration office. There is one in Los Angeles and one in New York. The cost is $10.00 per submission. Nonmembers may take advantage of the system for $20.00 per submission. The Guild will place a copy of your screenplay in its files and give you a record of the time of registration. For more information, contact the Writers Guild of America, west (Telephone: 323-782-4500) or Writers Guild of America, east (Telephone: 212-767-7800).

SECTION 501(C)

In all television agreements, you will see a provision that the writer must acknowledge that it is a criminal offense under Section 501(c) of the U.S. Federal Communications Act for any person to accept or pay any money, service, or other valuable consideration for the inclusion of any plug, reference, product identification, or other matter as part of a television program, without disclosure in the manner required by law. The purpose of this provision is to distinguish television programming from advertising, in which product identification is specifically labeled as an advertisement. Otherwise, the program is subliminally selling a product without labeling it as such. The provision usually goes on to further state that the writer understands it is the producer's policy to prohibit the acceptance or payment of any such consideration and the writer represents that the writer has not accepted or paid, and agrees that the writer shall not accept or pay, any such consideration.

16

The Role of the Producer

I have included this chapter in this book because it is important for you to understand the function of the producer of your project and her continuing rights to your material.

THE PRODUCER'S RELATIONSHIP TO THE MATERIAL

Producers who work for studios are employees just like you. And unless a project gets made, they make much less than you. The average studio development fee for a producer of a feature film is $25,000. Producers often have agents. Keep in mind that it is a common practice for agents to earn a commission on the producer's salary, as well as the writer's compensation, when the agent delivers a piece of material to a producer who decides to take on that project. If you deduct the agent's commission plus legal fees, the producer is left with less than $20,000 to supervise the development of a script. Half of the $25,000 is paid on commencement of the writer's services for the studio; the other half is paid when the studio decides to make the picture or abandon it. That could take years. So producers who are not independently wealthy have to set up many projects just to make a living. As studios cut down on the number of pictures in development, it makes it difficult for producers to survive.

Producers (and, on rare occasion, writers) are usually able to negotiate some sort of "progress to production" clause in their own contracts with the studios. In other words, the studios cannot just hold onto a piece of material forever if they do not do something with it. "Doing something" is defined rather generally. A typical clause looks like this: "Notwithstanding the foregoing, if for any consecutive six (6) month period there is no active development (e.g., all reading and writing periods have expired, there are no offers outstanding with respect to the writer, principal cast, or director, nor any budgeting or location surveying taking place), Producer may give studio notice and if studio fails to resume active development within ten (10) business days, the Picture shall be deemed abandoned."

Thus, the studio must actively hire a writer, look for a writer, determine a budget, look for a star, and the like. If, after notice, the studio fails to do something, then the project will be abandoned and it goes into turnaround to the producer.

"Turnaround" means that the studio gives the producer the right to take the project to another studio. If the producer does get another studio interested in the project, then the other studio must pay the first studio back its entire investment in the project (cost of writers, producer's development fee, messengers, producer's offices, and the like), plus interest, plus a small piece of the net profits of the picture if it is made (generally 5 percent). The more money a studio spends on a project, the more difficult it is to get the project set up elsewhere.

Some studios have arrangements among themselves allowing the second studio to pay a fraction of the costs involved when the project is set up there and the balance if the picture is made. Note that the producer's turnaround agreement does not allow this, and this is a side agreement between the studios. It is called a "reciprocal arrangement." Some studios, however, refuse to enter into these kinds of arrangements and insist on getting all their money back when the project is set up elsewhere. In other words, they will not wait until a picture is made to get all their money back. Either the second studio pays *all* costs when it gets involved or it doesn't get the project.

Turnarounds are limited in time, generally for one year, sometimes eighteen months. If the producer with the turnaround rights does not set up the project at another studio within that period of time, the project remains with the studio that originally developed it and the producer may be dismissed. In short, for all of his endeavors, he collects his $25,000 development fee and has no further legal rights in the project (although many studios will keep the producer on, notwithstanding the precarious legal position). On the other hand, if the producer is lucky to set up the project elsewhere during the turnaround period, then he can try to negotiate with the second studio for another development fee. In most cases, the studio will argue that he has already been paid a development fee by the first studio (a fee the second studio must reimburse to the first studio) and is therefore *not* entitled to more money. However, if the producer is important enough, he might be able to eke out another $12,500 for several more years of work on the project. As you can see, it is not very much money.

On the other hand, if the project gets made, producers do hit the jackpot. Studio salaries for top producers can soar to $750,000 to $1,000,000 (in some cases $1.25 million-plus), depending on the producer. But remember: Of all the projects developed, very few get made, so the odds are not good. As my mentor, Peter Dekom, said, "Being a producer is probably the worst job in Hollywood unless you are rich, a former studio head who makes a golden parachute deal with the studio after leaving, a manager/producer who can survive on the manager commissions, or a writer/producer who can survive on his/her writing compensation." Being a plain old producer today is not a great way to make a living. Thus, producers today tend to be the ones who are truly passionate about filmmaking (they have to be passionate in order to survive) or those that spend their own money—and if it is their own money, they also have a stake in making sure the project gets off the ground.

Within the studio system, a strong producer may be a great asset to the young writer. For instance, if you are hired to write, the producer may ask you to let him read the script before you turn it in to the studio. He will probably make suggestions. He has been there before, and he wants to make the best impression on the studio. Opinions are formed very quickly, and, if the first draft you turn in is not good, the odds of your staying with the project are greatly diminished. He will also help you fight your battles, as he has the relationship with the studio brass. It is important for you to build a strong bond with your producer and to get him in your corner. Simply put, he is in a better position to sway studio opinion, and you should use him for that purpose. That is not to say that you should not fight your own battles. But it takes time to build relationships, and, when you are beginning, you will not have the long-standing relationship that the producer may have with the studio executive assigned to your project.

Of course, when you are starting out in Hollywood, it is hard to know who's who—more specifically, who can be trusted and who cannot. You want to get your script made into a picture. Someone finally expresses interest. You jump. Always remember that Hollywood is a "glamorous" industry (once you are in it, you will also realize it is very hard work). It attracts many individuals who want to add a little glamour to their lives. Thus, there are a lot of would-be producer types. All kinds of folks call themselves producers. The real question is what they have produced and under what circumstances. You should be aware of what I call the "glue factor." Some people are producers because they have attached themselves, like glue, to a project and the only way to get the project made is to include them. They are like a nuisance suit. They are usually not the most respected producers in town.

Many young writers make mistakes. Here is an example. A young writer I know signed with a fledgling manager/producer. Believing that this person could be helpful to him, he agreed to sign a contract allowing this person to manage him for one year. The manager took a commission on all scripts sold or writing assignments obtained—not unusual. The manager also included a provision that he had the right to produce all projects that he set up. The problem with this provision is that he could technically block any deal if the studio/financier did not want to include him as a producer. Since this manager/producer had never produced, it was quite logical that the studio would consider him as excess baggage, and, indeed, in one such instance a studio did. That is when I was brought in. The writer wanted to try to make a deal with a studio/financier that had expressed interest in his project. The manager said that the writer could not make such a deal unless the studio/financier also agreed to let him be a producer. I called the manager and expressed my outrage. I also pointed out that he had a major conflict of interest—as a manager, he was supposed to promote his client's best interests. In his capacity as a "producer," he was not promoting those best interests, and he was effectively blocking any deal. He finally agreed that he would only ask for $50,000 and not take a commission. Because of the contract, there was a potential entanglement on the chain of title and my client agreed to try to get him $50,000, with the understanding that the producer could not block any deal if, at the end of the day, it turned out that the studio would break the deal over the producing salary. The moral: *Beware of would-be producers.*

If you want a career as a writer, you must remember that screenwriting is a business. As a businessperson, you should find out everything about the person with whom you are going into business. Ask questions. Find out the reputation of the producer. Do you know anyone who has worked with him, knows him, or knows of him? Do your research, and, most important, avoid the sleaze factor in Hollywood, the wannabe's who can only be someone by virtue of the "glue factor" and not by virtue of their own experience or talent.

Of course, even the most professional of producers will sometimes try to attach themselves to projects they do not own. This factor sometimes permeates even the highest levels of Hollywood. I was recently called by an agent friend who was trying to option one of her client's books. She had sent the book to a well-known producer and asked the producer to make an offer. The producer did not. When the agent was on the brink of selling the book to someone else, the producer in question surfaced and told the agent it was his understanding that he had been given a free option. He also said that he would be a nuisance about it. While there were many legal loopholes in her argument (you need a written agreement to perfect chain of title and no purchase price had been established), the producer's stance did indeed create another level of complications. Since studios/financiers tend to protect producers who first pitch them projects, the producer who is in favor with a studio could very well arrange it so that the producer has to be taken care of before the studio will make a deal, notwithstanding his weak legal position. In other words, the studio could say that a particular producer is attached or we do not make the deal. Believe me, it has happened. It is called politics and it exists in all businesses, most dramatically in Hollywood.

This producer had strong relationships around town. Luckily, he backed off.

In short, you can never be sure that even the most experienced of producers will not try to pull something. Then again, if a strong producer is making waves, at least you know you have arrived, in a sense, and that your project is hot. In the end, if it is that hot, it will get set up with a major company and it even has a chance of being made. The wanna-be producers are in a different league and there is very little chance for an upside if you become embroiled in a legal entanglement. Do your research. You have to if you want to survive.

YOUR RELATIONSHIP TO YOUR PRODUCER

I cannot emphasize enough the importance of relationships in Hollywood. Many contract disputes are settled because of relationships and not by lawsuits. It is important to build your relationships and keep them. Keep in mind that the studios have what they call "revolving doors." Today's executives may be out of work in a couple of years, only to surface again in more powerful positions. There is a saying in Hollywood that executives fail upwards. When studios are looking for new executives, they tend to pick people who have been in that position before, regardless of their track records. What they are interested in are their *relationships*.

The same holds true for writers. Executives and producers like to pick writers who have strong relationships with them and with others. They want to know that you are not a troublemaker and that you are not on someone's secret blacklist. The stakes are high for studio executives. It is nice work for those who can get it and they do not want to lose their jobs.

In tough times, the writers with good relationships survive. The ones who have not built strong relationships cannot find jobs. I know several talented writers with substantial credits who cannot land jobs. They have no one to call. They do not fit into the studio mold. They are perceived as pushy and unpleasant to work with. Remember: If you have strong relationships, you can pick up the phone, independent of your agent. If you do not have such relationships, you have to rely on your agent. And if you are cold at the studios, the agent cannot sell you. "Cold" means that no one wants to work with you again.

Producers and studios like to work with people they like, with people they think listen to their advice. If you have worked at a company and cannot get a job at that company again, you have obviously done something wrong and should ask yourself what it is and correct it before it happens again. Ideally, you will build one primary relationship with a major producer or company—become a "pet" writer. You want that level of relationship—to know that no matter how bad the times are, you can get some kind of writing assignment. Screenwriting is a business and you must apply business principles to this business just like any other.

17

The Art of Negotiation

The most important thing to remember when negotiating with studios is that they all tend to have the same philosophy: You need them more than they need you. They also like to base their offer on your last "quote." How much did you get on your last writing assignment? Was it for a studio? If not, then the studio will probably discount whatever the quote was. For how much did you sell your last screenplay? Again, did you sell it to a studio? Did it get made?

FLOODGATE THEORY

Unless there is a bidding war going on or unless at the end of the day you are willing to walk away from a deal, studios hold tight to previous quotes in their offers. For them to budge even a few thousand dollars is a big deal. While your representative and not you will be the person interfacing with the studio, you should understand the mentality of studio business affairs executives. Unless your request falls within the framework of an "acceptable request," you will categorically be turned down. Their objective is to make a deal based on your last deal and in most other respects to turn you down. The reason: Studios have precedents, and they do not like to break them. They all believe in the floodgate theory—which is that once they cave in on a certain point, everyone in Hollywood will find out, and they will be confronted with the request again. If they have given in once, it will not be easy to categorically reject another comparable request. So the first rule is that the request has to fall within the parameters of what is acceptable.

That is where your agent and lawyer come in. We know what we can get and it is our primary job to get what falls within the acceptable framework—that is, unless your last script was produced and it was a huge hit, you have a bidding war going on, or you are willing to walk away. In such situations, many of the "rules" by which the studios play are thrown out the window. Obviously, you have the least leverage when it comes to writing assignments. The offer is pretty much going to be pegged to your last quote. If you push too hard, the studio will simply move on to its next choice. Remember: The studio's attitude is that writers are expendable. That is not to say we cannot angle for some improvement. If successful, the improvement might be for features $25,000-plus on the up-front monies (do not expect $100,000 bumps), and there may be some increase in the bonuses as well (sole and shared screenplay bonuses). Again, the increases are not going to be overwhelming. But every little bit helps, because it not only increases the fee, it increases the all-important "quote."

If you have a spec script, then you can refuse to make the deal unless your price is met. But unless the script is one of the hottest properties in town, the offer is probably going to be based on your quotes.

Altering Boiler Plate Provisions

The changes to the "boiler plate" provisions are all fairly standard. Sometimes a business affairs executive will say no to changes that were given on another writer's deal if the other writer got paid more. The

>oiler plate provisions (indemnities, force majeure provisions, and the ike) have nothing to do with compensation, and this argument drives ne up the wall! For instance, in services agreements there is always a lisability clause, that is, the studio can terminate the contract if the writer is sick for *three* days. I always ask that this be increased to seven :o ten days, and usually there is no argument. But, sometimes, studio lawyers will try to argue that they are simply not going to make the same changes for a $100,000 writer that they will make for a $500,000 writer. My answer is that I am concerned with fairness. This has nothing to do with how much the writer is making. Anyone can get a cold and be out of it for three days. That is simply not a reason to terminate an agreement. These points can usually be won. It sometimes requires several calls and some time. The reality is that some studios simply try to wear you down and oftentimes they are successful, particularly if they know the client is anxious to close the deal, to start working, and to *get paid*.

PATIENCE

One of the most important aspects of any negotiation is patience. Studios are slow, in part, because in recent years they have scaled down their legal departments, and most lawyers are tied up with actual productions. Therefore, development deals come second. Further, as mentioned above, studios sometimes move slowly in an effort to wear you down. The longer it takes to finish the deal, the longer it is going to take for you to get paid. If you are in a hurry to get paid, that always affects your ability to negotiate effectively. If you are desperate for money, you might have to give up fighting for some of the changes that fall within acceptable parameters because the studio is going to put you through your paces to get what you want. Unfortunately, this is a reality, and when my clients are desperate for money, I cannot push for points that I might win if I had enough time to follow through. Rarely do studios agree to everything you want on the first round and there are usually several rounds in any negotiation. The more complicated the deal, the more negotiations, and the more rounds there are, the more time it takes to get questions answered. If a provision is rare, or the money is unusual, then it will have to be approved by the top executives at the studio. Any points that are out of the norm have to go this route, and the more people involved in making a decision, the longer it will take to get an answer. Again, patience is the key in any successful negotiation.

COMPROMISE

It is also important to give up on some points. You should not expect to win every point, and, if you do, you might very well leave a bad taste on the other side. Relationships are key in Hollywood. Whatever you do, you want to finish a negotiation without ill will or a bitter taste in anyone's mouth. Both sides, while not entirely satisfied, need to feel that the arrangement is palatable. So whatever you do, never force something down the other side's throat that they will regret forever. The art of negotiation involves compromise somewhere. Always leave yourself with some term that you are willing to give in on, even if it was one of your more outrageous requests. At the outset, you want the buyer to feel good about having bought your material or having procured your services. That is not to say that you should not fight hard to get the things you deserve, but do not be unrealistic about your demands. That can kill any negotiation. There are parameters, and you want to hire a lawyer who understands these parameters so you get the most you are entitled to. What you do not want is a negotiation by someone who does not know the turf, because he is bound to make some mistakes.

I was recently involved in a negotiation in which the deal almost fell apart when the lawyer on the other side refused to give in on a basic point that is accepted by all of the major studios, smaller studios, and almost every company with whom I have done business. My client was a producer/director who optioned the rights to a book. The author knew that the intention was for my well-known client to use his contacts to make a deal with a studio to develop the property and finance a picture. The author of this book was also being hired as a screenwriter. My client wanted to be assured that when he assigned his rights to the studio, the author would look to the studio if the studio failed to make a payment, and not to him. The studio would have to sign a WGA Assumption Agreement so the studio would not only be on the hook with the writer but with the Guild as well.

Indeed, the writer at that point would be in the same situation as if he had made his deal originally with the studio. The writer's lawyer insisted that my client should still be on the hook for the studio's default, citing the fact that some studios are now on shaky legs, even though we agreed that my client would only be off the hook if the assignment was to a major studio. The majors are a pretty safe bet these days and the purchase of the book would not be effective unless the purchase price was paid. In my opinion, this lawyer missed the point of the deal. The writer, a new screenwriter, needed to be sponsored by a well-known talent in Hollywood—first, in order to be assured that he would have a chance to write the script, and second, his chances of getting the project made were greatly enhanced because a well-known Hollywood director was to be attached. He was much farther ahead than if he had optioned his book to the studio directly.

My client simply did not want to take the risk of a studio's default, and it was unfair to put him in that position in this case, given the motivation for involving him in the first place. Had the "off the hook" language been more expansive than a major studio, that would have been a different issue. We made it a deal breaker and the writer caved in on the point. My point is that the lawyer almost lost his client a deal.

KNOW THE PARAMETERS

On the other hand, a knowledgeable attorney can greatly facilitate a difficult negotiation by not wasting time on points that are simply not acceptable. I represented a producer who was acquiring life-story rights to the life story of a very famous artist. The artist's estate had engaged the services of an out-of-state attorney who knew nothing about the film business.

The main issue centered around merchandising rights. As the artist's estate makes a lot of money from posters and reproductions of the artist's work, the heirs did not want to give away their income in this area. The out-of-state attorney insisted that no rights to reproduce the artist's works be conveyed. I told him that I would not be able to make a deal with a studio without the ability, at least, to reproduce a limited number of works for the poster, T-shirts, the album cover, videocassette box, book jackets, and tie-in publications.

With the help of a Hollywood attorney that the estate finally engaged, we agreed that (1) the works would be limited; (2) they would be mutually approved; and (3) the uses would be limited to the uses I have outlined above. While not entirely satisfactory, at least I knew I would be able to meet the studio's very *minimal* requirements. With the help of a Hollywood attorney who knew what had to be included as part of the deal, at least I had a shot at making the deal with a major financier. Knowing the parameters is key to any deal. There are certain rules that are unchangeable by *anyone*, and it is important to know what they are. On the other hand, what is acceptable for John Hughes, William Goldman, and Ron Bass is not necessarily going to be acceptable for you. Your attorney needs to distinguish between what is essential and what is wishful thinking.

While it is not possible for you to know all of the parameters of negotiation, once you have read this book, you will understand most of the standard requests. If your agent is asking for something that does not appear in this book, it is probably a point that falls outside the parameters of customary negotiation. Just make sure you do not lose a deal on account of it or leave a bad taste in the other side's mouth if you get it. I refer you again to my first negotiation as a producer, discussed in the introduction. By the time we finished the negotiations, I wanted nothing to do with the other side!

RENEGOTIATION

I am sure you have heard that contracts in Hollywood are sometimes renegotiated. This happens mostly with the star of a successful series, and in situations where the parties have an ongoing relationship and the studio wants to help keep the talent happy. When one of the pictures produced under a term deal is an overall hit, the studio has come to expect that lawyers and agents will routinely insist on better terms for the next picture under that deal, and the studio is usually willing to oblige, because naturally this is what studio executives are after—huge hits.

Even with contracts concerning one project, studios sometimes will reconsider their original position. I have a client who optioned his script to a studio and wrote one rewrite. They had him under contract or two rewrites. The rewrite experience was miserable for him. In the process of discussing the rewrite with the executives, he realized that they completely missed the point of his script, and it was clear this relationship was not working. He is a very talented and well-known writer. The studio accepted his first rewrite and excused him from his obligation to rewrite another (at the same time, he agreed not to accept the money for the second rewrite, which had been committed).

While you might consider this a renegotiation, the legal term is "waiver." The studio waived one of its requirements. Similarly, if the contract says you have to deliver your first draft in ten weeks, and you need twelve weeks, the studio may waive the ten-week requirement. Couching such changes in terms of waiver is much better for you because the studios hate the word *renegotiation*. Waivers are much more common than renegotiations, and as long as the subject is not more money, and as long as you have a good relationship, you might be able to discuss changes to the terms of your contract. Studio executives are willing to listen, particularly when it comes to delivery dates and terms of that nature. In the end, they want the best script for the money they are paying you and, in that sense, they are often reasonable.

REPRESENTATION

Finally, I want to add that under no circumstances should you negotiate your own deals, unless you simply cannot get a representative. First, studio executives do not like dealing directly with individuals. It is very awkward for them. Second, unless you are very experienced, you may forget to raise certain issues. It is simply better to use a professional in this regard. You also must be careful about going around your agent and lawyer to try to win points. Trust that your representatives are representing your best interests. If they are not, discuss it with them or get another representative. That is not to say that you will never be involved in a negotiation. Sometimes, on certain key points, it might be better for you to deal directly with the creative executive to win points. But this is strategy and it should be worked out very carefully with your representatives and with your representatives' full knowledge. You need to be a team and not working at cross-purposes.

304 THE SCREENWRITER'S LEGAL GUIDE

I had a client who did not listen to this advice. She wanted an office at the studio while she was writing a script for that studio. I asked. The studio told me they had no office space on the lot and told me to ask my client to find out how much it would cost to rent an office of the lot. They would reimburse her. Rather than doing so, she picked up the phone, called the plant manager at the studio, and found out that there were several vacant offices at the studio. The studio executives found out and were furious. She basically tried to prove that the studio was lying to her and they did not like being put in that position. She never got an office and never got reimbursement for office space. The moral: Don't try to go around your representatives. They are there to help you, but it is very difficult to do so when you try to negotiate you own deal without telling them. Coordinate you strategy. It is crucial.